Acclaim for RICH COHEN's

Lake Effect

"Cohen . . . has taken the everyday stuff of life and made it joyously readable. The mundane becomes richly evocative in his hands. The usual becomes unusual, the boring becomes interesting, the sweet becomes bittersweet, and *Lake Effect* becomes the proverbial book you can't put down."
　　　　　　　　　　　　　　　　　　　—*Milwaukee Journal Sentinel*

"Arresting and thoughtful. . . . Cohen brings back the flavor of the '80s culture with insight and humor."　　　—*The Washington Post*

"A rare book [with the] glint of a superb novel. . . . It contains lines so heartbreakingly apt and funny I stopped to reread constantly."　　　　　　　　　　　　　　　　—Jonathan Lethem

"Cohen has written a fine book."　　　　　　　—*Chicago Tribune*

"Elegiac, nostalgic and *Gatsby*-esque . . . Cohen's memoir is filled with tender moments . . . but never loses its realistic, hard edge. . . . Poignant and lyrical."　　　　　　　　　—*Publishers Weekly*

"A universal story of youth, maturity and love, *Lake Effect* is a probing meditation on the passage of time, an accomplished book."　　　　　　　　　　　　　　　　　　　—*Bookpage*

Meredith

RICH COHEN

Lake Effect

Rich Cohen is the author of *Tough Jews* and *The Avengers*. His work has appeared in *The New Yorker* and *Vanity Fair*, among many other publications. He is a contributing editor at *Rolling Stone*. He lives in New York City.

Lake Effect

Lake Effect

RICH COHEN

VINTAGE BOOKS

A DIVISION OF RANDOM HOUSE, INC.

NEW YORK

The Library of Congress has cataloged the Knopf edition as follows:
Cohen, Rich.
Lake effect / Rich Cohen.—1st ed.
p. cm.
ISBN 0-375-41132-1
1. Teenage boys. 2. Fathers and Sons. 3. Male Friendship. 4.Chicago (Ill.). I. Title
PS3603.048 L35 2002
813'.54—dc21   2001038605

Vintage ISBN: 0-375-72533-4

Author photograph © Jerry Bauer
Book design by Robert C. Olsson

www.vintagebooks.com

For my friends on the North Shore

While *Lake Effect* is, in essence, a true story, in telling it I have changed most names and many details and, in a few exceptional instances, the course of events. Otherwise, I might have given the impression, wrongly, that I was after a kind of objective truth; in reality, these stories are subjectively told through my eyes and through my memory. Nor have I tried to tell the full and complete story of any of the people in my life. After all, almost everyone I know, even my very oldest friends, remain, in important ways, a mystery to me. I was instead after the spirit of a certain season and the thrill of a certain kind of friendship and what happens to such friendships when the afternoon runs into the evening.

Lake Effect

Part One

In summer we slept on the beach. We would park our cars on a side street and hike through the trees to the ravine and then down to a secret little shore that only we knew about. We would get a fire going and drink red wine and look at the lights winding along the north coast and, to the south, at the haze above Chicago. Out on the lake, we could see the red hazards of ships, and sometimes a speedboat splashed its tiny wake onto the rocky sand. Jamie told stories about the lake, which he said was over a thousand feet deep, and about the ships that had gone down beyond the horizon, voices vanishing in the cold water. When the wine was gone, we sat talking about girls and fights, or what we would do next week or next month. Who could see beyond next month?

There were a lot of us on the beach, the usual crew.

Tom Pistone, who wished he had been a teenager in the fifties, drove a '61 Pontiac GTO, walked with a swagger, and dated girls in polka dots. Ronnie Flowers, who tagged after us like a mascot, was simpleminded and easy to fool and knew just one way to deal with people—as the butt of a joke. Tyler White, a genius or a fool, spent hours watching construction sites.

Of all those friends, the one I remember best is Jamie Drew. Looking back, I see that Jamie was the true hero of my youth, the most vivid presence, not only of my childhood but also for kids up and down the North Shore. Words he said, gestures he crafted, swept our school like a craze, imitated, in the end, even by the teachers. He was quick and dashing and honestly the smartest person I have ever known, and yet he seemed to hold his own talents in mean regard. My mother called him a lost soul. For a long time, I saw him as a tricked-out racer rusting in the garage—that part of each of us that did not survive the rough transition into adulthood.

When the fire burned down, we buried the embers and settled on the sand, which stayed warm for hours. In the morning, the sun appeared across the lake and, one by one, we climbed the hill to our cars and drove home to top off our sleep in our warm beds. Jamie and I often dozed late on the sand and then swam up the shore to the public beach, where our friends, showered and shaved, were waiting.

This was in the middle of the 1980s. It did not seem like it at the time, but that decade, as odorless and colorless as a noxious gas, came to inhabit every part of our lives. On the radio, we listened to "Scarecrow" by John Cougar Mellencamp, each of us worrying, in his own way, about the plight of the American farmer. In the fall, we wore jean jackets and chewed tobacco—Skoal long cut. On the weekends, we disappeared on end runs to Wisconsin, where the drinking age was eighteen, returning with a case of Pabst Blue Ribbon or Point beer. Jamie's favorite beer was Mickey's Big Mouth, which he drank in noisy, head-clearing slugs. We would hide the beer in my back-yard, bringing it inside only when my parents left town. A six pack might make a half dozen trips from the yard to the fridge. When a can was finally opened, it fizzled and foamed with the sweet skunk taste of summer. On televi-sion, we watched David Letterman, who was then still funny, and Ronald Reagan, whose smiling face beamed down on us. We knew that Reagan also was from Illinois, but his state and our state seemed far apart in time and place. My father called him the man with the very old face and the very young miracle hair. In school, Jamie and I studied all this in Popular Culture, a class where we also learned stereotypes from entertainment history. Our favorites were the Old Nat stereotype, which resulted in courtly black gentlemen dancing on white movie screens, and the Fu Manchu stereotype, featuring Oriental tyrants hellbent on world domination. Sometimes, as we sat on the beach, a Japanese kid would walk by and Jamie would say, "Think he suffers from the Fu Manchu stereotype?"

Most days ended with a dozen friends back at my house, sitting around the kitchen. I was at first flattered by the appeal I had for my friends, until I realized it had nothing to do with me; my friends were coming to see my father. My father was different from the other fathers in town: men in gray suits, newspaper under an arm, waiting for the train to the city. My father wore dirty brown pants and T-shirts crossed by lines and a watch on each wrist. "A man with one watch thinks he knows the time," he would say. "A man with two watches can never be sure." He had a job that kept him on the road. If not working, he was at home weeks at a stretch, wandering the house in reading glasses and boxer shorts. He often wore a suede cowboy hat, which, he said, identified him as a High Plains drifter. When a friend of mine, accustomed to the routines of his own father, crinkled his nose and asked, "Mr. Cohen, what is it you do?" my father wiped a plate and said, "Son, I am what you call a house husband."

A few years before I met Jamie, his father had been killed in one of those pointless high-speed tragedies that stain our national highways. Now and then, when Jamie mentioned the accident, he would curse under his breath. For this reason, he developed a special attachment to *my* father, who, rather than advise or instruct, simply treated him like a man. More than anything, Jamie was a boy raised by women, by his sister and his mother and his grandmother. I once warned him that a boy raised by girls had a greater chance of going fag. It was a stupid thing to say and a joke, but it turned into a big fight. I guess I was oblivious to the great fearful need in Jamie, the need for authority, someone to guide him. It was a need I would come to recognize in so many of my friends, kids who came of age during the divorce boom, in a nation seemingly without adults, a nation dedicated to the proposition that nothing counts except celebrity; it was this need that would later send us flitting from mentor to mentor, party to party, scene to scene, never resting, never settling, never satisfied with ourselves. For a time, it was a need Jamie and I filled in each other. One night, when he was lying in the twin bed across from mine, after we had each gone through the list of the girls in school we wanted to sleep with, Jamie said, "I wish I could be more like your father: you know, a High Plains drifter."

I laughed. "Jamie, it's just a fucking hat. He's from Brooklyn."

Jamie said, "Yeah, but still, I wish I could be that way."

In the autumn of 1972, my family moved to Glencoe from Libertyville, a farming town in northern Illinois. We were the only Jewish family in Libertyville. When I asked my father if he had met with much anti-Semitism, he smiled and said, "Are you kidding? When we moved in, the neighbors shook my hand and said, 'Thank God, we were afraid they would sell to Catholics.' They hadn't even worked their way down to us yet." Before Libertyville, my parents, newlyweds out of Brooklyn, had lived in New Jersey and Long Island, moving as my father was transferred. As a result, we came to have that special closeness of families on the go. I was four when we left Libertyville. My only memories of that town are of a sunny main drag of car dealerships and Dairy Queens and of the Des Plaines River, which wound by our house. Once, to convince my brother it was safe to walk on the frozen river (in school, my brother had been warned of black ice), my father jumped up and down, breaking through the ice into the swift current. The other things I remember are from stories later told to me: myself, in a red snowsuit, floating face down in a sewer of runoff, where my sister had dropped me; being crammed up the shirt of Tracy Hawkins, a neighborhood girl who wanted to pretend she was birthing me; driving with my mother to see a house she liked in Glencoe, which, in my mind, plays like a fancy movie dissolve into the next scene.

Glencoe is thirty miles up the lake from Chicago. It is a perfect town for a certain kind of dreamy kid, with just enough history to get your arms around. It was founded in the early 1800s by a blacksmith named Taylor, who walked out of the city, dark buildings and foundry flames at his back, into the great silence of the north, forests of oak and elm, Lake Michigan appearing and disappearing beyond the trees. He waded streams and passed through Indian settlements teeming in the open fields—settlements remembered today only in the names of country clubs that, until recently, did not allow blacks or Jews. In a flat place between the lake and the swamps to the west, he cleared trees and built a house and a dock and invited his friends and family to join him. He called the town Taylorsport, a name later changed to Glencoe. For a time, it was an industrial center, where lumber and coal were stacked on barges and towed down the lake. By the 1880s, it was a bustling country hamlet of unlit dirt roads. At night, the sky above the lake was a canvas of stars. In 1892, the town was destroyed in a cattle stampede, a thousand head of raging beef bound for the slaughter yards of Chicago. Ten years later Glencoe had reemerged as a prosperous village of feed stores, blacksmiths, and schoolhouses. When the railroad was built, with a station in Glencoe, the town was yoked to the city. The president of the railroad built a mansion in town.

When my family moved to Glencoe, it still had the character of a village, a life removed from urban turmoil. In the summer, we went without shoes under a canopy of trees along trim midwestern streets lined with Victorian and Tudor and ranch houses. In the woods, there was a bridge built by Frank Lloyd Wright, the only bridge he ever designed, that cut over a steep green gorge. In town, we would wander into stores where the owners knew our names and the names of our parents. Some considered Jamie a bad kid and followed him through the aisles.

There was Ray's Sport Shop, a dark cave cooled by an industrial-sized fan, naked metal blades cutting the air. Ray, in sweat-stained short sleeves, greasy brown hair, and a wispy mustache, thrived on fear, on the terror he spread to the kids in town. If he saw you in a brand of shoes not sold at Ray's Sport Shop, he waited for your mother to walk into a store, grabbed the meat of your arm, and said, "I run a family business. Maybe I don't sell the best stuff, but I sell it only to you kids. If you don't buy my stock, my family starves. Get it?" A few years later, when Ray sold out to a Korean immigrant, the kids of town, free at last, went on a magnificent mall spending spree. There was U-Name-It, a store that surfed the T-shirt craze, pressing decals of Arthur Fonzarelli or designs that said HOCKEY MOM or I'M THE GREATEST AND KNOW IT. I had two shirts that identified me as A WILD AND CRAZY GUY. There was Harry's Delicatessen, where my father often ducked out back to smoke a cigar with the owner. The walls of Harry's were lined with pictures of regulars, including Jamie's mom, who was a secretary in a doctor's office in the city. Once, when I wanted to complain that my father was not on the wall, Jamie said, "Why not let my mother enjoy this glory alone?" There was Sloppy Ed's, a hamburger stand where we stopped every day on the way home from the beach. Sloppy Ed himself was a sort of guru, sweating over the grill and cursing the kids who came in just to play the video games—Frogger and Donkey Kong.

We lived on a plateau north of town, in an upscale area known as the Bluffs, down a winding street buckled by tree roots, in a drafty brick house built in the 1920s. It was a rambling collection of back stairways and secret rooms. For years, my parents did not have enough money to furnish the rooms and every word echoed in the emptiness. As a result, the house felt like a piece of scratch paper, something you scribble on and throw away. When I was older I played floor hockey in the basement and, using markers and spray paint, filled the walls with the faces of spectators and scoreboards and dreaded hecklers. I covered the floor with the boulevards and buildings of a major city. Starting with a piece of Astroturf, I built a cemetery, with overturned garbage pails standing as tombstones, each recalling the life of another dead eight-year-old—my age at the time.

Soon after we moved in, my mother led me through the street, from house to house. I had to knock on each door and say, "Hello, I am new in the neighborhood. Are there any kids here I can be friends with?" It was torture. After several misses, we came to a blue wood house down the street. Before I knocked, the door opened. There was a short roly-poly kid: big mouth, giant teeth, bright eyes, dopey grin, fluttery hands. His voice was high, persistent, excited. It said, "My name is Ronnie. I'll be your friend. Best friend. I love friends, love 'em. Don't got many. See that car over there? That's a Valiant. It got top marks on the test track in Chamonix. My house is old. Let me get my stuff. My butt hurts. Can I sleep over?"

Ronnie was the first friend I ever made. Every day, before school or on weekends or after school, he would come over to our house, knock on the door, not leave. If the door was open, he did not bother to knock and you would come across him in the halls, smiling, waiting to say, "See that car out there?" Or "Want to hear the funny thing about this jar?"

Sometimes, my mom would find him in the kitchen and say, "Ronnie, Richard is not home."

Ronnie would say, "That's OK. I'll play with Herbie."

One afternoon, when Ronnie was standing in the downstairs foyer, my father—Herbie—spotted him from upstairs. Stepping into the shadows, my father cupped his hands and, in a voice that boomed through the empty halls, said, "Ronnie, this is the Lord thy God."

Ronnie looked up and said, "Yes, God. I hear you. Where are you, God?"

"Ronnie, I will not reveal myself to you yet. You are not ready. You must first go home and ask your mother to read to you from the Bible. Go home, Ronnie."

In town a few weeks later, my mother ran into Ronnie's mother, who said, "We've got Ronnie in counseling. He thinks he spoke to God."

I walked to school each day with Ronnie and my brother, Steven, who is five years older than me. In those days, my brother worshiped my father and imitated everything he did. When my father threw out an old briefcase, my brother fished it out of the trash, patched it, and cleaned it with a miracle product ordered from television. So there I was, between a roly-poly Ronnie and a twelve-year-old with a briefcase full of book reports. In this manner, I went grade to grade—from the Explorers to the study of mold. One morning, a gym teacher named Bowman, a crew-cut ex-Marine with whiskey breath and dark glasses—during lunch period, he sent me to buy him smokes in town—told my class, "In high school, you are in for a rude awakening. You'll be walking down the hall and a senior will hit ya and ya'll hit the floor and he'll keep on walking."

I remember thinking, At least he won't stay around to kick me.

Then I was at New Trier, a rambling high school backed by fields and running tracks. There were floors and floors of classrooms and a swimming pool and a theater and gymnasiums and a fenced-in smoking area for bad kids and an auto shop also for bad kids and a power plant with smokestacks rising in a winter sky. It was the typical American high school, with kids swimming by in tight schools—green schools of football players, black schools of theater geeks, tie-dyed schools of Deadheads. When a school of football players passed through a school of theater geeks, there was a flurry in the water, a commotion of charley horses and arm slugs. New Trier is where

John Hughes set his movies about teenage angst: *Sixteen Candles, The Breakfast Club, Ferris Bueller's Day Off.* We were often told that it is the best public school in America, a citadel of success, where every kid goes on to college and the good life. We were taught the names of the many celebrities who were graduates: Ann-Margret and Rock Hudson, Bruce Dern and Charlton Heston. We were warned of the pressure of such an environment—not everyone can be a Rock Hudson—and guidance counselors reminded us that our school district was the center of the teen suicide belt. I had a teacher named Tony Mancusi who introduced himself to us, saying, "Kids, my name is Tony Mancusi, but call me the Cooz. The door of the Cooz is always open; whether you want to discuss a grade or a teen pregnancy, do it with the Cooz."

There were more than four thousand kids in school. In those first months, people who had been stars in junior high school might rise quickly through the ranks and just as quickly flame out, sputter, and die away. Other kids simply vanished, falling to the bottom of the food chain— you might ask after them at the Dr. Who Club. For much of high school I just let myself be carried by the current, lost and drifting, searching for interesting faces. One of the best friends I made was Tom Pistone, whom I met junior year in gym class, first period swimming, toeing the line in our damp school-issued Speedos, taking orders from a mustachioed, comically vain teacher everyone called Magnum P.E. On the weekends, Tom built cars from scratch, and he loved the fifties. At my house, my father looked Tom up and down and said, "You remind me of a kid I grew up with: Bucko. Bucko was the coolest kid I knew."

Tom grinned and asked, "What is Bucko doing now?"

My father thought a moment, then said, "Last time I saw Bucko, he had a gun and was guarding a junkyard and listening to calls on his police radio."

One afternoon, as I was moping through another bleak winter day, Tom looked at me with his earnest drive-in stare and said, "You ever meet Jamie Drew?"

"Who?"

"Drew-licious. C'mon, you'll get a kick out of the kid. He's absolutely crazy."

Actually, I had already heard of Jamie. He had moved to Glencoe from one of those working class towns west of the city, a ragged collection of liquor stores and laser-straight streets tucked behind the slaughter yards. His name was Jamie Drew, but in the seventh grade the girls started calling him Drew-licious. He was preceded by a legend. He was the kid you see late at night, walking the streets of a town, shadowed by police cars. When he was eleven, he had been arrested for breaking into cigarette machines.

Tom led me to a homeroom on the far side of the school. We looked in the door. A teacher was sitting at a desk reading a newspaper. Some kids were in front doing homework. The rest of the class was in back, gathered around someone at a desk. This was Jamie. As he talked, the kids in front stopped doing their homework and the teacher put down his newspaper. Jamie had recently read *Tortilla Flat* by Steinbeck and so spoke in the mock-heroic manner of the characters, an errant knight of King Arthur's court. Rubbing his belly, he laughed and said, "Surely our friend will not begrudge us a single beer, for he is our friend and must certainly know that without beer we will not have the strength to fight evil."

Tom waved and said, "Drew-licious."

Jamie waited until the teacher was looking the other way, then ducked out of class. He put his arm around Tom and said, "Hey, buddy." We were just sixteen, but already you could see how handsome Jamie was going to be. He had high cheekbones and a long nose and his eyes were dark and restless; his hair fell to his shoulders in curls, and his skin was smooth and coppery. There was a tireless energy about him, an inquisitiveness that made him fill in the border of each scene. Before listening to a story, he had to know dozens of irrelevant details. "Where did it happen? How did you get there? Did you hitch? What did she look like? Does she have a sister? Cousins? A brother? How much can that dude bench? Who's from Waukegan?" If he was excited, he slapped his knee. If he was very excited, he slapped your knee.

Jamie looked at me and said, "So what's up?"

Tom introduced us. Jamie narrowed his eyes and said, "Yeah, I know you. You're from the Bluffs." He did not say how he knew me. It did not matter. We were already friends. Tom, having made the connection, now drifted into the back of the scene. And so began my adventure with Drew-licious, and with it a new stage in my life.

I began spending most of my days with Jamie. We met each morning outside the school rotunda, where hippie kids played hackey-sack. I told him stories about my house, things my father said, how my mother reacted, or else about the letters I received from my brother, who was then in his cool phase, which blew through our lives as brief and refreshing as a tropical wind. That fall my brother had entered New York University, where he hung around the Cedar Tavern, let his hair grow into a dizzying 'fro, rarely shaved, drank Jim Beam, and read Jack Kerouac. He sent pictures. Before first bell, Jamie would examine each shot, studying the facades of Greenwich Village. "How can you beat that," he would say. "Fucking New York!"

We often met during school, in front of the office of the student paper, the *New Trier News,* where I was a beat reporter. The room was filled with long tables where the newspaper was laid out, and the walls were lined with cubbyholes where, each Monday, I received my assignment. The assignments were made by Doc Tangier, the faculty sponsor, a strange old queen with a long face, pale skin, eyebrows shaped like boomerangs, and a goatee years before the return of the goatee. I was also in his English class, a seminar where, every morning, another classic (*The Secret Sharer, All the King's Men*) was picked apart to reveal its secret homoerotic theme. One day Doc Tangier asked us, "Do you still use the word 'tool' when referring to an erect penis?"

A football player said, "No, we use the word 'lilyrod.' "

Doc Tangier, who knew and approved of my sister years before, took an instant disliking to me. He selected me to cover the Ham Radio Club. When Jamie read my article about the uses of ham radio, including communication in the event of a nuclear apocalypse, he said, "So if Armageddon comes, the only remains of the human race will be these guys talking to each other?" On one occasion, I was suspended from the paper, punished for my story about a New Trier football game, during which the Glenbrook North marching band had been driven from the field by a hail of pennies. I defended the rowdy crowd on grounds that the marching band was wearing painfully funny hats. Doc Tangier fixed me in a cold stare and said, "Mr. Cohen, you are not the smartest person in the world, but then again you don't pretend to be."

Jamie would sit in the newspaper office, looking over my shoulder, saying, "No, man, compare the ham radio kids to visionaries trying to raise God by computer."

Doc Tangier did not mind having Jamie around, and I often caught the Doctor looking at him. "Your friend is not unlike one of those pained heroes of Greek literature," he told me. "One of those wondrous young boys who reach their potential only after a terrible fall from grace."

Sometimes, Doc Tangier gave us permission to walk the halls, to roam with the freedom of my press pass. The classrooms flashed by, rows of boys in oxford shirts, girls in stone-washed jeans, teachers who stepped into the hall and said, "Back to class, Drew-licious." Jamie talked mostly about sex, some new revelation, how he got a girl's shirt off. He was still smarting from his breakup with a senior, a girl with a car, a beautiful girl in jeans and lip gloss, who one day, as inexplicably as a change in the weather, went punk, turning up for school in a green Mohawk and black lipstick. Kids who envied Jamie the day before shook their heads and said, "Poor bastard." For my part, I envied Jamie even his pain. So what? He loved and lost. I had never even taken love out for a soda. Once, as we were crossing the parking lot behind school, a girl walking the other way smiled at Jamie and Jamie smiled back, and she flipped up her skirt and I could see her legs and her underwear and it was really something to see. Jamie grabbed my arm and said, "Don't worry, friend, you'll get in the game."

During free periods, I met Jamie in a basement common room, where you could buy doughnuts and soda. The walls were covered with murals painted by students during the Bicentennial—snare drums, flags, and flutes. At each table, kids chewed tobacco and spit into soda cans. When a kid, reaching for his Coke, grabbed the wrong can, a howling filled the room. There were also narcs on the prowl. A paraprofessional would sit at your table, rub his eyes, and say, "Fuck, man, I am harshed! Do you know where I can score some weed?"

For the most part, the talk was of sports, with betting pools on every game, or of girls. A kid named Randy Klein told a crowd how, anxious to lose his virginity, he had visited a prostitute in Chicago. Before Randy had sex, the prostitute asked if he wanted to do anything else. He said he wanted to "try that sixty-nine thing." As a result, Randy had to rush home, feeling ill and still very much a virgin.

Jamie and I sat at a table in back, where we were joined by Tom Pistone or Ronnie. Letting his gaze drift across the room, Jamie would give a name to each type of kid. He did this in the manner of Adam in the Garden of Eden naming God's animals. This gave us a sense of strength, of mastery over the school; by naming, we took possession of what we had named. There were, of course, the Football Players and the Cheerleaders and the Honor Students, but, according to Jamie, there were also the Big Dumb Guys, the Little Dumb Guys, the Girls of the Big Dumb Guys, and the Speed Walkers, who, with their minds fixed on college, did everything extremely fast. "Dig that," said Jamie. "Never a wasted move."

Then there were our friends, who also fell into categories. I had played hockey since I was young, so there were the kids I met on the ice in Squirt or Pee Wee. These friends liked to watch the Chicago Blackhawks on cable television or the video of *Slap Shot,* the Paul Newman movie about minor league hockey. They looked at Jamie with suspicion, a slickster never tested on the boards or on the field—Jamie had no talent for sports. As I came out of the locker room after a game, hair wet from the shower, carrying my bag and my sticks, Jamie was waiting, his hands thrust deep in his pockets. He would shrug and say, "Let's get away from these clowns."

Through Pistone, we were also friends with the gear-heads, who smoked cigarettes which they tossed away with a flick, lifted weights, and haunted the low-slung garages of West Wilmette. Leaning over engines, they would raise a hand and say, "Now really wind her out." These kids were strangely war-haunted. They wore fatigues to school and dog tags and talked about fighting Charley. A kid named Glenn Christian, who later joined the Marines, told me he was the reincarnation of an American who died in Khe Sanh. I laughed. The next day, he came to school with the death certificate of a soldier killed on August 15, 1968. "The day before I was born," said Christian darkly.

"Why the day before?" I asked. "Why not the same day?"

"Don't be an ass," said Christian. "Reincarnation takes at least a day."

In movies about high school, there is always the

shadow of something ahead, the Vietnam War or the threat of adulthood, but in our lives there was nothing but clear water into the distance.

And there were the girls from Glencoe, a pack roaming in the streets of town. Jannie Ruffan, who had blond hair, a freckled nose, and a laugh that climbed your spine like fingers; Carrie Sharp, a cute redhead who appeared in a touring company of the musical *Once Upon a Mattress;* Haley Seewall, whose mother thought I was a hoodlum and who, for no apparent reason, insisted on calling me "Deacon." These were our girls, who, like a free space in bingo, we did not have to work for or luck into or worry about. As a result, we came to see them as off limits to the general population—off limits even to each other. These were good girls, whose chastity, unbeknownst to them, we had vowed to protect.

Around this time, one of the football players, a squat mean-faced kid named Motu, met a man in a bar downtown, a man named Rizzo, who invited the football player to bring five boys and five girls to his house for a game, "Rizzo's Game." A week later, five football players took five girls down to Rizzo's, where they undressed, sprayed each other with whipped cream, rolled around on the floor, ate bananas, showered, and went home. The story of Rizzo's house spread through school. At the end of the month, the same five football players asked Haley Seewall, one of our girls, to play Rizzo's Game. Jamie begged Haley not to play. "If you go," he said, "I will never talk to you again."

Haley went to Rizzo's, and the school was soon filled with stories of the dirty things she had done. When Haley tried to talk to Jamie, he waved her away. A few days later, he told me there was too much talk in general. "What is all this chatter?" he asked. "I sit in class and listen and listen, and then a teacher asks me a question that she damn well knows the answer to and I gotta spit it back? I say no."

"You say what?"

"I say up to this point yes, beyond this point no."

The next morning, when I met Jamie outside the rotunda, he would not talk to me. I was offended until I realized he would not talk to anyone. For one week in March, Jamie did not say a word to his family, or friends, or teachers in school. When called on in class, the kid at the next desk would say, "To cleanse his system of the modern world, Drew-licious will not speak for five days." Even the teachers came to respect Jamie. When at last he opened his mouth, his voice was clear as a bell. "So this is how I sound," he said with wonder.

Haley ran over and hugged Jamie. He turned away. That was fifteen years ago and he has still not said a word to her.

A few months after I first met Jamie, he invited me to his house. As usual, we hitchhiked from school, getting off at Green Bay Road and cutting through town. In college, far from the Midwest, I would draw maps of Glencoe,

each avenue and throughway. Looking at those maps, I
would imagine Jamie and me walking that winter afternoon along the lake bluffs, the sailboats pulled up onto
the sand. It was very cold. Following the advice of parents
everywhere, I was dressed in layers. Jamie wore only a
T-shirt and a cloth jacket. He said it was important to look
cool, even if it meant freezing to death—an ethic he
brought with him from beyond the slaughter yards. Jamie
was a lower-middle-class kid living in an upper-middle-
class town. This made him seem authentic and interesting. In him, I found a vitality and an excitement that my
family's relative affluence had sealed me from. In me, he
found the stability missing from his own life. He also
found an audience. Shivering in the wind, he clapped his
hands and said, "In my mind, I'm on a beach in the
Azores."

Jamie lived within sight of town in a trim, two-story
wood house in a neighborhood of brick behemoths. It was
white with green shutters, and there was a backyard with
flowers and shade trees and a garage, where, a few nights a
week, Jamie and Pistone pieced together an old Mustang
convertible. Jamie lived on the porch, an extension built
under the trees—an arrangement that allowed him
incredible freedom. Late at night, if he was restless, Jamie
would climb out his window and into the street, where
Pistone was waiting in his GTO with the lights switched
off. Dropping the car into gear, Tom would coast off to a
college party or a double date or to Big Twist and the

Mellow Fellows, a band who played at Biddy Mulligan's, a bar on the North Side of Chicago. As the sun came up, Jamie was back in bed, drifting off to the whistle of the commuter train.

In Jamie's room, there was a desk covered with pictures. In one, Jamie was dressed as a priest. He had his pants pulled down and a beautiful Chinese girl was spanking him with a rubber chicken. Jamie looked at the picture and said, "Someday I'll tell you the story." Another picture showed a handsome man with powerful shoulders in jeans and a leather jacket and a cowboy hat pulled low. The sky behind him was filled with mountains. I assumed this was Jamie's father but did not ask. I have always found it difficult to bring up any subject that might make anyone, especially a friend, unhappy. As a result, I come to know people only over the course of time, and only by seeing their personalities played out in a dozen tiny incidents.

Jamie took the photo out of my hand and set it back down on his desk. He crossed the room and opened his closet. The shelves were like something from a downtown boutique, with shirts arranged by color, earth-tone to pastel, and button-downs in perfect rows. He bought these clothes in secondhand stores—silk shirts decorated with stripes or teardrops or painted designs. As we spoke, he stripped off his T-shirt, folded it neatly, and, for a moment, stood bare-chested, scanning the shelves. He was at ease with his body, which was as well formed as the hull of a ship. I became conscious of my own torso, which, in comparison, seemed to me a failed prototype. He smiled as he carefully took down a black shirt patterned with red dice. It draped smoothly across his shoulders. "My Dean Martin look," he said. "Brings me luck."

"Is there a reason you need luck?"

"Well, for one thing you're about to meet my grandma."

Since his mother worked downtown and his sister was never around, Jamie was often alone with his grandmother, Violet, a willful old lady with a puckered face and sharp blue eyes. Years before, Violet had moved to Illinois from a small town in Nebraska. To her, Jamie was a boy with too much spirit. To Jamie, Violet was big government, whose laws are best read as suggestions. "Yes, I love her, but she drives me nuts," he would say. "She has to have her hand in everything."

We sat at the kitchen table, where Violet set out pound cake and orange soda. In school, we studied Mikhail Gorbachev and the Russians and the nuclear stalemate we knew would go on forever. Jamie was one of the few kids who took none of it seriously. As I chewed, he leaned over and said, "Want to see a real Cold War?"

Jamie sipped his soda and set down the glass. Violet moved the glass an inch closer to the center of the table. Jamie took another sip, and again Violet moved his glass. Jamie winked at me and said, "Violet, I am now going to take a drink and return my glass to the spot which you have chosen. To prove you love me, do not move my glass."

"Why would I move your glass?"

Jamie took a swallow and set down his glass. I looked at Violet. I could see the battle she was fighting within herself. When Jamie looked the other way, she moved the glass. "Aha," said Jamie. "I have seen you. Why can't you just leave well enough alone?"

In a whispery voice that was like music, Violet said, "I don't know."

It was clear that Jamie was locked in a comic struggle with his grandma, a struggle that reached its apex years later, when Violet mistakenly believed she had won the Illinois State Lottery. Over the course of a summer day, she and Jamie, closed up in the house, traveled the spectrum of emotions from devotion to complete distrust. When I showed up, Jamie told me, "Though I am not ready to kill Violet for the money, I am prepared to convince her that it should be transferred to my name for tax purposes."

A few hours before dinner, Violet hid the ticket, saying, "No one will ever find it."

"You are an old lady," said Jamie. "What if you die? Then no one will ever get that ticket. Did you think of that?"

Violet looked at Jamie and said, "I don't know."

. . .

Whenever I think back on Jamie and the life of his house, it is Violet's voice I hear, a lyrical plea that pursued Jamie through the halls. "Jamie? Where are you, Jamie? Have you forgotten your grandma? Jamie." It was this voice that chased Jamie into the streets, in and out of a dozen stores, and through the spring slush to my house, where he began spending more and more time. You entered my house through the kitchen, where you might find my father in beetle boots and reading glasses, eating ribs or stone crabs or ice cream. When I brought Jamie home for the first time, the door opened on a strange scene: my mother in a neck brace, which she wore when suffering from one of a dozen mysterious ailments. Without a word of hello, she said, "Have you seen your father?"

"No," I told her. "I just got in."

She walked out, and a moment later my father came in, opened the fridge, and asked, "Is your mother looking for me?"

Before I could answer, he left with a chicken leg. Then my mother was back without the neck brace. She went to the freezer, took out a bottle of vodka, poured three fingers, tossed it off, and walked out. My father came in, smiling, sharing a joke with himself. He looked at Jamie and said, "Who is the new kid?"

"This is my friend Jamie."

"Richie has always had real trouble keeping friends," said my father. "I don't know why. But for God sakes, son, be careful."

Then my father went out and my mom came back in, wearing the neck brace. "Is your father looking for me?"

Without waiting for an answer, she left the room.

Jamie said, "Is it like this every time?"

I said, "It gets worse."

Ducking out of the kitchen, we made our way through the house, from the dining room to the living room, which had finally been furnished with chairs and tables that went out of style the moment they were delivered; to the library, filled with law books and plays by Eugene O'Neill; to the family room, that staple of suburban life, which had once been my bedroom but was now filled with couches and video games and an Apple II computer on which my father did not balance accounts, my mother did not store recipes, and I did not write term papers; through the red room which, before college, had been my brother's, and the pink room which, before college, had been my sister's—rooms as empty and forlorn as once-vibrant immigrant neighborhoods abandoned for better streets in the suburbs; through Dolmi's room, the live-in housekeeper from Ecuador, who had dressed up her wall with a tremendous crucifix, an exotic presence in our otherwise secular home; at last we made our way to my room in the attic, that wild terrain north of the second floor.

In my house, the attic had always been the frontier, the country where a man went in search of freedom. There was a couch, a television, a stereo, two single beds, and a window that opened onto a flat roof. In the summer, we would climb onto the roof, smoke cigarettes, and blow smoke over the gables and dormers of the Bluffs, the dark lawns and rusting basketball hoops, blue light flashing in windows where parents flipped from *The Tonight Show* to *M*A*S*H*. "This is the real Glencoe," Jamie would say. "And when I am old, this is how I want to live."

Since the situation at Jamie's house was less than ideal, he was soon sleeping at our house three or four times a week, in the single bed a few feet from my own. Sometimes, in the middle of the night, he would wake me up to talk about a dream or a girl he could not stop thinking of. Or else he would speak of his childhood, the years before his father died, long long days around the house, like they were some kind of Eden. He spoke too of the state trooper arriving with the tragic news, and of his sudden consciousness of the sadness of the world, which he called his own personal fall from grace, as tormented and anguished as the fall of Adam. "You see, every man inherits the Fall but every man relives it too," he told me. "Every man passes through all stages of man, as the embryo of a baby—and this is something doctors can actually see— passes again through all the stages of evolution."

One night, when Jamie excused himself from the dinner table, my father, home from a business trip and too tired to care much about anything, said, "It seems like that Drew-licious kid is here a lot."

My mother said, "Jamie lives here."

My mom began to treat Jamie like a member of the family, asking after his schoolwork, making sure he was home early on weeknights. We worked side by side in the attic, dashing off papers, clowning, and chewing tobacco. Now and then, after he had been around for several days, Jamie would simply disappear, meaning he had hooked up with a girl or stumbled upon some adventure. He might be gone for two or three days, but he always came back, in a clean shirt, smiling, telling stories. On those occasions, I was jealous of Jamie, of the places he went without me. My own existence, compared to his, seemed half lived. Often I greeted him with silence or cursed him for leaving me behind. "Oh, c'mon," he would say. "Your time will come."

"When?"

"When you're ready."

But I could not stay angry at Jamie and was soon laughing at his jokes or asking him to repeat some off-kilter observation. "When you watch an old movie and you see a dog, did you ever stop and think that every one of those dogs is dead?"

Finally, the last day of junior year, as kids tore up their textbooks and lit fireworks in the hallways at school, Jamie said, "Tell your mom you're sleeping at my house. I'm taking you out and getting you drunk for the first time. That way, even when you are an old man, you will still think of me."

After school, I showered and put on a blue shirt with yellow stripes. Looking in the mirror, I asked myself, "Will Jamie like this shirt?" I said good-bye to my mom and went outside. At seven o'clock, I heard Ronnie say good-bye to his mom, start his car, and then he was at my house.

A few years before, tired of taking schoolyard abuse, Ronnie had put himself on a strict weight-lifting program. Bit by bit, he had turned into a stocky, slow-moving monstrosity. He wore T-shirts that hugged his biceps and spoke mostly of cars, of turning radius and zero-to-sixty. When he got his license, he told us, he would soon be driving his mom's vintage Porsche Spyder. His father, a serious Christian, instead gave him a car that had once belonged to his church group, a roomy blue Plymouth with yellow vinyl seats. Rather than complain, Ronnie put a happy face on this development and spoke of the size of his engine block. To prove his point, he jammed the accelerator and sent the car flying. Driving with Ronnie was harrowing. In his car, people actually fought to not sit up front. Once, riding shotgun with Ronnie, I struggled to fasten my seat belt and did get it fastened the moment before we hit a tree. Walking around the smoking ruin, he said, "It is not nearly as bad as I thought." Jamie had asked Ronnie to drive only so we did not have to worry about drinking. In those days, Ronnie would do anything for Jamie. Like everyone else, he wanted to remake himself in the image of Drew-licious.

"What about this shirt?" Ronnie asked me. "Will Jamie like it?"

We drove through town to Jamie's house. When Ronnie hit the horn, I said, "Sounds like my grandma's horn."

Ronnie said, "Want to take a look at the engine block?"

After a while, he turned off the car and we went in. Violet was standing in the doorway. She asked Ronnie to sit down and then walked around him like he was a tree. "I cannot believe it," she said. "How did you get so big?"

Ronnie did a sort of aw shucks thing, then said, "The gym."

Violet put her hand to her mouth and said, "You mean you did this to yourself on purpose?"

As I walked upstairs, I could hear Ronnie ask for something to eat and Violet say, "You've had enough."

I found Jamie in the bathroom, sitting before a steamy mirror, brushing his hair. His reflection looked back through a porthole cleared in the mist. He was wet from the shower and his body glistened; he wore white boxer shorts covered with dollar signs. "What do you think," he asked. "Too boastful?"

I sat on the edge of the bathtub and watched as he ran a razor under his chin. He had no hair on his legs and his chest was smooth. He opened a bottle of cologne, smelled it, made a sour face, closed the top, and said, "I prefer my own smell."

He pulled on a pair of cloth pants and a shirt that was

the orange of the sky at sunset. He took a last look in the mirror and ran downstairs, where Violet was wide-eyed, head in hand, listening to Ronnie. "I do twenty reps of flies," he was saying. "Then squats, then bench. And I gotta find a spotter, 'cause the weight I lift is heavy duty. So you know what I do?"

"No," said Violet.

"I carbo-load."

Jamie grabbed Ronnie and a moment later we were in the Pontiac, heading south on Green Bay Road. We picked up Tom Pistone, whom we found in the garage behind his house, working on an engine with his father, who was young and blond-haired and handsome and wore a one-piece jumpsuit. Compared to my own parents, he was a strange comic-book creature.

Wiping grease from his hands, Mr. Pistone cleared his throat and said, "Boys, I know you're taking Tommy out for a big night, and why not? I also know that boys your age get hopped and blow your cool and, if a girl is present, maybe go off too soon, sometimes in your pants, to your shame and to the girl's endless frustration. What I am saying, boys, is: For Chrissakes, have patience!"

He reached into his jumpsuit and pulled out a hand-rolled cigarette.

"So to help you, I invite you to share this joint, a hit or two of which will keep you calm and loaded for bear."

"What is it?" I asked.

"It's the finest creeper weed, boy. Take a drag, and

twenty minutes from now it sneaks up on you and *pow*! Takes you where you want to be."

Tom said, "Dad, I asked you to stop pushing that shit on my friends."

Tom's father shrugged, lit up, and ducked under the hood, vanishing in a cloud of smoke.

And we were back on the road, heading east, flying by cookie-cutter houses and overgrown parks, by kids walking home from Little League, cleats clattering on the pavement, or else entire teams, in jerseys marked with the names of sponsors—Marcus Opticians, Olsky Jewelers, Bressler's 33 Flavors—celebrating a victory with two scoops. We rolled down the windows and a breeze blew off the lake, and it was sweet and filled with the summer ahead. Ronnie turned on the radio. We argued over the station. Tom wanted to listen to the oldies, Buddy Holly, the Everly Brothers. His favorite song was "Let's Live for Today," by The Grass Roots. Sometimes I caught him singing the words under his breath: "Sha na na na na, live for today. And don't worry 'bout tomorrow, hey, hey!" I liked WLUP, the Loop, which played music that made you feel good about being born in Middle America—Springsteen, Petty, Cougar. Jamie wanted WXRT, which was New Wave and Punk. Ronnie liked the Beach Boys, but Ronnie did not have a vote.

After a while, Jamie put his head out the window and looked at the sky. The stars were out. "Late enough," he said. "Let's go to McDonald's."

McDonald's was in the town just south of Glencoe; it had opened a few years before, amid much protest. The more staid elements of the community feared the fast food chain would upset the bucolic mood of the north suburbs. There were mass mailings, protests, meetings. In the end, the restaurant won approval in a referendum. To the kids it was VE Day, cheers and low-fives, uninvited kisses in high school hallways. In the first flush of victory, the owners of the restaurant agreed to build in the manner of the local architecture, with no golden arches and no big sign, the building as modest as a Swiss chalet. We called it Mickey's or McDick's or Mickey D's—a frequent stop on our aimless nocturnal rambles.

On weekend nights, kids from the shore turned up at the restaurant. They stood in the parking lot or sat on car hoods or crowded in front of the cash registers. There was endless conversation—what happened at school or what happened out front, a fight that had changed the social hierarchy. Mostly, there was talk of parties. You went to McDick's when you wanted to find out whose parents were out of town. Standing in the parking lot, you heard about a party, drove over, drank until the cops broke it up, and then headed back to McDick's.

"Let me do the scoping," Jamie said as we walked in. "I'm gonna move around and be careful and not hit on any party that is too soon to be overrun or that has been sniffed out by the McPig."

The McPig was Chico Ronga, an off-duty cop that McDonald's hired to manage the weekend crowds. Chico carried a blackjack and a walkie-talkie, wore polyester pants and a mustard yellow windbreaker, and greased his hair back. He had a skinny waist and a tremendous gut, which he carried like a pot of gold, saying, "Out of my way, you little fuckers, or I'll pulverize ya!" Chico was a working-class guy from the west suburbs. He hated the rich kids on the shore; he hated their manner, their clothes, their foreign cars; he hated their parents; mostly he hated that they called him the McPig. Each night he would eavesdrop. If he heard of a party, he called it in to the Winnetka police.

Chico liked Pistone because they raced their hot rods on the same track. As Jamie walked through the crowd, Chico threw his arm around Tom and said, "Tommy, boy, ain't seen you and your old man out at the course."

"Don't worry," said Tom. "When we come, we'll come heavy."

Chico laughed. "I'll pulverize ya!"

Jamie walked over.

"What about it?" asked Tom. "Any parties?"

Jamie looked at Chico and said, "Let's get something to eat."

Chico said, "The kid ain't talking in front of the McPig."

We took a booth. Jamie said there was a party in West Wilmette at a kid named Jake's house. "Good kid," said

Jamie. "And he has some kind of home-fermented shit we can try."

Ronnie said, "I can't drink. It inhibits muscle mass."

As we were talking, Terry Montback came over with a tray of McNuggets. Montback was a forty-year-old guidance counselor from school; it was his job to talk to kids, listen, gather information. Sliding into our booth, he said, "How's it hanging, Drew-licious?"

"What's going on, Mr. Montback?"

"Just thought I could take a chow with you guys."

Like so many adults, Montback admired Jamie, the kid he could never be. He asked about our final exams and about our families, then moved on to his only real subject—the difference between his generation and our generation. "Just look at almost anyone under twenty," he said. "What do they care about? In my time, we marched on Washington and protested Vietnam. Kids today care about nothing."

Jamie frowned and said, "It is not that young people now care less than young people then. We're just not as stupid."

"How do you mean?"

"In your time, you believed in your government, that it was good, that it would serve you," said Jamie. "So when you became adults and saw that the world is corrupt, you took it as a personal insult. You thought, 'My God! The world is corrupt! I must cure the world!' So now, when you look back and see people like me who have no interest in being shocked or in curing the world, which, as you yourself learned, cannot be cured, you think we are lazy. But we're not lazy. We're smart. We know that the world is corrupt, that it always has been, and that it always will be."

"So you'll do nothing?"

"Well, I won't become hysterical," said Jamie. "I won't convince myself that my personal discoveries are like the discoveries of Columbus. I won't insult a generation of strangers by calling them lazy."

Montback got up and walked away.

A few minutes later, we were back in the car, driving into the flat, featureless towns west of the lake. We sped through open fields, the soft wind whispering in the cattails. As we crossed the highway, looking south we could see Chicago on the horizon like a thunderhead. The west faces of the tallest buildings glowed in the sunset. When we reached Wilmette, Jamie guided Ronnie, saying, "Left. Past the gas station. Cut through the cemetery. Think of the dead lying in the ground. Watch for the speed trap."

So the cops would not be tipped off by a street filled with cars, we parked a few blocks from the party, walked through backyards, and made our way to a wood house, as simple and insubstantial as a drawing in crayon. We knocked. For a time, we stood looking at each other in the porch light. A girl opened the door and said, "Drew-licious!" She led us down a hall to a room filled with music and conversation, boys holding bottles of beer by the neck, girls angling glasses to cut down on foam. It was like stepping into a speakeasy. I felt the excitement of being away from my parents, with new friends, far from the pettiness and humiliations of my past. Jamie said, "I'm gonna find Jake."

Tom wandered off, and for a time, I was left alone with Ronnie. He pretended to talk (brake pads), and I pretended to listen, but both of us were really watching Jamie. The party had broken up into smaller parties, groups of people in the kitchen and in the living room, gearheads around a car in the garage—the engine racing, falling silent, racing. Jamie danced from crowd to crowd, welcome in every group, too restless for any single conversation. We were still years away from cocaine, and yet, as he ran through the rooms, he looked like a speed freak, determined to let nothing pass him by. He wanted it all and he wanted it now.

He found Jake in the garage and brought him over to me, saying, "This is Jake. This is Jake's house. In the basement of Jake's house is a bottle of home-brewed whiskey fermented by Jake's brother, who is off in the city with the big kids. Jake has invited us to drink this poison together with him."

Ronnie said, "Is it safe?"

"Nothing is safe," said Jamie. "That's why we do it."

Ronnie said, "My body is my temple."

Jake said, "It won't kill you."

Jake wore overalls with nothing underneath and greasy hair pushed back and no shoes. His front tooth was chipped. He struck me as a sort of suburban Huck Finn, fiddling under the hoods of abandoned cars, sleeping on the beach. To him, everything was comical, and he laughed at the slightest suggestion of a joke. That night, he made me feel like the funniest kid alive, guffawing at my observations on the suburbs, house parties, the nature of man. Jamie said, "OK, funny boy, are you ready to drink this hooch?"

The basement was standard issue: damp, spooky, pachinko machine, board games (Risk, Pit, Sorry), washer-dryer. Reaching behind the dryer, Jake retrieved an unlabeled bottle filled with murky yellow liquid. He unscrewed the cap, breathed in the fumes, and grimaced. He took a deep breath, as if he were about to dive into cold water, and drank. He wiped his mouth on his forearm and handed the bottle to Jamie, who took a slug and passed the bottle to Tom, who said, "No fucking way," and passed the bottle to me. The whiskey had a rotten smell that I recognized from car trips through Gary, Indiana.

Jamie said, "Hey, Richie, whatever you want to do, that's cool."

I closed my eyes and took a swallow. It was sharp and clear and I could feel it burn going down. I imagined it glowing in my stomach. When I passed the bottle to Jake, he said, "One's enough." Jamie took the bottle, drank, handed it to me. I drank and handed it to Jamie. He drank. I took the bottle back and downed a big slug.

Jamie said, "Go easy."

He balanced the bottle on his leg. I grabbed it away and started to drink. Jamie grabbed me, saying, "Enough." He pulled the bottle out of my hand and smiled and said, "Jeez, you want to go blind?"

In my memory, the next several hours are as ragged and gap-filled as a home movie shot on super eight: I am in a kitchen, talking to a girl, who holds my hand and says, "Go on, please go on"; I am on a weedy lawn, looking at the stars, tears running down my face, saying, "None of it means anything"; I am in a parking lot, shoving a kid, throwing a punch, and getting knocked down; I am on a public beach, kids gathered around a bonfire, which sends smoke into the sky; I am wading into water so cold I cannot feel my feet; I am rolling in the sand. And all the while I am aware of Jamie, never more than a few feet away, watching me. Though I am stupid and helpless, he keeps me close and protects me from the bad things that can happen to a young kid drunk on moonshine.

Jamie carried me up the steps to the parking lot and gently laid me in the backseat of Ronnie's car. In those days, Ronnie was mostly interested in driving fast. He often used the term *red-line*. "I red-lined this baby at one-twenty-five." At the same time, he was petrified of getting a ticket or of any other run-in with the cops, who he feared would abuse him as he had been abused on the schoolyard. So, believing a patrol car hid on every side street, Ronnie would gun his car up to a hundred miles an hour and then brake down to thirty-five in time for the intersection. That night, hanging out the window, my head rattled around like a Ping-Pong ball. When we reached Jamie's house, I crawled out of the car and puked in the bushes. Jamie took me behind the garage and stood me against a tree and took off my clothes. When I opened my eyes, I saw Jamie ten feet away, aiming a hose at me. The water came in a cold blast and I hugged myself and coughed and shouted, "I am not an animal!"

Jamie dried me with towels. "My mom and Violet are asleep," he said. "So be quiet as you walk through the kitchen." When he opened the door, I ran naked through the house, threw open the door to his room, and dove into his bed. Even before I landed, I was fast asleep.

When I opened my eyes, it was eleven in the morning, the sun was shining, the windows were open, and a warm breeze carried the smell of cut grass. I was a seventeen-year-old kid the morning after his first drunk, and I felt fantastic.

I asked Jamie for my clothes.

"I put them in a bag," he said, "and threw them very far away."

"Even my shoes?"

"Especially your shoes."

Jamie gave me a shirt and a pair of shorts and we walked to town. The doors of the stores were open and the merchants stood in the sun. We ducked into Ray's Sport Shop, which had been failing since Ray sold out. The new owner, Lee Ho, a Korean in his forties, was extremely happy to see us. As we walked the aisles, Lee pushed his glasses up his nose and, in a singsong voice, said, "Best nylon, two-ply," or "Cross training, training two sport," or "Racket wins while you enjoy tennis."

I picked out a shirt, a bathing suit, and shoes. I asked Lee to send the bill to my parents, a service performed by every store in Glencoe, making life, for the kids of town, the very best dream of communism.

As Lee put my shorts in a bag, he said, "OK, do you want to wear your old shoes or your new ones?"

I said, "I have no old shoes."

Lee tossed his head back, burst out laughing, and through his laughter shouted, "No shoes? You really need new shoes!"

Jamie and I started laughing, and we were still laughing as we stumbled out onto the warm sidewalks of town. And all at once, I realized this was a windy June morning, the first day of vacation, the entire summer before me, a new country waiting to be explored.

Jamie said, "Let's go to the beach."

So we turned onto Hazel Avenue and started east, the lake waiting at the end of the road. I thanked Jamie for taking care of me the night before and told him I was embarrassed about how I acted. "It's not your fault," he said. "It's these towns. There's nothing to do so you go and get blind drunk and then suffer the remorse. No. There is only one way for us. As soon as I get the Mustang running, we're heading down to the city. That's the place. That is where it will all happen. In the city."

Of course, we could get a lift into the city from Ronnie, but that would mean having Ronnie along with us, and in that case we would be better off in the suburbs where the inanity of Ronnie at least had its proper context. It was not just me who believed that, in a showdown with Ronnie, Chicago would be in some way diminished. So we waited, kicked around, followed my father through the backyard, gleaning his routine for some pearl of wisdom— "Remember, boys, if you don't know where you're going, any road will get you there"—as each night Jamie and Tom, whispering and passing tools and opening beers and stepping into the street to watch the moon set over the low roofs of town, worked on the car, bringing it around, piece by piece, gear by gear, like a great holy ark that would carry us to another world. "Look at her," Tom would say. "I can see my face in the fender, my god-damned beautiful face."

One afternoon, as I was standing in my driveway, throwing a tennis ball at the garage, practicing the many trick pitches that my father had taught me (screwball, knuckler), I heard what sounded like a gunshot followed by laughter and a beautiful hum. When I turned around, Jamie and Tom, side by side in the Mustang, were daz-zling under the overhanging trees. Across the street, an old man was watering his yard. In the spray, I could see a thousand tiny rainbows. When the Mustang pulled up, I could hear, blasting from the speakers, the opening words of "Let's Live for Today." *When I think of all the trouble people seem to find, and how they're in a hurry to complicate their minds...*

Tom turned it up and shouted, "I even got the fucking tape deck to work."

Inside, the car was like a cockpit, the low-slung driver's seat surrounded by dials and warning lights. Behind the stick shift, Jamie had installed a phone, an old piece of junk found in his garage. It connected to nothing. At stoplights, if he pulled alongside a car full of girls, he would hold the phone to his ear and take up a conversation left off at the last stoplight, a never-ending argument with his agent. "No more openings," he would shout. "I'm only human."

Jamie looked at me, alone in my driveway, and said, "Let's go."

"Where to?"

"The city."

I ran inside, changed my shirt, pulled on a pair of clean pants, ran some water though my hair, looked in the mirror—not bad—told my mother I was going to Jamie's house...

"When will you be back, honey?"

"I'm sleeping over."

. . . ran outside, climbed into the backseat, and said, "Onward."

Jamie threw the car into drive, scooted past Ronnie's house—I could see him in the window, watching with his sad, sleepy eyes—and then we rolled through town. We went by Ray's Sport Shop and Harry's Delicatessen. There was a line outside Sloppy Ed's, the girls in constellations, moving through their galaxies. To the kids of town, Chicago was a place seen two or three times a year from the window of a Town Car or from inside a restaurant; now here we were, lighting out on our own. Under my breath, I said, "Going to the city. Got business in the city."

We followed Green Bay Road to Sunset Ridge, which took us through the lagoons of the Forest Preserve and then onto the Edens Expressway. With the shudder and pace of the passing cars, I at once felt I had slipped the bonds into another world. To this day, I feel the same on an airplane bound for a foreign country. I am on the ground in New York but, surrounded by accents and a mood of excitement, I'm already on the far side of the ocean. I never saw Jamie look in the rearview mirror or check his blind spot or look in the side mirrors, and still he seemed to know just where we were on the highway. He dodged the slower traffic like it was standing still.

We sang along with the radio and talked about the girls in school and the difference between the juniors and the sophomores; then about white women and black women and which is better in bed (Jamie said he definitely wanted to sleep with a woman of every race); and then the best kind of beer, Mickey's or Point; then nuclear war and would it be better to be at the epicenter of the blast or out in the suburbs, where you would stumble around for a few days and then die. Jamie said he hoped to be vaporized and leave behind nothing but his shadow.

About thirty minutes south of Glencoe, the trees along the road gave way to factory yards, billboards, and smokestacks. Jamie turned down the radio and there was only the sound of the wind. I looked at the passing neighborhoods—neon signs, pool halls, apartment houses, clothes strung over yards, fathers over barbecues, smoke mounting into the clear summer sky. I thought of the families sitting to dinner and wondered why I had been born where I was born and why my parents were my parents, and I was soon imagining the life I might have led in one of these town houses, the elevated train rattling past, the city at the end of every street.

Up ahead the sun was going down and the skyline of the city looked like a paper cutout against pink marble. We got off the highway at Ohio Street and rolled by apartment houses and traffic lights to Michigan Avenue, gliding between the tall buildings, coasting along the canyon bottoms. Tom knew the name of each building; he pointed out the Playboy Club, roguish with its peaked cap; the Tribune Tower, a sandcastle at the mouth of the

Chicago River, and the John Hancock Center, saying, "That's the sixteenth biggest building in the world." Tom already had that brand of pride characteristic of Chicago, a pride built on insecurity, a fear that people in the East are laughing at you. For this reason, anyone from Chicago can give you a tour organized around the phrase *Biggest in the world.*

"See that fountain, Buckingham Fountain? Biggest in the world. Even bigger than the one they got over in England. See there, those stockyards? Biggest in the world. And it's not even close. See that? It's the Sears Tower, biggest building in the world."

Looking up to where the sky was still blue, I felt like a reef fish peering at the surface of the water.

"Where are we going?" I asked.

"The South Side," said Jamie. "The Checkerboard Lounge."

Everyone I knew was afraid of the South Side. The name itself was a curse, a slander; it struck fear in the heart of every kid from the northern suburbs. It had once been the home of our grandfathers, a haven for immigrants from Poland, Russia, and Greece. On weekend nights, the air had filled with fumes from their grills—souvlaki, bratwurst, sausage—and the streets had soaked up the warm midwestern rain. But drib by drab the sons of those immigrants had moved to the manicured pastures of Rogers Park or Bucktown, or even farther north to Winnetka, Evanston, Glencoe. And so the South Side had become a great American slum, a ramble of burned-out buildings and tenements, the hunting grounds of black and Puerto Rican street gangs, the Latin Kings, the El Rukins. It was where TV reporters filed their most troubling reports, where cops went for kickbacks. It was where you headed if you had nothing to lose, if things could get no worse, if you were out of ideas and did not mind being beaten or robbed or kidnapped or killed. It is where, on our first night in the city, Jamie had decided to take us.

"Why?" asked Tom. "In the name of God, why?"

Jamie parked on the shoulder of Michigan Avenue, put an arm around Tom, and explained how, on the South Side, we could mingle and carouse with the true aristocrats of the city, and also we would not be carded.

"That's your reason?" asked Tom.

"That, and because we are going to hear the blues, and there is no place to hear the blues but on the South Side, and because there is really nothing closer to my heart tonight than the blues."

Before Tom could think of an answer, Jamie started the car and made the wide turn onto Lake Shore Drive. It was the moment when the chain catches hold on the roller coaster. Tom whispered, "Oh, fuck," and the buildings flew past, following the curve of the shore. We ghosted by the Shedd Aquarium and Soldier Field and exited in one of those featureless neighborhoods just beyond the Loop, rocky little beaches and grimy apartment towers, and

then we were into the real South Side, gliding down endless avenues of storefronts, boarded brick buildings, and
check-cashing joints with one light burning.

We turned onto 43rd Street and pulled up before a
dilapidated house—the Checkerboard Lounge. If only I
make it inside, I thought. There was a steel chain strung
across the front door. A big man in a black coat looked me
up and down and said, "Five bucks." I handed over the
money and stepped into a rank-smelling room just big
enough for a stage, warped under weak lights, a few dozen
chairs, and some long narrow linoleum-topped tables.
The room was crowded with hipsters from another era,
black men of the 1940s celebrating the end of the Second
World War, in velvet pants and candy-colored jackets and
wide-brimmed hats and, below the hats, smiles filled with
gold teeth. The women wore jumpsuits and tottering-high
heels. Walking to the bar, in groups of two or three, their
asses swung like metronomes. They returned with glasses
of syrupy red wine called Ripple and ice-chilled shots of
Chivas Regal. There were a lot of beauty products in the
air. If the storm fronts of perfume and cigarette smoke had
met, it would surely have rained inside the club. Now and
then, the men burst into laughter.

"What are they laughing at?" I asked.

"Us," said Tom, who was making eye contact with a bus
of a man with long Jheri Curls. On his right hand, he wore
one of those rings which says a name (Terrence) and

stretches across three knuckles and is just the best thing for fighting.

"We're not such a big noise that they need to talk about us," said Jamie. "These men talk about rivers."

Jamie ordered three glasses of Ripple and three shots of Chivas. I swallowed a mouthful of Ripple. When it reached my knees, I was happy. I smiled at a woman and she smiled back. Tom rolled his eyes. Jamie said, "No, it's OK. He's just feeling it and there is nothing less real in feeling it than in not feeling it."

And then Jamie was feeling it too, and so was Tom, and a few of the fellows got on stage and picked up instruments and started to play. The singer sat on a stool, a big man in overalls. His voice was scratchy and his belly shook as he shouted, "Some folk built like this, some folk built like that, but the way I'm built, don't ya call me fat, 'cause I'm built for comfort, baby, I ain't built for speed."

When I went to the bathroom, I saw Jamie in a corner talking to a guy in a green suit. Jamie followed me into the toilet and said, "C'mon, we're leaving."

"I just ordered another Chivas."

"Finish your Chivas and we're gone. There's a guitar player on the West Side, a place called Rosa's, supposed to be the best guitar player in the city. His name is Melvin Taylor."

And then we were back on the road, rushing past row houses frozen in the moonlight. Jamie fooled with the radio, then shut it off. He spoke about the blues. He said the blues had come from the South, from farms and plantations where field hands strummed acoustic guitars. He said the blues had followed the Mississippi River north, picking up the rhythm of the cities as it went. He said, "That is why, in the best songs, like 'Bring It on Home,' by Sonny Boy Williamson, you can hear the freight train and the highway." He said the blues eventually reached Chicago, where Howlin' Wolf and Johnny Shines worked as night watchmen in factories and added to the music the sound of the slaughter yards and the assembly lines. He said major innovations came in downtown clubs where it was too noisy to hear acoustic instruments, so the musicians plugged into speakers. He spoke specifically of Muddy Waters, who ran a Coke bottle up and down his guitar strings, and of Little Walter, who electrified his harmonica, giving it a lonely late-night sound. He told us the names of his favorite singers: Robert Nighthawk, Johnny Littlejohn, Lafayette Thomas, Hound Dog Taylor, Little Milton. When he stopped talking, we were in front of Rosa's, a neon sign flickering in the window.

Rosa's was dank, a bar running down one side, a stage in back. Drinks were being served by a quarrelsome old lady with a shock of white hair. The place was empty, a few aficionados lazing in their cigarette smoke. Onstage Melvin Taylor was playing guitar with his band. He wore a beautiful shirt and dark blue pants, a hat pushed back on his head. On the guitar strings, his hands blurred like propellers. With each guitar burst, his eyes widened. His fine-

boned face opened and closed. He sang about drinking
and chasing girls, being chased by girls, and satisfying
many women at once. His music was like nothing I had
ever heard—guitar solos cool and precise and running
out like surf.

We finished our beers and ordered more and then the
music had us on our feet. Jamie threw an arm around me,
the lights of the city spinning behind him like a trick in
an old movie. His breath was hot and beery. He said,
"Check out the bass player, the ass on him. He's got big
pants not as a statement of fashion, you understand, but
because those are the only pants that can handle that
tremendous ass—an ass handed down from generation to
generation—and it is awesome and majestic, like a state
flower, by which I mean a symbol of something else, a
whole republic of guys out playing the blues in bars."
Then he said, "What would Chicago be like without black
people? A wasteland. And to me that big ass is a symbol of
this other city thirty miles from home, but we never see it,
and that is something I will drink to."

In that moment I understood, for the first time, that
Jamie and I had come together on a quest. I suppose we
were searching for grittier terrain, a world more real to us
than the suburbs, a place where the paint and paper had
stripped away. Jamie was my guide on this search, for his
life seemed more genuine than my own, more genuine
and more interesting.

Melvin Taylor finished his set, went behind the bar,

and poured himself a drink. Jamie walked outside and came back with the car. We drove to the Edens Expressway and headed north. The morning fog was rolling in. The buildings of the city were lost in the fog, and I could see the tops of the towers suspended. Jamie's eyes glazed over, but when I nudged him he said, "I'm just fine." And soon we were back in Glencoe, on empty roads, streetlights shining in the fog.

That summer we had no jobs and no desire to find jobs and did nothing but try to impress each other. It was our work. Hours, days, weeks went by with nothing but a perfect sense of stillness. There would always be time—time to wander, time to waste. Most days, we slept late, walked to town, met at the counter of Sloppy Ed's, filled up on hamburgers, and then went to the lake.

There was a pier called Ming Lee's, a broken-down dock with boards missing and, at the end, a steel structure that must have once been a house. I was never sure why it was called Ming Lee's, but some kids spoke of a crazy old Chinaman who had been seen emerging from the water stone dry. We would sit at the end of the dock smoking or drinking. Kids climbed the ruined house and dove off into the lake.

One afternoon, Darren Faulkner, one of nine brothers, the red-haired bullies of our town, made the climb. It seemed that there was a Faulkner for every grade and a brother was assigned to you along with a homeroom. *Mr. Evans is your advisor, Kyle will be beating you up.* There was Kyle and Kit and Tim and Buddy, who formed a club called "The Committee to Derail the Train" and who actually went to work on the problem. We always half-hoped something terrible would happen to the Faulkners, and that afternoon Darren jumped into the water and did not come back up. He hit a pole hidden beneath the surface. It broke his neck. The accident cursed Ming Lee's and made it into one of the mystical places along the shore.

A few hundred yards down the beach, we had a favorite spot, a spit of land that ran out into the clear water. Stretching a towel on the sand, Jamie would watch girls go by and talk about Ronnie Flowers. Jamie had a talent for studying people, picking apart their behavior. It was as if, by studying other people, he hoped to find clues to his own life. He might discuss the tribulations of Ronnie, or his chances of future success, or his prospects of love. Jamie's favorite subject was the destruction of the old Flowers house, which had burned down years before—a fire spotted by my brother, who noticed, on a hot summer day, smoke coming from the Flowerses' incinerator chimney. My father rushed over to the house, rang the bell, banged on the doors, and then, trying to get inside but also because it must have been fun, tossed a heavy piece of lawn furniture through a picture window.

Within a few hours, while the Flowerses, at the Ice Capades, watched a Smurf turn a double axel, their house was consumed. In its place, the family built a behemoth, a New Age shoe box of a house set amid gardens of bad sculpture.

"I have a theory, controversial, so bear with me," said Jamie. "I think Ronnie's father, Bob, Bob Flowers—I think Bob set that fire. Think about it. The Flowerses were in their forties, shackled to a very tired routine. Life was behind them. Then their house burns down. Heirlooms, antiques, photographs—all of it, the whole past with its cargo of failure and disappointment—gone. They are free! So what do they do? The dumb bastards, they build another house, another trap, and they think they can finesse it by building a house that is absolutely modern, up to the minute and all that. So now they are stuck with a new life that was new in 1976.

"It must have been tough for that kid," Jamie went on. "It must have been like growing up on the set of *Kojak*. Never allowed to touch anything. I've probably been in that house five times, and never once have I seen Bob Flowers. I mean, I've heard his voice: 'Ronnie, tell your friends it's time to go home!' When Bob drew up the plans he must have engineered it acoustically so that, while lying in bed, he could yell at Ronnie no matter where he was in the house."

In the afternoons, we piled into Jamie's car and just

drove around. Sometimes we went to one of the underground record stores we discovered in that gray area
where the city shades into the suburbs: Round Records
or Vintage Vinyl or Wax Tracks, dingy head shops with
hookahs and water pipes and know-it-all clerks. There
was always a good record on the stereo, but you were too
proud to ask for its name. Jamie went straight to the racks
of funk and blues, too cool for his own time. Standing over
the records, hair falling below his eyes, he would say,
"Reverend Davis! Man, that's it! The true gen!"

I searched for imports by the Kinks or the Rolling
Stones or the Who. In this, I was pretty typical. I also liked
Bruce Springsteen and was forever on the lookout for
bootlegs of his legendary shows at the Bottom Line in
New York or at the Roxy in San Francisco. On those
records, you could hear the voices of people in the audience, and it was not hard to imagine the smoky clubs. I
liked it when Springsteen drifted in and out of a song,
telling the boardwalk stories of his boyhood on the Jersey
shore. I believed he was singing about the life we were
living—the summer life.

We went back to my house, sat around the attic, and
listened to our records. In the summer, the floor creaked
and the wind blew. Sometimes, as Jamie talked about the
meaning of some obscure verse, I would record him on
video tape. (I had borrowed the camera from C. C. Durst,
a tough fireplug of a kid, and returned it years later when
it broke.) Onscreen, Jamie looked like a second-tier movie

star, the vehicle of a late night mystery. I featured him in a movie called *The Humiliator,* in which he played a white-collar bully. In the course of the action, I am paid to humiliate him and do so with nothing but a cup of luke-warm water and impeccable timing. I used Jamie in *Cross Now,* based on *Apocalypse Now,* in which Jamie, once a promising young crossing guard, has gone wild in the forest, giving people bad directions and crossing them into the very teeth of traffic. In the last scene, I termi-nate Jamie's command. And then *The Embarrasser,* a sequel to *The Humiliator,* in which Jamie and I humiliate the Embarrasser. I am especially proud of the training sequence.

When Ronnie went on a vacation, we filmed *Ronnie Doesn't Live Here Anymore,* in which several people remi-nisce about Ronnie, including a postal worker, who says, "I hardly knew him. Sometimes I saw him playing basket-ball. Do I miss him? It would be unfair to say, but I do wish he were here." When Ronnie returned from his vacation, we filmed *I'm Sorry,* in which Ronnie apologizes over fifty times: to his parents, to his friends, to his teach-ers ("It was my fault I couldn't learn; I'm sorry") to his neighbors, to himself, to his cousin ("You should've been born first, anyone can see that; I'm sorry"), to a toll booth attendant, to a man on the street, to a guy on a road crew ("It's not the jackhammer, it's me, I'm a light sleeper; I'm sorry"). In each movie, I tried to capture a true piece of my world and to show the laymen, if the laymen were interested, what it is like to grow up down the street from a kid like Ronnie.

When it was too hot for the beach, we went to the city to see the Cubs. This was more me than Jamie; he was not really a fan. The notion of being an observer, of sitting and rooting for someone else—well, that was just not Jamie. To him, spectator sports were a kind of mass hysteria during which regular people turn themselves into a crowd. "There is nothing worse than a crowd," he said. "Everything bad that happens happens in a crowd." I told him there is a lot to learn from a crowd. It always seemed to me that you got closest to the real Chicago in the stands of its stadiums. After a Bears game in January, a playoff that the Bears lost, which therefore marked the onset of true winter, I was in a crowd of fans crossing Lake Shore Drive in gloomy end-of-the-season silence. The mood lifted only when, out of nowhere, a gruff cop with a tremendous mustache said, "Get your heads up. Tomorrow's another fucking day."

One afternoon at the end of the summer, I took Jamie to see the Cubs play the St. Louis Cardinals. We met in town, caught a bus to Evanston, and stood on the platform waiting for the train. Jamie handed me a silver flask, which he had tucked into his pants. It was dinged up with impressions left by fingers and marked with the initials J. D. "It was my father's," said Jamie. "It was his before the tragically unfair accident that ended his promising young life." Whenever Jamie spoke of his father, it was in a kind of heroic tone that often struck me as a put-on.

There was whiskey in the flask. When the train came, we sat in the last car getting drunk. At each stop, more fans crowded aboard with pennants and spongy WE'RE NUMBER ONE fingers. Heading south, the train threaded its way through a private world of red brick and fire escapes, curving in and out of apartment houses with quick glimpses of kitchens and living rooms. Jamie opened a window—you could do that on the El—and stuck his head out. Behind him, the images of the city spun past: street signs, billboards, aerials. He closed his eyes. I asked a question. He ignored me. I asked again. He ignored me. I grabbed his shoulder and pulled him inside. An instant later, a brick wall dashed by the window, not two inches away.

Jamie turned pale. It took him several seconds to find his voice. He said, "I would have been cut in two. Right now, my head would be bouncing around somebody's yard. You saved my life." He was quiet for the rest of the trip, looking out the window. When the doors opened, we followed the crowd.

Wrigley Field is at the intersection of Addison and Sheffield avenues on the North Side of Chicago. It is a tight configuration of brick and wood, an heirloom of the last century. It was first home to the Chicago Whales, of the old Federal League. I told Jamie about the great athletes who, over the years, had played in the stadium. Mike Kelly was a hard-drinking Irishman from the South Side, the first catcher to think of communicating with his pitcher in a code of often comical hand signals. Cap Anson, a true racist, described a minority hire in his autobiography as "A little darkey that I met in Philadelphia, a singer and a dancer of no mean ability, and a little coon whose skill in handling the baton would have put to blush many a bandmaster of national reputation. I togged him out in a suit of navy blue with brass buttons, at my own expense, and engaged him as a mascot." Grover Cleveland Alexander, a once-great pitcher, came back from the trenches of the First World War shell-shocked and broken. A heavy drinker, Alexander fell into seizures on the mound. On such occasions, the infielders shielded him from view and made certain he did not choke on his own tongue. In the bio pic, Alexander was played by Ronald Reagan.

My favorite old-timer was Hack Wilson, a squat alcoholic power hitter who still holds many offensive records. After a storied career, Hack Wilson became a drifter, wandering from job to job until his death in 1948. His body went unclaimed for three days. Years before, in 1929, when the Cubs lost the World Series, he had told a train terminal of reporters, "Let me alone now, fellows, I haven't anything to say except that I am heartbroken and that we did get some awful breaks."

Jamie and I bought bleacher tickets. The sun beat

down. There were shouts from the concessionaires. In the distance, the empty train rumbled off to the city. We stepped into the shadowy depths of the stadium, a post-card view—grass, dirt, players—at the mouth of each tunnel. Jamie laughed. I suppose he was happy to be alive.

The bleachers are home to the most belligerent fans in Chicago, a mob seated directly above the action. In the course of a game, the hecklers shout and curse. It's a signal achievement to so incense an enemy outfielder that he climbs the ivy—scrambling up the vines that pad the out-field wall to reach the heckler. I was at a game in which Omar Moreno, of the Pittsburgh Pirates, started up the trellis only to be pummeled and covered in beer. One minute he was on his way up; the next minute he was flat on his back. After a game in which the home team was heckled, the Cubs manager, Lee Elia, blew up in a press conference, calling the bleachers "a playground for the cocksuckers." There was even a theatrical production set entirely in the bleachers called *Bleacher Bums*, a play co-written by the actor Joe Mantegna in which, in the course of nine innings, a man falls in love, a kid learns the meaning of life, a bully gets his comeuppance, and the Cubs lose.

Jamie and I found a spot on a bench in left field. The fans in the right-field bleachers were shouting, "Left field sucks!" I could see the broad back of Gary Matthews, the Cubs left fielder whom everyone called "The Sarge," a pot-bellied, pigeon-toed veteran. He was warming up, playing catch with the center fielder, releasing the ball in an easy motion that sent it across the field on a tight line. I watched dozens of games that summer, some on television, some in person; in the course of the season, the Cubs lived a lifetime. I saw blown leads, comebacks, seesaw battles. What I did not read in the *Chicago Tribune* I learned from Harry Caray, who announced the games on TV and radio for WGN.

Harry Caray had waxy white hair and a pink face with a high plastic shine. His heavy black glasses were a trademark, and he slurred in a way that made you think, The old boy has had one too many. His most famous exclamation, "Holy cow!" was used on home runs and double-plays but also on strange and wonderful sightings around the ballpark. Spotting the right sort of woman in the right sort of bikini, he would interrupt himself to shout, "Holy cow!" Or, on another occasion: "Check out the kid in the sombrero! Holy cow!" At times, he seemed to ignore the game altogether and instead talked about a favorite bar or restaurant or a sausage that had set his stomach ablaze. Between anecdotes, he might make brief mention of a spectacular development: "So anyway, this joint, it has a great jalapeño burger—*there's a triple play*—but, Cub fans, this thing *will* repeat on you. Holy cow!"

In the mid-eighties, when the Cubs seemed sure to win their first World Series since 1908 (they blew it), it was Harry Caray who created my sense of the team. He spoke of their all-animal infield. "It's a zoo out there," he would say. "Leon 'the Bull' Durham at first base, Ryne Sandberg, 'the Ryno,' at second base, Larry Bowa 'Constrictor' over at shortstop, and Ron Cey, 'the Penguin,' at third." He said this was not only the most competent infield in the game but also the best-looking. "Sandberg, classical good looks. Bowa: scrappy, sinewy, sexy. Ron Cey: just look at that guy! Bull Durham: what woman would not want to make love to Bull Durham?"

Jamie ordered two beers and struck up a conversation with the girls in the seats next to us. These girls were from one of the towns out near Santa's Village, a stark nowhere by the airport. They wore tight shirts, denim skirts, and white boots—outfits that triggered certain socioeconomic half-truths that I could not put into words. Here is what Jamie was saying: "On the way up here, I almost died. My head, the very head you see sitting atop my shoulders, this one talking to you, it was almost sheared clean off. For all I know, it *was* sheared clean off and this is just a crazy postlude for my brain, which is too dumb to know it is sitting in the bushes in some backyard."

"What are you saying?"

"I might be dead."

"You think you are dead?"

"Can you prove to me otherwise?"

I was irritated. Jamie was letting his attention be drawn from the game. He was mixing up sex with the sacred. I took a slug of beer and reached for his hand. I held it tight. I spoke of my father and how he had told me again and again not to be a fan of the Cubs. He hoped I would instead follow the New York Yankees or the Los Angeles Dodgers, teams he had loved as a kid. He worried that, in following the Cubs, who almost never won, I would come to accept failure as the natural condition. The better the Cubs look, he told me, the bigger the heartbreak.

"So you see what this means," I told Jamie. "If the Cubbies win, I will at last emerge from the old man's shadow."

But Jamie had already drifted back to the girls, who were rubbing his neck and head, assuring him that he was still very much alive. He made a joke and they sipped his beer. One of the girls climbed on his lap. Jamie had a hole in the crotch of his jeans. The girl stuck her finger in the hole and Jamie said, "Be careful, you could get shocked." In this manner, the game drifted by, fly balls carried on the wind, clearing the wall, landing on Waveland Avenue, where a passerby would look up and shout, "Ours or theirs?" If the ball had been hit by the Cardinals it would be thrown into the bleachers, from where it was tossed back onto the field.

In the seventh inning, Harry Caray stuck his head out of the press box and sang "Take Me Out to the Ball Game." Though he had performed this ritual at thousands of games, he mangled the words, singing, "Buy some peanuts and popcorn too!" It did not matter. It was still terrific.

By the top of the ninth inning, dark clouds had rolled in and we could see flashes of lightning. The city glowering in the distance looked like something from a painting by El Greco. With two outs, the Cardinals, who were ahead by a run, loaded the bases. The third baseman came to the plate, banged the mud off his cleats, and waved his bat. It got quiet. You could hear the flags snapping on the flagpoles. The pitcher went through his windup, the batter swung, the ball jumped. The Cubs center fielder, Bob Dernier, standing a few feet behind the infield, ran with the swing. At the end of his run he dove, reached out, and caught the ball. He waved to the kids in the bleachers. From that moment, Bob Dernier was my favorite player, this wiry dude with curly blond hair spilling out from under his hat. He was not an icon. No one will remember his name. He was just one of the boys who flashes for a summer and then drifts back to his shit-kicker town to work in an office by the highway, coach Little League, and grow paunchy. "So I could see this, " said Jamie. "That is why I did not die on the train."

In the bottom of the ninth inning, two Cubs reached base. The wind picked up. Trash blew along the ground. A hot-dog wrapper danced out of my fingers and onto the field. It blew through the legs of the outfielder and was kicked away by the shortstop. The lights blinked on in the press box. The left fielder looked at the sky. A raindrop fell. It stained the dirt on the warning track. Spectators headed for the tunnels. The ground crew stood at the edge of the field. Jody Davis, a Cub with big freckled arms, came to the plate, watched two pitches go by, plucked at his jersey. The next pitch was inside. Jody swung. A flashbulb went off and the moment was frozen in the light: this big kid swinging from his heels, the catcher rising out of his crouch, the sky a moment before the cloudburst. The ball landed a few rows behind us in the bleachers. A guy with a huge gut held it aloft. Jamie said this guy would no doubt open a restaurant and call it The Guy Who Caught the Ball's Place. "People will come in and ask, 'Is the guy who caught the ball here?' And the hostess will say, 'Sorry, he only comes in on weekends.'"

The Cubs spilled out of the dugout and stood around home plate waiting for Jody Davis—just a kid living one of those moments that sports can deliver, a tiny epic, like a feat from a storybook. When Jody reached home plate, he vanished into a shower of back slaps, and the sky opened and it started to rain.

Jamie and I followed the crowd through the tunnels and into the rain. People were cheering and high-fiving. I asked Jamie what happened to the girls. He shrugged. To me, situations like that never mean anything unless they lead to other situations. Jamie said that no other situations were necessary—those girls had already been as much fun as they were ever going to be. As he said this, we were following a sea of wet backs across Addison Avenue to the El. Water ran in channels along the curb. Jamie threw his head back. His shirt was soaked and it clung to the folds of his body, each as carefully drawn as the shadings on a blueprint. I shook the water from my hair and slicked it back. I saw my reflection in the glass of the station door. I felt sinister. Jamie said I looked like a gangster. In the distance, I could hear a roll of thunder. A train was waiting. We piled on and tottered off into the storm. The windows were steamy, and through the glass the passing yards were lush and green. We sped by the wall that almost took off Jamie's head. When I pointed it out, he said, "Are you crazy? Nothing can kill me." With each stop, some more people got off, until the train was just us and a few old-timers heading to the suburbs in the rain.

Jamie and I got off the train in Evanston and stood in front of a liquor store until a guy in the parking lot agreed to go in and buy us beer. He came out with a six-pack of Budweiser. I offered him an extra five bucks, but he refused it. Walking down Green Bay Road, we took turns holding the bag. Cars had on their headlights. Jamie stuck out his thumb. A Volvo stopped and we ran to the car, each with our own fantasies about some lonely housewife, but inside were two girls from school, a year younger than us and cute.

We drove through the little towns along the shore. Jamie talked about the summer and the summer parties and told the girls we had a six-pack and wanted to be dropped off at the Glencoe beach. He asked if they wanted to come along.

One of them said, "In the rain?"

When the girls dropped us off, we could see patches of blue sky. The girls said they would try to come by later.

We walked to the gate where on most afternoons a lifeguard checked beach tags, but the rain had closed the beach and the gate was locked. No one was around. We climbed over the fence and followed a steep road down to the water, walking between the thick oak trees, the leaves dripping with rain. Between the trunks I could see the stormy surface of the lake.

We left our shoes on the road and went across the beach. It was damp and firm. The sand was cool between my toes. In the distance, there was a group of those Midwestern kids who think of themselves as surfers, even though they live a thousand miles from a decent wave. These kids were dreamers, listening to the Ventures and Dick Dale, reading surf magazines, driving around in station wagons loaded with surfboards, and hoping for even a modest storm that might generate a chop. Just now, they were in wetsuits, paddling out into the water. We went the other way, past closed-up food concessions and boats that had been pulled up onto the sand. Jamie went out onto Ming Lee, lay on his stomach, and looked into the water. It was very clear. He dropped the beer and it fell to the bottom, sending up a plume of sand. A gull wheeled far above. The lake smelled fresh and clean.

We walked along the beach. Jamie left his pants and shirt on the sand. His body was like carved wood, with broad shoulders and a slender waist. He was tan. I followed him out into the water. The rain started, drops jumping off the surface. I dove under the water and swam along the sandy bottom. It was quiet and cool. When I came up, Jamie was far ahead, swimming against the current. A few minutes later, I climbed onto the raft, wooden planks with a diving board. Jamie was stretched out on the raft in the rain. It drummed against his body.

The rain let up and I sat on the edge of the raft, my feet in the water. The sun shone through the clouds and beams of light went far down into the lake. I could see mossy rocks on the bottom. On the surface, the water was as smooth as glass. Fish jumped. Looking north, I could see the shore and the houses built into the ravine, white houses with black roofs, and the wet road with traffic going along it. Far away, I could see the haze over the city. In that moment, the lake seemed to me a great ocean, rimmed by cities and towns, Chicago and Milwaukee on its western shore, the colleges of Michigan on its eastern shore, the industrial wastes of Gary and Hammond, Indiana, on its southern shore, and, on its northern shore, the blue-black forests of the Upper Peninsula, with its sawmills and ragged docks. I thought of the ships sunk deep in its canyons, skeletons in the galleys.

Jamie sat up and said, "Over there."

Far up the beach, holding a shopping bag, were the two girls who had dropped us off. Jamie called out to them, waved, and went off the diving board. I could see his body knife through the water, sharp and clear, gliding along the bottom. He came up once, took a breath, and dived back down. The next time he came up holding the beer, which by now was cold. He walked along the shore, hugging himself. He called to the girls. I slid off the raft and swam to the beach.

And those strange overcast afternoons that would come in the middle of the summer, in the very hottest part of the season, as a respite or a remission, with the lake churned up and a cold wind, so much colder for being out of place and unexpected, blowing in from some far-off north country. The kids would wander through town in sweatshirts and long pants and flip-flops, huddling in the diners and the record shops; or stand on the beach in the damp wind, the kind of wind that has always made me certain there is no God or, in another mood, that there is a God; or wade into the surf—yes, in the Midwest, we call it surf—which on those cold days always felt so wonderfully warm. It was those afternoons that made you see the summer as fragile and precious and transient, and compared to them the hot days were a mindless idyll.

One evening, as I was driving home, coming up the rise that climbs into the Bluffs, moving into the thicket of houses, each with its own story and its own parents and its own kids—and at this stage in my life I considered it my job to know every one of those stories—I forgot, for one strange moment, just who I was. I am not suggesting that my mind failed, or that I suffered from some kind of amnesia; it was only that, for a moment, coming into this lane of familiar houses, the things of my life—my name, my parents, my siblings, my sports, my friends, my pastimes—became detached from me; it was as if I could see them at a distance. It was a wonderful moment. I thought to myself, If I am not those things, what am I? And I knew at once that I was the one who was driving this car, and that I was the one thinking these thoughts—that I was something more than the sum of my parts. For that moment, I was afraid of nothing, because I knew I would survive even when the details of my life had faded away.

By the time I reached the house, with the lights in the windows and my father in the garden, my life had already reclaimed me.

In September, the nights were cool and the leaves on the trees began to turn color. At school, it was talk of exams and college visits to the Big Ten. (On a trip to the University of Illinois, I slept in a frat house, saw strippers, watched college football, and vomited.) Every Saturday morning, I went to a prep class for the SATs, a big play late in the game to make up for years of bad grades. The class, in a humdrum brick house in Northfield, was taught by a high school English teacher who had retired to tend to the needs of her husband, Ernie. Two hours into each session, we would hear a yawn and a belch. A moment later, the man himself would emerge in his bathrobe.

He would say, "You kids getting any smarter?"

We took a break while our teacher cooked some eggs for Ernie.

The class was taught around the dining room table, and after the break we made room for Ernie, who, as he ate, watched us as you watch a TV game show, calling out the answers. He argued over the meaning of antonyms and synonyms, shouting, "Bullshit! I call bullshit!"

Jamie met me after each class, or else he was waiting back at my house, watching my father watch football. We would then head to the attic, where we listened to music and he asked what I had learned in class. For the first time, I began to feel a strain between Jamie and myself. It was as if our futures were taking hold of us. He did not have the grades or the money for the colleges where most of our friends would apply. He had only himself. I, on the other hand, had a father and a mother who were busily charting and scheming my next step. On occasion, I felt like one of those trees my father planted in his garden, a fragile tree, like the pink flowering dogwood, that the books said would not survive the northern wind; a tree that, by sheer force of will, my father had brought to bloom.

When I asked my father why he was going to such trouble, he spoke of the world and how it is organized into tracks, inside and outside. Get on the inside track, he said, and there's less distance to travel. On the inside track, you will find jobs and homes and upward mobility. On the outside track, you will cover more ground but still not get as far. My father was not one of those fathers who spoke of hard work as its own reward. History and his own experience had taught him that the world is often run on connections and that, in such a world, the best you can do is be on the inside of those connections. Jamie had no such sense of the world and no one to teach him. So side by side we walked into meetings with halfwit guidance counselors, but we carried ourselves quite differently. I was looking to the years ahead with trepidation but also hope. Jamie did not talk of the future, or of college, though he said he would find somewhere to go. He was simply enjoying his last months of high school, untouched by the ups and downs and heartbreaks of his own past, living in a pocket cut by his style and gestures. If questioned, he would say, "I'm taking it, little brother, one heartbeat at a time."

We took the SATs on a Saturday in October. "This test will be the end of me," said Jamie. In a room on the second floor of our school, I checked the tips of my pencils. Very sharp. In that moment, I had a vision of kids all across America crowding into high schools, sitting at desks, checking pencil points, passing back exams, and waiting for the proctor to say, "Ready, begin!" And then the heart-pounding moment when you turn over the sheet and spot that forest of empty circles. I recognized myself as part of a generation, a nationwide collection of kids, each the product of the same songs and jokes, each facing something like the same future. We were the kids who grew up after disco, which taught us, even more than communism, to fear big ideas.

I could hear the pencil scratches of students getting ahead. Boys and girls at desks, heads down. In a flash, I glimpsed the Reaper moving among them, cutting down the chaff, saving many for lives of quiet desperation, selecting a precious few for summer homes and private jets. I thought, These bastards are out to get me! Take my spot, go to my college, be loved by my parents. I believed I was at last seeing the real world. But just then I spotted Jamie, dark-eyed and grinning as he filled in the boxes. He looked up at me and shrugged. I smiled, read the first question, and in a moment was just another kid at another desk in America.

After the exam, a bunch of us drove to Sloppy Ed's. The hamburger stand stood at the end of a damp street, the windows steamed over. Inside, the air was humid and warm. Ed was behind the counter, his thick hands buried in his apron. He had a tough old-world face. Whenever I saw him, I heard accordions. "You took that test today," he said. "So I'm feeding you for free."

I asked why.

He said, "Oh, because I hate crap like that."

We ate at the counter as Sloppy Ed told us lies about his days in the navy, fighting in 'Nam, and his stint as a circus strongman, about alligator wrestling and how to tell a real blond from a fake: "Look at the mother." Then we went outside to watch the sunset. In Illinois, night comes on slowly, the sun dying into the fields, light on the horizon separating like the contents of an unstirred cocktail. Jamie said, "See it now, because when it goes, it's gone."

Weeks went by, each day shorter than the day before. Our tests were off wherever ungraded tests go. For the moment, the future left us to settle back into our old lives. In November came the first mornings of frost, each blade of grass glistening with ice and casting a shadow. One day, the sky filled with clouds and gusts rattled the windows and the first flakes of snow fell onto the fields. Everything looked strange in the snow, the branches of the big trees weighted down, front yards as crusty as birthday cakes. After school, we stood in the road, fishing for rides. Creeping up behind an idling car, we would take hold of a bumper, bend our knees and skitch off through the slush. A well-chosen truck might carry you for over a mile. It was like flying. When we got home, our faces were wind-burned and we drank hot chocolate or stole sips from the whiskey bottles my parents received as gifts but hardly ever drank. Sometimes we ducked into the shed behind the house and smoked a joint, the acrid smoke hanging in the cold air. Then, filled with profound thoughts, we stretched out before the living room fireplace and watched our shadows dance. Jamie said, "This summer, after school, I think I'll just take off. We live in this great big country, so why settle for this flat little corner of it?"

The winter went that way. I do not remember much else about the days except that they were very cold and we had to wear many layers of clothes and sometimes my hair froze stiffly on my head. By March, the snow turned gray along the roads, and walking in the fields your boots broke through the crusts of ice, and at night the windows filled up with your own reflection, pale and sickly in the dead months of static electricity and random shocks. Winter in Chicago is dark and lonely, and we survived it by going to house parties and studying calendars, imagining the solstice swinging toward us in the night. Then one day it was not so cold, and the next day was even warmer, and the snow turned soupy by afternoon and we were certain that spring was coming. As we walked in the streets of town, the sound of snow melt was everywhere. Jamie said, "With my help, you will now find a girlfriend."

Over the next several weeks, Jamie set up double dates with every kind of girl at school—smart girls and not-so-smart girls, stoned-out girls and girls bound for Harvard or Yale, marching-band girls and girls with nothing much going at all—a plethora, a poo-poo platter, a buffet of nights that began with Jamie racing from his house in some new outfit: linen pants, leather jacket, a cotton shirt with the sleeves rolled, leather shoes, a fisherman's cap, pointy black cowboy boots. And then we were off to Highwood or Lake Forest, girls peeking out from a living room window.

In a sense, it was the same night again and again, with only a change in backdrop—Beinlich's on the highway, where we ate cheeseburgers and apple pie; the second-run dollar-a-pop movie theater in Highland Park, where we watched *Lost in America*, three times; Sam and Hy's in Skokie, dreary old Jewish Skokie, for my all-time favorite, a root-beer float, a scoop of vanilla ice cream melting into its own foam; or just flying through those sleepy little towns that spill down to the dark water of the lake. In the rearview, Jamie whispered to his girl as the split-levels and convenience stores tumbled by.

And later, walking the girl to her door, or along the shore of the secret beach, and the strange sensation of a hand resting in my own, sometimes dry, sometimes damp, the perfume, kissing or being kissed. (It was a great surprise that a girl would let me kiss her, as it would later be an even greater surprise that a girl would let me sleep with her. I still believe it's only convention that convinces a girl to sleep with a boy. After making love, or what on *The Newlywed Game* they used to call whoopee—"Where is the strangest place you and your wife ever made whoopee?"—I would sometimes hug a girl and say, "Thank you, thank you. That is the nicest thing anyone has ever let me do!") Then the drive home, tipsy and reeling. If I was stoned, Jamie would set the cruise control to prevent me from slowing to a crawl. Halfway down my street, I would flick off the headlights and drift into the driveway. We would then sneak up to the attic, climb into the twin beds, and go over the night scene by scene, Jamie giving advice.

Here is what he told me: Greet girls with a broad smile; be engaged at the beginning, indifferent at the end; never be too nice to the parents; talk sometimes about poetry, sometimes about fights; be friendly to the loneliest kid in school because the loneliest kid in school needs friends; now and then, when you are out having fun, ask yourself, "What is Ronnie doing tonight?" Be humble in the knowledge that Ronnie is doing nothing, or else he is in his basement lifting weights, which Jamie called "heavy things in no need of lifting." One night, Jamie, reaching across the space between the beds, touched my arm and said, "Here is the most important thing—do not work too hard. Sit back and let people paint themselves onto you. Don't fight it. Let them see in you whatever they want to see. Let them do the work."

I found myself slipping into a new vocabulary, which I spoke with a clubby ease: Jamie and I talked of prospects, scores, dry spells, long stretches in which you could not find a date, nothing on the plate, nothing on the horizon. Once, when Jamie was in the midst of such a dry spell, he told me he had had a wet dream, which he called a rain dance; he said a rain dance is brought by the rain god, the sweetest and most charitable god of all. Jamie was teaching me a way of life, a habit of moving from girl to girl, never leaving the old girl without a new girl in the wings—each new girl the next hold on the jungle gym, carrying you higher. With each new girl, I could again tell my favorite stories and execute my favorite tricks; with each new girl, I could again see myself reflected as if for the first time; with each new girl, I could again showcase only my best qualities. If I failed and the many bad qualities were showcased accidentally, I could simply switch girls. Each new girl had the power to mint me like a coin.

One night, Jamie and I took our dates to Greek Town. For the kids on the North Shore, Greek Town was Shanghai before the Revolution, or Hot Springs, Arkansas, before Repeal, or Paris between the Wars. It was the port dreamed of by long-haul sailors, a haven of vice. Just off the highway and just west of the Loop, it was a tumbledown strip of seedy immigrant dives. Each restaurant had the same menu of overstewed beef and cheap red wine served by waiters in dinner jackets. There was Santorini and The Greek Isles and half a dozen other joints, but our favorite was Diana's. Driving my parents' car, I picked up Jamie and the girls, got on the highway, and did my best to keep quiet. I did not laugh or smile. If I had to say something—"If we don't get gas, the night is ruined"—I made sure it was gloomy.

I had been set up with Heather Blunt, a serious-minded blond girl with long legs, green eyes, good grades, and smart friends. I had had a crush on Heather since sophomore year, when we shared a lab table in biology. The teacher, a kindly old white-haired gentleman, had opened the class by saying, "Over break, I had heart valve surgery, so I may die at any time; let's begin." In class, I made many smart-ass remarks and talked back to the movies (*Why Planet Earth? Zinc and You!*) that ran before us like propaganda. Sometimes, with my safety goggles in place, I caused the Bunsen burners to spark up like factory vents.

Two years later, when I set my mind on a date with Heather and so sent word through that network of high school girls that is even more effective than the pneumatic tubes that once carried messages to the far-flung corners of vast office buildings, word shot back: Heather says no; she is afraid a date with you will play like a sitcom. "You're too much of a clown," Pistone explained. "She thinks, in the middle of messing around, you'll stop to make some dumb joke."

It was a crushing response and certainly true, so I took it to heart. Even years later I still believed a person could be either serious or funny but never both. I thought any joke you told, no matter how well-turned, would shoot holes in the serious impression you might be trying to make. After that, whenever I saw Heather at school, I frowned and spoke of continental drift, of nuclear war, of my general sense of dread. I often used the phrase "To hell in a handbasket" or said "It will get worse before it gets to worse." One day, when Heather mentioned a millionaire who had been caught bilking other millionaires, I said, "It is easier for a camel to pass through the eye of a needle than it is for a rich man to enter the kingdom of God." The next day, Heather agreed to go on a date with me. In the car, I did my best to stay in character—a serious young man weighed down by the problems of the world. When Jamie asked if I had seen David Letterman the night before, I said, "I do not watch that kind of television."

He said, "What kind of television do you watch?"

I said, "Public television."

A few minutes later, when Jamie asked what I thought of the new Tom Petty record, I said, "When you consider the fact that, at any moment, whether by design or by some absurd accident, we might well die in a fiery conflagration, does Tom Petty really matter?"

I found a parking spot in front of Diana's. The sun had gone down. The sky was that cool shade of blue often used as a background in passport photos. Jamie said, "C'mon, little brother, let's get a table."

We found a booth in back of the restaurant. We ordered a bottle of red wine. The waiter asked if we were twenty-one.

Jamie said, "Sir, I will kindly ask you not to insult me or my friends."

The waiter shrugged and came back with a bottle. And soon we were eating stringy meat and fried bread from silver platters. The room was filled with chattering voices, singing, and dishes breaking as waiters shouted *"Opa!"* and set fire to plates of cheese. We finished the bottle and ordered another. With each glass, the floor, which was made of that kind of black-and-white checkered tile you see in old Italian kitchens, danced and shimmered before my eyes. On the way to the bathroom, to steady myself, I had to look at my shoes. I said, "I am buzzed, I am loaded, I am drunk." It seemed exciting and dangerous as slowly, drink by drink, Heather opened up like a flower, sitting close and holding my hand as I said, "See how serious I am? Serious, serious motherfucker. Like Kissinger I am so serious."

From there, my memory is a blocked station on cable, an occasional image flickering through the static: Jamie leading me to the car and taking away my keys; me sitting in back with Heather, kissing Heather, saying, "I love you, I love you, I love you"; highway signs spinning past like lemons in a slot machine; my stomach turning over and me shouting, "Pull over!" I ran into the trees and puked into the Skokie lagoon, that lonesome swamp where the mob dumps its bodies. We must have dropped off the girls, because the next thing I knew Jamie and I were in the front hall of my house, looking up the stairs, where my mother, in a sheer nightgown, stood on the landing, eyes clouded with sleep, saying, "Honey, is that you? Are you home?"

I felt the bile rise inside me and rushed into the bathroom. I could hear my mother repeat her question—"Honey, is that you? Are you home?"—and the instant before I started to panic, before I thought, All is lost, I heard Jamie's voice, slow and steady, say, "Yes, I am home."

My mother said, "Good night, honey, I love you."

And, in a response that even then I registered as symbolic, Jamie said, "Good night, Mom. I love you too."

In April, we went to a party thrown by Rink Anderson, a handsome kid with a broad smile and a cool reserve I recognized from sixties movies about surfing. Rink was the big blond kid on the periphery. His speech was wide-open and breezy and sprinkled with trademark phrases. If, for example, a party went south, he said, "Let's bail." If a friend smoked some bad dope and started to panic, he said, "Take a breath and ride down the crest." If you got dumped by your girlfriend, he said, "You will always have country music."

Rink was a strange hybrid, a sweet and melancholy popular kid. In junior high, after years of being the coolest kid in grade school, Rink gained a bunch of weight, his prepubescent body fueling up for the blastoff that would carry it above six feet; for a time, he was ridiculed by the very kids who had once worshiped him. In high school, when Rink resumed his place atop the social order, he cherished the memory of his chubby years; in the story of Rink Anderson, I've always felt his brief stint as a fat kid played a role similar to the role polio played in the life of FDR—it gave him depth; it gave him empathy with the masses.

The Andersons lived in the kind of house you might see in an Alfred Hitchcock movie, a marble slab built into the side of a ravine overhanging the lake. Every window was filled with water and sky. We stood on the back porch as night crept across the waves. Rink had the radio tuned to a weekly show called *Blues Breakers*. He hummed along with Sonny Boy Williamson. Every few minutes, the doorbell rang and another group of kids came in. When it got dark, Jamie and I went to the living room, where I saw the kind of cute little blond girl that has always made my heart fly into my mouth. She was talking to friends, and now and then she looked over at me. Jamie saw me looking at her, went over, and introduced himself. I went into the kitchen. When I got back, Jamie said, "I have it all worked out."

Jamie arranged it so the girl and I were left alone on the back porch. As I looked at her, I wondered what my face was doing. She smiled. She said her name was Molly. We went into a back room and sat on a bed in the dark. There were other couples on other beds. After a while, we walked down to the beach. We talked. I said something romantic. I drove her home. A few nights later, we went on a date with Jamie and a friend of Molly's. Then we went out alone. Then she was my girlfriend.

Molly was just another suburban girl with a room full of stuffed animals and snapshots, but to me she was a Gypsy from the steppes, wild and exotic. I came to know her secrets and to fill in the gaps of her stories. In her place, I built a figure of romance, standing in a fog at the end of the platform. My brother, home from college, said, "I did not know they made human beings that white." Pistone said, "Like so many nice girls, she is plain." Jamie thought of her as a starter kit, a demo to introduce me to the toggles and joysticks. Still, she was my girlfriend, and for this reason alone I cherished her and cared about her.

We met during free periods in the student commons. Around my friends, she was shy. She would nod and blush and look away. But after school, when we were alone, she burned with a low fever, saying my name, guiding my hand. Since I had no experience of sex, I found my way by trial and error, hoping to inflict as little pain as possible. Looking for the sweet spot, we rubbed each other raw. On spring nights, we worked our way from stage to stage— from kissing and squeezing, to undoing and unclasping, to holding and stroking. We fooled around in her bedroom when her parents were at dinner, in my bedroom when my parents were out of town, at the houses of friends, in wood-paneled family rooms in the flickering light of rented movies—*Stripes, Volunteers.* We did not have sex, but instead lived in the gray land of the dry hump and the hand job, where your mind is capable of imagining nothing grander than the blow job, the great mystical blow job that stands as the crowning jewel of any truly worthy high school relationship.

One night, in the attic, with the windows open to the cool breeze, with Bo Diddley on the stereo shouting his fast, dirty version of "My Babe"— "My babe, when she gets hot, she gets hot like an oven"—I was crowned, brought from the shallows of boyhood into the wavery depths; and all the while, my parents just downstairs watching *Dynasty.* After I dropped Molly off at home, I went into their room. My father asked me about colleges. As I answered his questions, part of me marveled: The fool! How he talks! As if I am the same boy that he knew this morning!

When Jamie told me he would not go to the senior prom, I said I would not go either. The truth is, I had already begun to tire of Molly. In those weeks, I had time only for myself—my own worries, the riddle of my own future. Each day, a few more kids came to school waving envelopes, saying they had been accepted by the college of their choice, second choice, safety; and just like that, they were relieved, for another four years anyway, of the dread fact of having no idea what to do.

You see, for the most part, the kids I grew up with had been taught that being a success means doing better than your parents, and that doing better than your parents means making more money—but our parents were rich. So what chance did we have of making more money, and why should we want to? What mattered to our parents could never matter to us. What mattered to us—a sense of style, of experience-collecting—seemed so simple and pure we were afraid even to talk about it.

As a result, most of the kids in towns like Glencoe and Winnetka just went along, high school to college to whatever, hoping they might someday, as if by magic, understand the longing of their fathers, who themselves had made a mistake known to successful fathers throughout history—they had raised rich kids. For the kids on the North Shore this meant seeing college as a hack politician sees another term—four more years, a reprieve, an escape—as it would later mean trying to lose their inheritance in one grand post-college spree, or indeed trying to make even more money than their parents, or trying to spend more, or devising some entirely new notion of success. Of course, to a degree, Jamie and I were immune from such concerns. My father and mother were in no way conventional, and Jamie's father was not even in the picture. Still, this was the world where we grew up, and it marked us. As we got older, we became increasingly interested in the idea of success and in how to make our way, without too much injury, into the thicket of the adult world.

One by one, my friends caught the reprieve—Tom

Pistone to Illinois State University at Normal, Tyler White
to Michigan State University at Lansing, Rink Anderson
to the University of Montana at Missoula, Ronnie Flowers to the University of Iowa at Iowa City, where, though
he could start over, he would still be Ronnie Flowers. In
addition to an acceptance letter, Ronnie had also landed
himself Casey Cassidy, a girl he met at the health club, a
female Ronnie, choppy red hair, scattershot, hopeful.
Ronnie drove Casey's car as if it were his own—a green
Jaguar. Once, when Jamie and I were in the car, a phone
rang and Ronnie answered it, saying, "Yes, Casey. . . . No,
Casey. . . . Of course, Casey. . . . I love you, Casey."

A few days later, my father asked to speak to Ronnie
alone. He began by asking about Casey: "Where is she
from? What does her father do? Does she have a sister? Is
she nice? How many miles are on that Jaguar? How does it
handle? What does her house look like on the inside?"
After Ronnie had answered each of these questions, my
father said, "Ronnie, you know I care about you, right? I
want only what is in your best interest? You know that I
am thinking only of you?"

"Yes, Herbie."

"Good, Ronnie. Because I don't want you to take this in
the wrong way. Ronnie, marry that girl! Marry her now
while you still have the chance. You will never do better,
Ronnie. And this is no insult. Believe me, if she had a sister, which, sadly, she does not, I would urge Richard to
marry the sister."

·　　·　　·

In May, I was accepted to Tulane University in New Orleans. My parents were not home when the letter came, so I went down the street to tell Ronnie. His mother, Chris Flowers, who was baking cookies, said, "Oh, really? I went to Tulane."

At the same moment, in unison, Ronnie and I said, "You did?"

"For a year," said Chris. "Then I dropped out."

Again in unison, Ronnie and I said, "You dropped out?"

"Yes," said Chris. "To get married to my first husband, the one before Bob."

From there, Ronnie was on his own.

He said, "You were married before you were married to Dad?"

Ronnie asked some more questions and then dropped the subject. He actually seemed to lose interest. That is the amazing thing about Ronnie—his inability to wonder, to worry, to suffer. As I got older, I realized this would be his ticket to true happiness. Ronnie Flowers is a kid who gets hit in the head with a baseball bat, but the moment before he gets hit is still the greatest moment of his life.

When I told Jamie my news, the results were far less gothic. He smiled and shook my hand and said he would now have a reason to visit the South. "It will be like we're still together," he said. When I asked if he had heard from any schools, he told me that, come to think of it, he had not applied to any. In the past, if questioned, Jamie had always spoken in a vague way of the university in Indiana or Wisconsin, and I guess I had assumed he had applied to some of the big state schools. Now I didn't know what he would do.

Some weeks later, Jamie and my father were working in our garden: Jamie in shorts, no shirt, dirt-smeared; my father like a cavalry officer in an old war movie: High Plains drifter hat, stubbly beard, cigar. A pilgrim and a wild Indian talking on the naked prairie.

"What is this about you not going to college?"

"Didn't say not going. Just didn't apply. Up in the air. Figure to figure."

"The world is full of morons, Jamie. Don't be one of them. Mistakes you make now, these are real mistakes."

"I'm just taking my time."

"Is this about money?"

"No, it has nothing to do with money."

"Because if it does I can help. I'll pay your tuition. I don't want you to make a stupid mistake."

"Don't worry," said Jamie. "I'll be fine."

In June, the *New Trier News,* for which, on occasion, I still wrote, ran a list of the colleges that each senior would attend. Taken together with your class rank, this list was thought to tell the entire story of your life. In the paper, next to Jamie's name, there was an empty space. When I thought of it later, Jamie's decision not to apply seemed brave. He was the only kid I knew with the personality to face that spring without an acceptance letter. You see, in those weeks, I had a sense that life after graduation was already beginning to claim my classmates, that the kids in school were being defined by their future. Pistone walked the halls with shoulders slumped, as if every passing hour brought him closer to his unpleasant fate—Bucko, fallen idol of my father's youth, was calling. Pistone, at least, went easy, without much fuss or complaint. Other kids— and here I am thinking of a big kid named Will Tickle— had to be dragged kicking and screaming from their glory. Will peaked freshman year. He went downhill from there. By senior year, he no longer had success with girls, or sports, or friends. He seemed to sense that the world outside of school would be even more cruel. He was like a stock that gets devalued and devalued until one day it just drops off the big board.

The future wanted to define Jamie too—people could not look at him without seeing that empty space next to his name—but he would not let it. To him, the coming years were a trap he would find his way out of. He walked the halls with confidence, a plain sentence in fancy script, a bird puffed up with air. He wanted only a life free of other people's dreams, open to the sensations of a greater world.

One afternoon, as I sat in Earth Science, a class everyone called Rocks for Jocks, and I looked at Ronnie—who, due to the mockeries of fate, shared my lab table—Jamie appeared in the doorway in jeans and the sort of colorful shirt Sammy Davis Jr. wore in his prime. When the teacher turned to the blackboard, I ducked into the hall, and Ronnie followed.

Blues Fest was being held downtown at Grant Park. Jamie unfolded a schedule of the festival and said, "Melvin Taylor is playing. Let's go."

"How can we just go?" asked Ronnie.

"Easy," said Jamie. "We drive."

We met Pistone in the commons and ducked out the back door. There was a shaggy-haired school official in the parking lot, a narc in a Members Only jacket, and as we climbed into Tom's car he shouted at us, but Jamie turned up the radio and gunned the engine out onto the main road. We followed the lake past the big coast mansions. It was a thrill driving away from school, the red-brick behemoth fading in the rearview mirror.

Tom put the top down. The sun beat on my arms. Jamie smiled at me and said, "We must all do as the Buddhists do and live in the now—in the great glorious here and now." For Jamie, this was, of course, a joke. He was making fun of all that New Age garbage we watched on late-night TV, but doing so in a way that said, Hold on, maybe there is something of use here. However, realizing that, since our minds were always racing ahead, it was impossible for people like us to actually live in the now ("For one thing," he said, "not one of us has the right clothes"), he decided we should instead be satisfied to live in the five-minutes-from-now. "Keep your mind tuned to the moment just beyond this moment," he said, smiling, "and that is where you will live, and that is where I will look for you."

When we reached Chicago, it was windswept and golden. We stood at the foot of the John Hancock tower. It is almost a hundred stories tall. It goes up and up. If you look up too long, it makes you dizzy.

When we got to Grant Park, Tom, using his fake ID, bought drinks. We walked from stage to stage, sipping foam. The city, following the curve of the shore, rose and fell like the notes on a music staff. The water stretched to the horizon, as cool and clean as a sheet of marble.

Melvin Taylor came on at 3 p.m. We stood in the crowd, watching his fingers move up and down the neck of his guitar. Jamie was at my side. "This is my music," he said. "It makes me feel like swaggering." Then he was gone. A moment later, he was up on the stage—I still don't know how this happened—dancing with one of the backup singers.

Tom said, "He's not bad."

Later on, we stood under the trees, thumping Jamie on the back, saying, "Fuck college, just dance."

It was getting to be late afternoon, and behind us someone set off a bottle rocket. It climbed into the sky and then it sputtered and fell into the lake. We stood at the edge of the crowd, listening to horns and guitars, the cries of a singer. It was sad and not sad. In daylight, you always have a much sharper sense of what you are leaving behind.

I graduated from high school on a Wednesday night in June. The boys wore tuxedo pants and white dinner jackets and moved with the grace of lounge singers. Since there were a thousand kids in my class, the ceremony was divided into two sessions. Heading into the gym for the late session, I ran into Jamie, who was coming from the early session. He had already graduated and was being fussed over by his mother and grandmother. Isn't it funny how people still make such a big deal out of a high school graduation? Pulling me aside, he said, "See how it works? With all your plans and even that acceptance letter riding in your pocket, it is me who graduates first. If the world ends right now—and don't laugh, because the Bible is full of shit like that—I get the degree and you get nothing!"

He opened his jacket and showed me the flask tucked inside. "When you're out, grab Molly and meet me down at Ming Lee."

A few hours later, when we got to the lake, Jamie was on the shore, a bottle in his hand, a cigarette dangling from his mouth. Smoke hung in his wake and he had an arm around Allison Drake, a girl he had been dating for maybe two weeks. He shook my hand. Allison laughed. Allison laughed all the time, but really she had one of the saddest faces I have ever seen—a long upper lip, high cheekbones, murky green eyes. Her brother was a few years older than us, owned a hearse, and drove it around with the windows open, blasting The Dead Kennedys. One night, Allison borrowed the hearse and parked it behind her church. She and Jamie had sex in back where they put the coffins. In the morning, when the Methodists of Winnetka turned up in their Sunday clothes to pray, Jamie was exhilarated. "So you know what I did," he said. "I went in and I prayed right along with them—only I was different. God was up there winking at me, saying, 'There you go, boy, go forth and multiply!'"

We built a fire on the beach and passed around a bottle of cheap wine. The night turned cold and there were whitecaps on the dark water. I do not remember what Jamie and I talked about, but I think we were very happy and spoke of our friendship and how it would go on and on. This was the age of irony, and people dared not show genuine affection. Between expressions of love, we would dismiss it all with a wave of the hand or say something like "Don't go fag on me." Now and then, I looked across the fire at Molly. We had been running downhill since I did not ask her to that big dance. I had decided to break up with her in the morning. And I missed her already. When I told Jamie, he said, "Ever notice how, whichever direction you walk, you're walking away?"

An incident later that night delayed my plans. As Molly and I settled on a blanket near the fire, a strange warmth climbed up my legs. I felt sleepy and started to doze off, but Molly shouted, "You're on fire! You're on fire!" I jumped. The blanket was in flames and so were the cheap pants of my rented tuxedo. I danced down the beach hollering like Richard Pryor. Jamie coughed out the stink of burning polyester. Then, just as I accepted my long future in the burn ward, Molly knocked me down and buried me in sand. In other words, she put me out. How can you break up with a girl who has put you out? So instead we just kept on dating until it was clear to both of us that our fling had lost its flavor; it had been chewed out like gum. A few years later, I heard that Molly had fallen in with the football players and had even gone downtown to Rizzo's to play the game. But by then I no longer cared.

Just before dawn, Jamie and I went for a swim. It is exhilarating to go swimming in the dark with the moon on the water. Past the pier, we turned and looked back at the shore. Jamie said, "You want to hear my plan? I call it Reach the Beach. I'll hitchhike west, not stopping until the road ends, and I'll swim in the ocean, which I've never seen, and the salt water will wash me clean. And on the way I'll see some of America, and to tell you the truth I'm thinking of it as a kind of baptism, a second baptism, but this one I'll give to myself."

He then explained how, growing up in Illinois, we were buffeted, in every direction, by a thousand miles of rest stops. "It's a part of our identity," he said, "being the kids in the middle—in the middle of the country, in the middle of the road, in the middle of nothing." By swimming in the sea, he hoped to return, in time for the last big summer parties, as a man of western sunsets and western skies. That is what he told me, anyway, and I admired him for it.

A few days later, I went to Jamie's house and watched him pack. Shirts and pants stuffed in a duffel bag. Every few minutes, his grandmother poked her face in the door and said, "Why, Jamie?"

On our way out, his mother said, "You do not know the first thing about it, and you have no idea of the coldness you will meet."

In the car, I asked Jamie what his mother had been talking about.

He said, "Not even she knows."

I drove out to the expressway and dropped him near the on-ramp. He promised to call and write, keeping me informed of every adventure. Then I watched him scramble down the embankment onto the shoulder of the road. He was wearing jeans and a faded work shirt. He stuck out his thumb, and in a few minutes an eighteen-wheeler pulled over. Jamie threw his bag on his shoulder and ran for it, climbing into the cab, and a moment later he was gone.

That summer, while Jamie was away, some friends and I organized a softball team to play in the local gasoline league. As the name suggests, many of the teams were

sponsored by filling stations—Jean's 76 was a dynasty—
and were fleshed out by rough boys who spent their days
under the hoods of cars. These were big fellas from the
west suburbs, several years older than us, with greasy fingers and thick torsos. My friends and I were still smooth-
faced, slender-hipped boys. Since the games could get
rough, we only recruited kids we knew could play—high
school athletes in search of a summer fling. We practiced
on a field behind our old junior high, a rocky expanse a
few blocks from town. Sometimes a group of girls would
watch us practice. After driving a ball or making a
highlight-film grab, you would turn and smile at the girls.

In my mind I can still run down the roster of our team,
just as many Chicagoans can name the entire '69 Cubs. At
first base was Reed Cole, a big bear of a kid with a wide
back and an ambling, doe-dee-doe-here-I-go walk. At
second base was Tyler White, who later became a commercial prop pilot out of a regional airport that was
described to me as "The O'Hare of northern Wisconsin."
At shortstop was Jordie McQuaid, who, when buying a
pair of running shoes, told the saleslady, "I don't care
about all that shit, just tell me, Do they look cool?" On the
bench during a hockey game, McQuaid once said, "After
that goal, I could've had any girl in the stands, including
the mothers." At third base was Tom Pistone, who played
in a daredevil style that featured many head-first slides. I
played left field. In center field was Chick Young, whose

face was as neatly cut as a copper penny. Rink Anderson was in right field. Our pitcher was a wannabe fire spotter who actually pulled off a pickoff play that requires the first baseman to hide the ball under his shirt. The catcher was whoever we could pick up at the last minute. On the bench to fill out the roster was Ronnie Flowers.

We called our team the North Shore Screen Doors. To us, the screen door was a lyrical symbol of summer. We had jerseys made up that showed a screen door with wide eyes and a spooky smile. On the backs were our nicknames. For myself I chose the nickname Desoto Andujar, which sounded (to me) like a Dominican prospect not quite good enough for the major leagues. This was the year of the Super Bowl Shuffle, so we even wrote up a little song to make clear our intentions: "We ain't out there just to get a tan,/we're out there doin' the screen door slam!" On a schedule, however, the name read like just another one of the industrial concerns that played in the league: Wilmette Tread & Tire, Gary's Sunoco, North Shore Screen Doors. As a result, upon first spotting us, opposition players always burst out laughing: "Look at these pretty boys from the North Shore! We'll slaughter 'em!" Most of the games were played after dinner on a field at the edge of Glencoe under floodlights that could be seen across town. On a good night, a few hundred people packed into the rickety bleachers and followed the action on the hand-turned scoreboard. Beyond the lights was a stretch of oak trees. Train tracks ran through the trees, and now and then you could hear the whistle and see the light of the engine playing across the trunks.

Before games, as we took batting practice, Tom and I talked about Drew-licious. He had promised to write long description-filled letters, but I had heard almost nothing from him. One night, he had telephoned—a collect call from a bar, dead drunk, proclaiming the beauty of everything. Another time, he called collect and said he was in Las Vegas and a cocktail waitress was hot for him but he was too drunk to know how to proceed. I told him to write his room number on a napkin. It seemed like something Wayne Newton might do. Jamie said, "Yeah, yeah," and hung up. Tom showed up to one game with a postcard, a few salutations scribbled on the back of a picture of Dinosaur Park. And that was it.

"Where do you think he is right now?" I asked.

"I bet he is walking down the road with his pack," said Tom. "I bet it is hot as hell and he is parched and hoping for a ride."

"Does he get one?"

"Hell, yes, here comes a pickup truck loaded with girls."

The Screen Doors had gotten off to a rabbit start, winning four games in the first three weeks. It was a real pleasure to beat up on these big brawlers from behind the pumps. I still have a clear memory of Jordie McQuaid fielding a ball with a neat stutter step and flipping it to first base with a sidearm; of Tom Pistone tearing around third and diving into home plate in a cloud of dirt; of Ronnie Flowers reaching for a water bottle and spilling Gatorade across his gut. After each game we went out celebrating.

The summer before college was a summer of parties, cars parked up and down side streets, kids passed out in back lawns, sneaking with girls into locked master bedrooms, swiping booze from locked liquor cabinets, getting stoned in basements finished and unfinished, climbing chain-link fences, pool hopping, splashy cannonballs, and cops. Beer was a constant at these parties, sloshing in kegs, foaming in cups, turning the heads of beautiful girls who went dancing off into the lake. Beer, whatever we could get, Mickey's or Pabst or Schlitz, pervaded each night like a dirty wind. The big song on the radio, much to our national shame, was "Wang Chung," with the endlessly recurring chorus: "Everyone have fun tonight! Everyone Wang Chung tonight!" Before I took a slug, a friend would warn, "If you plan to Wang Chung tonight, please don't drive!" Staggering to his feet, raising his cup, Pistone said, "Toast with me. To our friend Drew-licious, who at this moment is stepping across the Continental Divide."

In July, the Screen Doors began to lose, sometimes in back-and-forth down-to-the-wire nail-biters, sometimes in blowouts. On occasion, the slaughter rule had to be invoked. I was the captain of the team. I responded by juggling the lineup, bringing beer to practice, banning beer

from practice. Nothing worked. As we lost to filling stations from up and down the turnpike, as the wind carried
each ball over our heads, as squalls from the east stalled
each rally, I felt like the Fisher King of myth, suffering
through a season of drought. To lose like this, week after
week, seemed the worst kind of bad luck. When all else
failed, I spoke to my father, who knew everything about
baseball. He promised to come to our next practice.

He walked over from town, cigar in his mouth. He
leaned against the backstop and watched us field and hit.
His eyes followed the play. He made notes on a yellow
legal pad. At the end of practice, he told me we were
undisciplined, stupid, reckless. "Can I help you?" he said.
"Yes, I can. But you must do exactly as I say. I will not have
two coaches of this team."

In those days, my father looked a great deal like Walter
Matthau, a fact often commented on by minor acquain-
tances and strangers. For these people, my father was
touched by the mystery of that minor deity, the celebrity
look-alike. On a flight to Roanoke, West Virginia, he overheard a couple arguing across the aisle, the woman saying,
"No, it's not him."

"It certainly is him," said the man.

"Then why is he flying coach?"

"How should I know? Maybe he's researching a role."

To prove his point, the man then shouted, "Walter!
Walter! Walter!"

It was this resemblance—the same jowls, fleshy face,

high forehead, grand nose, humorous eyes—that convinced my friends to accept my father as their leader. Since Walter Matthau made such an excellent coach in *The Bad News Bears,* a movie we had grown up with and still loved, it was decided that Herbie could lead the Screen Doors back to glory. Before his first game, we gave him a jersey that said BOILERMAKER, Matthau's nickname in the film. Of course, it was a kind of joke, but my father took it quite seriously. At the next practice, he made us run wind sprints. "It's all about conditioning," he explained. "Late in the game, when those other guys are sucking air, you'll have your legs." There were double-play drills and triple-play drills, and we had to practice hitting to the opposite field. For the most part, my friends just shrugged off these drills. The only person who would do just as my father said was Ronnie Flowers. So my father worked with Ronnie, hitting fungoes, shouting out words of encouragement. "Thatta boy, Ronnie! Now throw, damn you, throw!" When I told my father he was wasting time, that Ronnie would never play in a game, he said, "We will see."

And still, we kept losing. I could tell it was bothering my father. When, after an especially poor performance, he saw some of our players clowning in the parking lot, he said, "Of course they are Cub fans, nobody told them there is nothing good about being bad." My father took a special interest in Tom Pistone, who he said was the best pure athlete on the Screen Doors. By helping Tom was he trying to turn back the clock? Was he trying to save his old pal Bucko? Tom was forever swinging for the fences, driving the ball hundreds of feet, where it died harmlessly in the glove of an outfielder. "So look what you have," my father would say. "You have a long out." He urged Tom to hit the ball on the ground, saying, "You will beat it out every time." Tom followed this advice for a few weeks, smacking balls all over the infield, recording dozens of singles. In the end, however, swayed by the girls in the stands, Tom went back to the long ball. "That is the problem with your generation," said my father. "You each want to do it alone by yourselves, and so you will each fail alone by yourselves."

"Yes," said Jordie McQuaid. "But we will look cool doing it."

My father reached his breaking point at the end of July. He had flown home early from a business trip to make our game against Jean's 76. He dropped his bags at the house and walked over to the field in his business suit and loafers. It was a blustery summer night. The floodlights cut a neat piece of green out of the darkness. Beyond the lights, trees strained in the breeze. Beyond the trees were streets lined with houses. The field was soft and moist, and there was the wonderful smell of cut grass. Now and then, the wind blew dust across the ground. Pistone, at third base, was yelling, "A little pepper, boys! A little pepper!" The bleachers were filled with people from town, some in shorts, some in khakis, and our girls were there, and so were some of the kids we knew from school. Ronnie's father, Bob Flowers, was there and so was Sloppy Ed and the Korean guy who owned Ray's Sports Shop, who shouted, "No shoes? You really need new shoes, huh?"

In the first inning, Jean's 76 collected three quick runs, mostly on drives down the left-field line. When we came up, Tom tried to smack the ball into the trees, then I did the same, and so did Jordie McQuaid. My father shook his head, turned to Ronnie, and said, "Be ready." Jean's tacked on a few runs each inning, until we were on the verge of the slaughter rule. As we ran out for the fifth inning, my father shouted to Tyler White. He told him to move from second base and reposition himself behind the shortstop; the center fielder was to shade into left; the right fielder was to move into center. It was something like the old Ted Williams shift—my father said it would counteract the other team's deadly pull hitting. I said his plan was idiotic and embarrassing. We would not do it. He walked out onto the field and said, "What did I tell you about two coaches?"

He was standing near the pitcher's mound, and soon we were shouting at each other in front of the entire town. The players on the bench for Jean's 76 were laughing. "Desoto Andujar," one of them yelled. "Look at Desoto Andujar!" The umpire threatened to call a delay of game. My father said to me, "You're out! Get on the bench!" He turned to the dugout and called for Ronnie, who raced over like a frisky retriever. My father said, "Ronnie, get into left field."

"Ronnie doesn't play," I said.

"He's playing now," said my father.

From the seats, Bob Flowers shouted, "Go get 'em, Ronnie."

I said, "No."

My father said, "What?"

I said, "You're fired."

My father looked at me, and I could not tell if he was hurt or if he was smiling. Maybe both. He turned and walked out of the lights. He walked home. Ronnie trotted back to the dugout. The next inning, the other team's catcher, a huge fat man, hammered a pitch high into the air. I watched it vanish into the black sky and a moment later I heard it drop into the trees. I had never seen a softball hit that hard. Three runs scored. The slaughter rule was invoked. The season was over.

A few days later, I went by Jamie's house. I told Violet that Jamie had borrowed something of mine, that I knew where it was, and that I needed it back. She held open the door. Of course, this was a lie. I just felt like looking around. I walked out to the porch. Everything was as he left it, his bed neatly made and his books stacked evenly on their shelves. I opened his closet and looked at his pants and at the neat row of shoes and at the neat pile of shirts. I looked at his desk, at the pictures he had set out: his father backed by mountains, the skyline of Chicago, Little Walter in a crisp white suit, blowing his harmonica.

In a drawer, I found a stack of notebooks. I sat down and looked through the pages. These were journals, hundreds of entries, some long paragraphs, some sketchy descriptions of feelings or moods, some just a single phrase or word. The pages were written in the same style as Jamie's speech, with each sentence running on and on, circling toward some greater truth. There were theories and ideas in the notebooks, and notions and descriptions and anecdotes and dreams and predictions and stories. Sloppy Ed Carter was in it, and so was the lake ten minutes after sundown ("the sky red and the water so blue it hurt my eyes"), and Ronnie was in it and so was my father, stumbling through the garden like a High Plains drifter, and I was in it, and so was Tom, raising a beer, and God was there, and so too were about a thousand clocks, each ticking off the hours, and there were short little poems and lists, which read to me like something from the diaries of old Ben Franklin, just another experience-crazed American dead set to reinvent himself, and there were stories, one about a Mexican landscaping crew that worked in the yards up and down the North Shore, their broken-down pickup truck rattling with tools and stink-

ing of manure, "the most wretched, hardworking out-
siders in the world," and in the back of each story was
Jamie's father, ambling the great green pastures of heaven.
On the last page, there was an entry written a week before
Jamie left on his trip:

> I live in the suburbs with my mother and my sister and
> my grandmother, almost a prisoner but full of road
> dreams and the constant anticipation of adventures in
> strange cities. At night, I pore over maps and imagine
> every highway and hill and out of the way town. I
> approach big cities in my mind. I explore every back
> street and alley. From the tops of tall buildings I enjoy
> crystal views of streets spilling into the country.
> Sometimes the streets are filled with traffic and some-
> times they are deserted and I am alone.

As I was reading, Violet came in. I never thought of
myself as a snoop, as someone who looks through closets
and reads the diaries of other people, but then again—
here I was. Violet said, "I have fixed you lunch."

"I can't stay."

I ran through the house and out to my car. I drove
through town and into the fields. I cannot say just how I
was feeling. Like a creep, I guess, empty too. In such
moments, I feel that everything is spinning and everyone
is changing; even the universe is spinning, so the loss of
this moment and this mood and these friends will be so

utterly complete that no one, not even me, will be around to remember it. I don't know. It's kind of impossible to explain. I pushed the accelerator to the floor. I love to speed through the country, flying past cornstalks and telephone poles. Whatever is bothering me, whatever is under my skin—a pain which, like the houses beyond the horizon, I can sense but not yet see—is blown away, and my head clears, and my heart races.

One afternoon in August I was sitting at the counter of Sloppy Ed's, eating a charburger and reading Mike Royko's column in the *Sun-Times*, when I overheard a conversation between two kids I knew in a vague way—kids who drifted on the edge of school life, riding skateboards and hanging out in the smoking area, emerging, like strange tropical birds, in only the hottest days of summer. One kid was named Chester, but everyone called him Chester the Molester, because he had once dropped his pants and displayed himself to a busload of Catholic schoolgirls. The other kid was also named Chester, but everyone called him Chester the Ingestor, because he would swallow anything. In the course of one summer afternoon, Chester swallowed two Valiums, a cockroach, a piece of broken glass, a butterfly, and an entire bottle of Tylenol. The Chesters were talking as they took turns on Donkey Kong, a video game that filled the hamburger stand with a cartoon collection of chirps and beeps.

Here is what they were saying:

Chester the Molester: No way, man, catch it, he is way fucking different. I heard he saw some crazy shit out there and that it *fried* his brain.

Chester the Ingestor: I heard he saw a Swami. Fucking Swami gave him a whole shitload of healing crystals. At the airport, they made him put the fucking crystals through the X-ray machine, and the crystals lost maybe fifty percent of their healing power. Maybe that's what fried him.

Chester the Molester: Bullshit, he hitched back. No. It was the whole fucking thing, man. It did him in! He was gonna Jack Kerouac it out there, swim in the ocean, and Jack Kerouac it back. But something went all screwy.

Chester the Ingestor: I heard he took a medicine cabinet full of pills.

Chester the Molester: I heard he banged a hundred hot chicks.

Chester the Ingestor: Maybe that's what fried him. He has eaten everything on the menu, and now there is nothing left to taste.

Chester the Molester: And he is stuck back here where there is nothing but takeout and skank.

Chester the Ingestor: Hey, you ever make it to the third cartoon on this machine?

I went over and asked who the hell they were talking about. Chester the Ingestor kept his eyes on the video screen. Chester the Molester looked at me.

"What do you mean?" he said. "Drew-licious."

"What? Is he home?"

"Fuck, yeah, he's been home for at least a week."

I did not believe it at first. I thought one or both of the Chesters were lying. Then I did believe it and I was really happy. Jamie is back! Then I still believed it, but I was hurt. Why had Jamie slipped back into town without a word? Why had he ditched me? These were my thoughts as I walked to his house. I found him on the stoop, smoking, looking at the streets of town, his hair swept back, his face tawny. He said, "Hey, little brother, I was wondering when you would show up."

"What the fuck? Why didn't you call me?"

"C'mon," he said. "Don't do the obvious thing and be mad at me."

For a moment, I was actually too mad to say anything. In addition, I felt like a fool for being so obvious in my anger. I said, "Fine. Tell me what I should be?"

"Well, I guess you should just be happy to see me."

I waited a moment, then said, "Yes. I am happy to see you. Welcome home."

Jamie threw open his arms and smiled his great big smile, but it was only his mouth smiling. The rest of his face was gloomy. Despite the fineness of his features, and his broad shoulders, and his clear eyes, he looked washed out, defeated. I asked about his trip and he said, "There is nothing much to talk about." I asked if he had made it to the Pacific Ocean and he said, "Can't you tell? I'm a new man." I asked if he had reached any decision about his immediate future; had he decided on a college? He said, "Don't hustle me, son, the future is not yet in view."

I had known Jamie in hundreds of situations, at hundreds of parties, on hundreds of afternoons, when he was raised up and when he was beaten down, when he was drunk and when he was hung over, when the sun was shining and when his mood was black. But this was more than a bad mood. The light in him, that great mischievous glimmer, had gone out. I wondered what happened out west. What was he not telling me? I thought of my favorite movies (*Lawrence of Arabia, Sullivan's Travels*), and how in each of those films the action is structured around a pivotal scene, an event that forever alters the hero, that fills him with meaning or sets him on the path to glory or on the road to ruin. But in this film, Jamie's film, the pivotal scene had taken place off-camera, on the other side of the country. So here I was, left to re-create that moment from a few scraps of circumstantial evidence: the slump of his

shoulders, the drag of his voice, his end-of-the-world sadness, and how everything in him seemed dead. "What
about Las Vegas?" I asked. "How did my napkin trick
work?"

He said, "Oh, yeah, fine. " Then he stubbed out his cigarette, sighed, and said, "Let's get out of here."

Jamie had lost his interest in the variety of life. He
would sit for hours on his porch staring at his toes. He
spoke under his breath, or in clipped sentences without
meaning, or blandly of great events. The color had gone
out of his face. His eyes were as cold as embers. Even in
the same room, he was far away. He said nothing about his
trip. Everyone was worried about him. It was an epic of
sadness, and it overwhelmed our little world. We decided,
in the last week of the summer, since my parents were out
of town, to throw a marathon party for Jamie, which we
hoped would lift him from his funk. I filled the refrigerator with food and sangria and made up the beds in the
guest bedrooms and set out pictures I had taken in happier times: one showed me and Jamie with linked arms at
Wrigley Field, another showed us in a toy store battling
with croquet mallets.

Late in the afternoon Ronnie drove me to Evanston,
where we bought beer from an Indian who, because we
were young and stupid and knew just a little of the history
of the world, we called Gandhi. On the way, talking about

the real Gandhi, Ronnie said, "Some people are nice and some people are good, but Gandhi, now that was a great guy!" Then Ronnie grew very somber. "Maybe there is something seriously wrong with Jamie," he said. "Maybe it is something that even a marathon party cannot fix."

I said, "Ronnie, there is nothing that a marathon party cannot fix."

When we got home, the street was lined with cars and my house was filled with people. Some were girls from school, some were friends from the beach, but most were people we had never seen. It was a windy end-of-summer night, and I could smell pine needles burning. I found Jamie in the backyard laughing and drinking a beer. Tom put the speakers in the windows so we could listen to R.E.M. and the blues. Ronnie came out of the house with a glass of Old Grandad. He had never tasted alcohol before. Ever since he began lifting weights, which he had done in hopes of escaping abuse, he refused cocktails, saying, "My body is my temple." Again in hopes of escaping abuse, he now wanted a drink. He was soon going to college and so planned to advance into that club of whiskey drinkers he was certain existed out there in the world. He threw back his head and swallowed. He wiped his mouth and said, "OK if I have one of those beers?"

Within just a few minutes, I could see the liquor take its effect. Ronnie slouched into his own shoulders and his movements turned loose and easy. Then something truly strange happened; it is something I have never read about, or seen on television, or anything. Ronnie Flowers, who had never been east of Fort Wayne, Indiana, began to speak with a British accent. A Yorkshire accent, really, slang from the factory towns of northern England. He slapped Jamie on the back and said, "Eight boys, eight for nine and they as shy as heifers. You'll never fill a bag, but the ones you land you'll be glad you landed." We were mystified. At last, Jamie surmised that, late one night, Ronnie must have fallen asleep before a television set that was airing an old John Ford movie. "It must have gone straight down into his subconscious," said Jamie. "Besides, that is how Ronnie has always wanted to live. Just another one of the blokes yammering away in the pub."

I had intended to look after Jamie, to care for him, to nurture him, but I got drunk and started to have fun and then really worried about no one but myself.

Now and then, Ronnie shotgunned a beer or threw back three fingers of whiskey, shouting, "Aye, mate, ain't we friends after all!" Tom did back flips to impress the girls. If ever he learned the truth—that these flips impressed the boys far more than they ever did the girls— he would have been horrified. Tyler White was in the bathroom, adding and dividing floor tiles. Rink Anderson kissed a girl like someone in a Norman Rockwell painting—leaning forward, hands behind his back, lips outstretched. I was with Jamie in the attic listening to music as the party raged below. In the manner of Roman senators, we occasionally entertained a visitor from the lower floors. "Tell me," Jamie would ask, "are the people happy?" The party waxed and waned, ebbed and flowed; in the mornings, my friends slept in guest beds or on floors. In the afternoons, when I took a shower, I set a vodka and orange juice on the sink, which I sipped as I shaved. I felt like Bobby Darin.

On the third night of the party, Jamie and I drove to the town dump, to throw out several Hefty Bags of empty beer cans. As I parked alongside the Dumpster, a cop pulled in behind me, party lights flashing. A moment later, he was at the window. I could see only his uniform and the brim of his hat. In an ominous cop voice, he said, "What are you boys doing out here?"

I said, "We have come to throw away some trash."

The cop said, "Where is this so-called trash?"

I said, "In the hatchback, sir."

The cop said, "Can I see this so-called trash?"

I said, "Be my guest."

A moment later, I heard the cop poking through our empties. He said, "Oh-ho-ho, *that* kind of trash!" I looked at Jamie. He was laughing. Then the cop was back in the window, saying, "Who bought you this trash?"

I said, "We made it ourselves, sir."

"Look at it from my point of view," said the cop. "I got underage kids driving around with a load of trash they are not authorized to have."

He took out a note pad and wrote down our names. "I am not letting you discharge this trash at this site," he said. "Furthermore, if I find this trash in any public Dumpster at any time over the next two weeks—and I will be looking, boys, believe that—then I am coming after you with all of my power. Take this trash home and show it to your parents."

Jamie and I drove to the Sheraton Hotel by the highway and dumped the bags in the parking lot.

As the week dragged on, friends began to drift away. The party was a train making stops in the country, and at each stop a few people got off. It was strange. One minute, a friend would be just as ragged and poorly drawn as me, and the next minute he was as fresh as a new painting, hair still wet from the shower, chinos and button-down shirt, holding a suitcase. He walks from room to room, shaking hands, saying his good-byes. "Well, it's been an honor to know you!" And he is off to college: North Dakota, or Indiana, or Minnesota, or Iowa. Tyler White was gone, and then Rink Anderson, and then Jordie McQuaid, and then Ronnie Flowers, saying, "Good day to you, chaps. Good day!" One afternoon, as I was sitting in the yard, Tom Pistone came out in pleated pants and a cloth coat, a bag slung over his shoulder. He said, "So long, boys, I'm off to Normal." And then it was just me and Jamie, laughing and drinking, spinning through the night. And then Jamie was shaking me awake and I was looking up at him as if I were on an operating table hazy with anesthetic and he was showered and neatly dressed, saying, "Hey, little brother, I'm off. Gonna catch a ride and see if I can enroll in that big school they got out there in Kansas. I stashed the last six-pack in the wall. William Burroughs lives in Lawrence, so it can't be all bad."

I fell back asleep. When I woke up, the sun was low in the sky. I walked though the empty house. The rooms had been scrubbed clean. Jamie is a neat freak. He often said, "Destroy what you must but clean what you can." I stood in the driveway. After a while, my parents came home. We had a farewell dinner. That night, I lay awake in bed listening to the wind and to the message it was carving out of the dead air. It was speaking of farewells and voyages, how roads lead on to roads. In the morning, I showered, put on clean clothes, and left for college.

Part Two

In the fall of 1986, I arrived in New Orleans. I had left a gray, sober, Germanic city and all at once found myself in a drunken, weedy greenhouse of a town. New Orleans looks like a capital in the French Antilles, a port backed by swamps. Tulane is in the English quarter of the city, and the houses are ramshackle and Victorian. The leaves cast spiky shadows, and the vines running up the carports glisten in the drenching tropical rain. Each afternoon, I would climb up to the roof of my dorm, where I could look out over the neat greens of campus to the twisting coil of the river, tugboats heading toward the Gulf of Mexico. In the evening, the sun dropped through bands of dust and the sky passed through the colors of a mood ring—placid, agitated, angry.

I fell in with a group of boys from the dorms, prep

schoolers from the South with names like Whit and Ricky and Trey, who wore white bucks and backwards baseball caps, who loved Hank Williams Jr. even more than Hank Williams Sr., and who greeted you from a distance, shouting, "All right, son, let's go drink a couple!" After class, we would wander past the rundown mansions of the Garden District, with open doors offering a quick glimpse of marble and velvet. We talked about music or sports or high school, and I told stories about Jamie, which, late at night, grew into legends. On Saturdays, we walked down flat streets to the levee, the Mississippi River catching and reflecting the midday sun, so muddy the water looked like chocolate, and on the other side the smokestacks and industry of Algiers. We sat on the grass and imagined each other's hometowns, but I knew these friendships were just a temporary alliance. Whenever I found the chance, I slipped away.

Jamie was still very much at the center of my thoughts. I knew he had gone to Kansas, or so he had said, but I could not really imagine his life there. He did not write in those first weeks, and his mother, when I called, had also not heard from him. Once, in a bar, I met a girl who was visiting from the University of Kansas and, when I asked if she had heard of Jamie Drew, she said, "Drew-licious?" So somehow the nickname had tagged along. Well, that was good news, anyway. He was staking out his legend. Also, I knew some other kids that went to KU and from them there were rumors that Jamie had moved on to serious drugs, or was drunk all the time, or was seen with the worst kind of people in the worst kind of dives. And then there was still that other life that he lived in my mind. I thought of him whenever things went badly for me, when a girl shut me down, say, because in such moments Jamie gave me that special loser's solace: "Oh, baby, you've made a terrible mistake. You should meet my friend Jamie; he and I are superstars back on the shore." Just the memory of Jamie could make me feel that way. And of course I thought of him on those great nights that just went clicking along. At times, I felt like a fisherman, netting colorful experiences that I would enjoy not now so much as later, back at home, in some dark bar, where I would share them with my best friend.

A few nights a week, I would ride down to the French Quarter. The streetcar ran past brick walls painted over with advertisements, my favorite being the sign for HERMAN AND SON PAINTERS, benevolent old white-haired Herman over the words TWENTY YEARS' EXPERIENCE, next to his son, dark-eyed and mischievous, over the words FULLY INSURED. I would ride to the end of the line and then walk into the narrow, twisting streets of the French Quarter. The French came here first, settling at the end of the seventeenth century, building a haven for Jesuits and businessmen fifty miles from the mouth of the Mississippi River. Then came the Spanish, then the French again, then the Americans. The city has always been the great drain of the continent. It stinks with the sadness of the last century. From open doors you hear foot-stomping and horn-blowing. Is there anything better than standing in the street and listening to horns? Or going around the corner to Felix's Oyster Bar for turtle soup, or having a drink at the Napoleon House with its open shutters and its ceiling fans? Like Venice, New Orleans is a monument that has been allowed to dilapidate, an aristocrat pulled from her horse and gawked at by men with money belts.

Of course, some people feel that if a pleasure or a place such as Royal Street has been discovered by yokels, by happy idiots, by guys on convention, then it is ruined and must be abandoned. Or, worse yet, it is ruined and so can be enjoyed only through a heavy filter of irony, a cheesecloth thrown up between yourself and the world. To me, this response is cowardly, an excuse to abandon the field to the yokels. It is running in the face of fire. So while other kids at Tulane avoided the Quarter, I spent many nights there, drawn to the same world that Jamie and I once looked for in the blues. From each trip I brought back some image or impression—a parrot-colored house glistening in the rain, a sloop plowing through the coffee-colored river—that I could turn over in my mind.

But most of the time I was just another kid on campus, far from home, lonely. There was a sense of abandon at Tulane that struck me as slightly insane. It seemed that many of these kids had come here on a spree, hoping at last to test the lessons of their parents or simply to flush them away. Of the twenty or so people on my freshman floor, only about five were around to graduate. The rest transferred or dropped out or burned away like debris on reentry. In Spanish class, I sat next to a kid who, on his desk, in addition to his notebook and pencils, set down a fruity cocktail—bright blue in a curvy souvenir glass, with straws, umbrellas, and a slice of pineapple. The teacher, a bug-eyed Honduran, spotted the drink and said in Spanish—everything in Spanish—"And what is that?"

"A Blue Hawaii."

The teacher ordered the kid to throw out the drink. The kid said that, since he was eighteen, his drink was legal, and since it was a Blue Hawaii it was refreshing, adding, "And, of course, it is delicious."

The teacher told the kid he would have to make a choice, so the kid gathered his notebooks and pencils and left with the cocktail.

Another day, I came to the same class after sharing a joint in the dorms. I was late and the chairs had been arranged in a circle, and this was confusing. As I sat down, the teacher said something to me in Spanish. It sounded like gibberish. I said, "Come again?"

He said *"Tengo"* or *"Tenga"* or "Tony," and there was something about *"la luz."* I somehow got the idea that I was being asked to turn off the lights. I reached over and flipped the switch. The room was in the basement, so all at once we were plunged into darkness. I could hear the other kids laughing. The teacher said something in angry gibberish.

I said, *"¿Cualo?"*
He said, "Richard, turn on the damn lights."

By November, I had at last found my way into a group
of friends, most of whom lived in a house a few blocks
from campus. The house had crooked shutters and a sag-
ging porch and was set before a curtain of swaying pine. If
you stopped by the house, you might find rooms alive
with conversation, or a party about to spill over, or just
kids sleeping it off. The boys in the house were pitied and
envied by the other kids on campus, because they were
idle and lawless and wild. They dressed in torn jeans
or dirty shorts, in shirts with no buttons and torn cuffs. In
the winter, some wore chewed-up black overcoats that
dragged along the ground. They went to class only if
moved to do so and slept where they fell, on couches or in
yards; now and then, when they tired of the city, they
headed north to the forests of Mississippi, emerging a few
days later with stories and game, and shared both in big
cookouts behind the house.

I would stand in the backyard, talking to each of the
boys, trying to find a way into the world they had built.
There was Joseph Rivers, a gloomy, dark-eyed Texan,
who wandered far from the familiar haunts, seeking out
desolate places. When Joseph fell into a black mood, he
would walk to a fraternity bar and pick a fight with a guy
twice his size, and the beating he took always made him

feel much better. There was Kip Clawdell, whom everyone called Crawdad, a creature of the great indoors, of skunky rooms, gossip, late-night talks. There was Tim Tree, so tall and sallow he looked like he had stepped from a painting by Velázquez. Tree spoke of binges and bar fights. Fog seemed to roll from the pauses between his sentences. There was Magna Para, short and stocky, with a glass eye. Now and then, Magna Para dropped his eye into a beer, chugged the beer, and caught the eye between his teeth. He called himself Cyclops. There was "Handsome" Hansen Jackson, the only son of a local judge, who, each February, so they could play at his Mardi Gras party, furloughed a combo of jazz musicians. Hansen was clever enough never to say anything anyone could understand. He spoke of the inanity of college professors, the portentousness of Hegel, the insipidness of rock lyrics. I did not like him at all. There was Maximilian Franco, a sophomore who failed out the semester before. In the middle of the year, Franco's father hired two goons to kidnap Franco and return him to his home in Paraguay. In addition to a blue blanket and a student ID, Franco left behind a Nintendo, which, over the next three years, traveled from room to room, driving down grades and ruining friendships. It was called the curse of Maximilian Franco. One afternoon, Joseph Rivers, a liberator whose name should be remembered with that of Simón Bolívar, hurled the game off the second-floor balcony, smashing it to pieces and freeing the house.

For the most part, these kids had met in the dorms, or at parties, or out at the bars, and they had been drawn together by a shared sense of style. This was not necessarily something they themselves possessed or even understood; it was instead something they badly wanted to *be.* Some of them called it *keek,* as in "He has keek," or "Very keek," or "Feel the keekness." If you asked them to explain *keek,* they would say, "Explain *jazz.*" I suppose *keek* was a way of carrying yourself, of looking at life: of never being wrong-footed or buried by a situation or suckered by fake writing, or fake music, or fake anything. It was being in the right place at the right time, or creating the right place simply by being there; it was enjoying whatever moment you were living without judging it for its value. Did they drink, did they take drugs? Yes, yes of course, but not with that tired old hippie idea of enlightenment. They took drugs because there were drugs to be taken and because drugs were fun to take. In keek, I recognized a quality I had first seen in Jamie, whom I came to think of as the complete possessor of keek, a natural aristocrat who, whether he knows it or not, is down here slumming with the rabble.

The creators of keek, those who brought the ideal of it to Tulane, anyway, were three guys from Missouri: Waxey James, Eli Tenafly, and Matt Congress, called Congolese, or Congo. Congress would often say, "If you can talk you can sing, if you can walk you can dance—a saying from the Congo." These friends had known each other as kids, and they had with each other a total ease. Each of them had been a successful high school athlete, and there was something gone to seed in even their smallest gestures. Eli Tenafly had dropped out of school years before and was simply hanging around, drawling in an accent of no known territory. He was crafty and could read weakness. Once, when my friend Billy had, for the first time, taken a tab of acid and was wavering between here and there, he met Eli Tenafly, who said, "Billy, I want you to know something: you are never coming down." Waxey James wore leather pants and snakeskin boots with steel tips. Though he was not yet twenty-two, his hair had gone completely white. Once, driving by late at night, I saw him skulking around the Desire Projects. And Congo? Well, Congo was going crazy; anyone could see that.

It was Congo who brought me to the house in the first place. We met in a bar, drinking side by side, talking about the beauties of back home. From the start, he spotted me as another kid lonely for the Middle West. He had the face of old America—sharp cheekbones, wide eyes. We would meet at the house, then go out to the clubs. At one point, he told me he was drinking too much and so had decided to cut back to three cocktails per night, which sounded like a good idea until he told me the cocktails—a pitcher of beer, a sixty-four-ounce daiquiri, a double bourbon. After a fight with Eli Tenafly, he moved into his own apartment. He often lost his keys. Rather than hire a locksmith, he would sleep for weeks on the couches of friends. Someone bought him a key chain with a beeper: clap three times and it beeps. Once, after I had not seen Congo for several weeks, he came into my dorm room, clapped three times *(beep-beep-beep)*, collected his keys, and went home. He wore one set of clothes until they wore out. He used to stand in the back of bars, face to the wall, drinking alone, saying, "Why, yes; yes of course."

In the early evenings, we went to Miss Mae's Place, a dive by the river where the drinks were cheap. From there we went on to Frankie & Johnny's for oyster or shrimp po-boys and pitchers of beer. And then to one of the music clubs uptown—Tyler's or the Maple Leaf or Tipitina's. Up front at Tipitina's there was a cast-iron bust of Professor Longhair, and we used to joke that, miraculously, the 'fro on the Longhair sculpture seemed to be growing. We often went to Jimmy's, a converted warehouse in a sketchy part of town. Dozens of local bands played at Jimmy's, the Uptown All Stars and Charmaine Neville, and good out-of-town bands, too, like Drivin' N Cryin' and the Pogues, but my favorite band was Dash Rip Rock, three young guys from Baton Rouge whose shows were always furious and wild. Their music was a combination of country and punk, what the band called cowpunk, with an occasional ballad for the girls. You always felt, at a Dash Rip Rock show, that you had stumbled onto the real thing. Now and then, the band played a parody of an old hit, including "(What the Fuck Is?) La Bamba," and a lightning-fast version of Jim Croce's "Time in a Bottle." Their own songs were always about something I had actually experienced ("All Liquored Up") or hoped to experience ("Shake That Girl"). I once saw the lead singer, Bill Davis, perform an entire set in nothing but an Indian headdress; this was during Mardi Gras.

Between sets, we wandered outside into streets lined with shanties, creaky iron dwellings blue with the light of flashing televisions. Underground bars were run out of some of these shanties, a slab of wood polished to a high shine, serving Thunderbird and King Cobra, a knockout malt liquor. Inside were black dudes in pimp-colored clothes. I never got up the courage to go in for a drink. Instead we went around the corner to Carrollton Station, a cavernous hall that twice a week staged a chicken drop.

You crowd into the bar with the country boys and the rednecks and the college professors and the sociology students and the girls from Loyola as the juke box blasts Merle Haggard ("Two Lane Highway"), or David Allan Coe ("You Don't Have to Call Me Darlin', Darlin' "), or George Jones ("White Lightning"), or Willie Nelson ("Blue Eyes Crying in the Rain"), or Johnny Cash ("A Boy Named Sue"), or Hank Williams Jr. ("A Country Boy Can Survive"), and wait.

The floor of the bar has been divided with tape into one hundred squares, each numbered. For a dollar, you buy a square; you can buy as many as you want. When every square has been sold, the crowd starts to chant. The cigarette smoke is so thick the faces in the crowd dull into a smear of color. At last, a chicken is set down in the middle of the floor; you watch as, to cheers and boos, the chicken bops its way across this arena of drunken faces. The chicken hesitates, scampers, clucks, pecks, feints, scratches. And at last the chicken defecates. If the chicken defecates on your square, the square you hold deed to, you walk away with the pot—one hundred bucks, a fortune. You always feel a little bad for the chicken, of course, and you never do win, except when you win, and at such times you feel only admiration for the chicken as you set off on a night of pleasure, every man your friend, every woman too. But usually you are back at Jimmy's for the second set.

Much later we would go to Bennie's, an after-hours club in one of those clapboard shacks built for poor families before the Second World War. From a distance, the bar looked like a music box, alone on its dark street, bursting with noise. In a comic strip, it would be surrounded by jagged lines. On the outside, it was no different from the other houses near Magazine Street, but it had been gutted and there was a stage in what had been the kitchen. The crowd squeezed in, no more than twenty or thirty people at a time. There was no cover charge and the music did not get going before 3 a.m., but on that makeshift stage you might see the greatest musicians in the world. They came from gigs at the big arenas; their shows had ended and still they wanted to play. During the Jazz Fest, when musicians came to New Orleans from all across the country, you might see a local guitar hero playing with Michael Stipe, or Marcia Ball backed by Stevie Ray Vaughn, or who knows. Between songs, an empty water bottle was passed around. Patrons stuffed in dollar bills, quarters, watches, rings. When we left Bennie's, we were always surprised to discover that the sun had risen and people were on their way to work.

At some point each night, we would stop by the house where the boys lived and try to scare up some action. If there was a bit of foolishness I did not want to engage in, Congo would say, "Son, these are just adventures. Now, wouldn't you agree that a young man needs his adventures?"

We often sat around talking to Eli Tenafly, who lived in a room in the corner of the house, in which everything, even the stains, were stained with some other kind of liquor, backwash, or fluid. Tenafly would sit there, rubbing his forehead, smiling. He was keek as hell, of course, and full of great stories, and not wrecked by ambition. He was just getting stoned until his money ran out. And, as I said, he was low-down and cunning and absolutely able to read fear. The ceiling of his room was strung with a web of Mardi Gras beads. This was the playing court for a game he had invented called Jake the Snake. Sitting on one of the room's low couches, you would throw a rubber snake up onto the net of beads; if the snake landed safely on top of the net, you got to give out a drink, or a hit, or a line of cocaine, or whatever you were playing for. There were dozens of rules, which you could learn only by breaking; each broken rule incurred a penalty drink or whatever. Some of the rules included Roughing the Jake (knocking loose a strand of beads), Banking the Jake (rebounding the snake off the wall), premature eJakeulation (throwing the snake before someone has finished their drink, line, hit, whatever). The Jake Court was strung with Christmas lights, and when it was dark the lights were shut off for a game of Night Jake. Some questioned the purity of Night Jake, which, they argued, lacked tradition.

For the most part, however, Tenafly preferred to play straight pool: that is, to sit alone in his room and get stoned or drunk, or else he liked to sit with just one other person whose mind he could manipulate. Perhaps because I am an open book, he took an instant liking to me and was forever asking me to hang out in his room. One night, I gave in and agreed to match him hit for hit, drink for drink, line for line. Even Congo was surprised. "Why would you want to do that?"

"Adventures," I said.

"That's not adventures," said Congo. "That's stupid."

I sat in that room smoking with Tenafly for hours, as again and again he loaded his pipe. At one point I began to shiver, and I could feel the curve of my spine and the fluids moving in and out of my organs and I knew for certain that I was going to die, so I looked up at Tenafly, who was breaking up marijuana on a tray, and he felt my eyes and he looked at me and smiled and said, "No, sir, we still gonna get a lot higher than this!"

When I closed my eyes, it was like being carried away in a swift river. Me on my back, swept by the current, looking at trees and cliffs and a faraway sky. I was certain I would never make it out of that room, out of the maze of rooms and streets that had become my life. Even now, years later, in my bed in New York, I sometimes wonder if I ever did make it out or if I am still in one of those rooms, head back, eyes glassy, dreaming.

In those weeks, it felt as if I were actually growing younger. Day by day, I was shedding that premature little-brother wisdom that had once—to some degree, anyway—kept me on the straight and narrow and so protected me and cheated me from that simple, pointless foolishness that is, after all, at the very core of keek. I guess I was never older than I had been at age thirteen.

In the morning, however, it was like the tide had washed out, leaving nothing but debris and headache and dry mouth and regret. OK, maybe not regret, but at least that sense of surprise that goes by the phrase, "How did I do that?" In this mood, I felt empty and sick for the Midwest, for the change of seasons, the sound of fallen leaves, the smell of coming snow, friends and family. I called my parents. As my father spoke, I could hear his office chair creak and the scene quickly arranged itself in my head: Herbie, in a bathrobe and beetle boots—the only shoes wide enough for his too-wide feet—at his desk on the second floor, looking out at the yard, the leaves turning red with the autumn. "Keep your options open," he might say. "If you work hard, you can still get the hell out of there and transfer to a decent school."

And, yes, I called Jamie but just about never got him, and I wrote him dozens of letters, filling him in on each detail, each development of my life. If he wrote back, it was a homemade postcard, a picture of himself: on a dusty street, in the window of an abandoned house, in a yellow field. I studied the foreground and background of each shot, imagining the life my friend lived just before and just after the shutter snap, how he bundled up on the first cold days of winter.

Our relationship had changed, of course; it was now less coherent and more episodic, following the inevitable course of childhood friendships when those friends have left home. No longer an unbroken current, the drama now played as a series of scenes, jump cuts. Jamie would come, Jamie would go, and the seasons would spin off into years.

Four or five months went by, and there was a knock on my door. I was lying in bed, looking out the window at the strange hazy tropical sky that settles over New Orleans. I crossed the room and opened the door. A voice said, "Hey, little brother, think you can let me in?" It was Jamie. He was wearing a wool coat for that cold Kansas wind, and his face was chapped and raw. He looked like he had crossed from the other side of the world. I was surprised to see him, so I hung back. I have always been shy on first meeting people, even friends. Jamie knew I meant nothing by it. He just smiled at me. I caught my reflection in his pupils—a convex little man, hands thrust deep in his pockets. Jamie said, "I came here to see you and to see the Mardi Gras, so c'mon, man, show me around."

He dropped his bag on the empty bed—with the use of some old-school shenanigans, I had been able to score myself my own room, the much-dreamed of single—and we set off across campus. It was like crossing the deck of a great ship, heaving with the waves, nodding to the other members of the crew. I was proud just to be out walking with Jamie, showing everyone I had such an interesting high school friend. It was like coming from good stock. People stared at Jamie—his loping stride, how he socked himself and said, "So here I am!" Or, "Little brother, we got some things to do!" Or, "Look at these trees, man, do you realize you go to school in the land of palm trees?"

To come down here, Jamie had ditched a week of classes at the University of Kansas, but he said it was OK because it was "field research." I asked how he made the trip. He said he had caught a ride from a friend of a friend as far as Jackson, Mississippi, and hitchhiked from there. When I asked his opinion of Lawrence, Kansas, where his school was, he shrugged and said, "It's a half-ass town full of forward-thinking types and a grocery list of alternative scenes. Its parents have declared a war on drugs."

We went to the house where the boys lived, and I took him from room to room. We found Congo at a desk near a window. It looked out on the backyard and the Dumpster. He was writing in his journal. As he stood to greet us, I stole a glance; the entire page was covered with the sentence, "Yes, yes of course." Congo shook Jamie's hand and then asked Jamie several random questions: "Have you ever made anyone cry?" "Do you follow anything that you call *policies*?" "What do you think of the term *pet peeve*?" "Have you ever sold anything to a friend?" "What is better, a roller coaster, a haunted house, or a water ride?"

Congo then turned to me and said, "I really like Jamie."

When you introduce an old friend to a new friend and they don't judge each other, or hate each other, but actually like each other—that is one of the greatest pleasures in the world. "Why don't you head over to Fat Harry's?" said Congo. "You can even take my car."

"What about you?"

"I'm gonna get back to the writing," he said.

Fat Harry's is a rundown dump, as dank and ominous as a bear's cave. Hours drift by, people come and go, but nothing really changes. Even on clear windswept mornings, it feels like the middle of the night. There is a bar in front and a grill in back. From the door you can see St. Charles Avenue shadowed by a lacy canopy of Spanish moss. Streetcars clatter past, washed-out faces in the windows. And then it is night at Fat's, regulars wandering in from odd jobs, the jukebox switching from Miles Davis to the Rolling Stones.

Jamie and I had a few beers and a few glasses of whiskey. Every third song on the jukebox was the "Mardi Gras Mambo"—"Down in New Orleans, where the blues were born, it takes a cool cat to blow a horn"—a scratchy trumpet-filled tune by the Hawketts, which is the true anthem of the New Orleans Mardi Gras, heralding the storm as surely as a covey of birds flapping across a thunderhead.

There was a strange moment of silence. Then everyone at the bar ran into the street. People lined St. Charles Avenue for miles, some seated in rickety bleachers, most on foot. Soon we spotted the parade, the Crewe of Bacchus, another one of those restricted old-white-boy clubs putting on its show for the drunken peasants of the city. First came the majorettes, batons playing tricks in the air, then the swaggering horn players in starchy white uniforms, marching hats and chin straps, and white boots. Black boys from all-black high schools razzmatazzing it down the street, shuffling side to side, swinging trumpets and trombones. Each marching band had the name of its school on its uniform: De la Salle, Brother Martin, Cabrini. One was called Cohen. Jamie convinced a majorette to give him a shirt—COHEN stitched in red lettering across the chest.

The street vibrated with footsteps; the horns shud-

dered through my limbs. It was spectacular. Then came
the grotesque, vulgar, billowy, Day-Glo floats and the
members of the Crewe in white clanlike hoods and masks,
and the women as fluttery as French queens in petticoats,
tossing out plastic beads, which the crowd fought over and
prized. Behind the floats came the torch carriers, shabbily
dressed black men on foot, shuffling under a shower of
coins, grimacing in the orange gaslight, a haunting throw-
back to the days of Reconstruction. "It presents a
dilemma," said Jamie. "If you throw a nickel, you are a
bastard. And if you don't?" Then came the last marching
band, a caboose of a kid in back, sleepy-eyed, maybe
failed two grades, raising his cymbals: *crash!* The sound
swept over the crowd. Mardi Gras had begun.

We did not see my room for many days. We slept on
couches, or on floors, or in backyards. We were often in the
French Quarter, in the street or in hotel lobbies, a drink in
hand, blue or red, juleps or Hurricanes. Rounding a corner, we would stumble upon noisy crowds, girls hanging
from balconies. There was no sense of cause-and-effect to
any of this, no logic. It was a train wreck of images—a run-
on sentence, a puzzle pieced together wrong.

At one point, we stood in a biker bar downtown called
the Dungeon, laughing and slurring and holding each
other up. Some old guy bought us a drink. He was alone
and full of talk. "You boys are damn young," he said, "so I
just hope your generation is better than mine. My generation has done nothing. We did not survive a depression or

win a war, we did not lose a war or go on pilgrimage, we did not immigrate or emigrate. Our lives have been just a collection of aimless conversations in smoky bars." He thought for a moment, then said, "Just like this one."

We hitched back up to Jimmy's, where Dash Rip Rock was playing. It was night. It was always night. The night went on and on. Mardi Gras is a night that lasts six days. When morning comes, it is not morning but just another version of night. Jamie said, "Let's take drugs."

I said I could get us a joint.

Jamie said, "No, real drugs."

We went to the house, where we found Tenafly getting stoned. He took us into his room. We smoked. Touching Jamie, he said, "Feel the keek coming off this kid." I found a book Tenafly had stashed behind his bed. It was filled with pictures. I read a story written in a fairy-tale type. A voice actually seemed to be reading the words into my ear:

In a land on the other side of the Black Sea lived a powerful King. One day, a peasant visited the court of the King, who gave the peasant a duck and said, "Kill this duck where no one sees." Many years later the King found the peasant, who was still holding the duck. The King said, "I told you to kill the duck where no one sees." The peasant said, "Yes, but the duck sees."

For some reason, maybe because I had been up for days, or because I had been drinking and drinking, or because I was just feeling the effects of the joint, the kicker of the story sent me into a swoon. In my head, over and over, I heard that voice say, "Yes, but the duck sees. Yes, but the duck sees. Yes, but the duck sees." For a moment, I felt I would never do anything with my life; there would be no escapes, and no guilt-free moments, and no end to my wandering, because wherever I went I would find the duck, and the duck sees. As I teetered on the edge of the abyss, Jamie yanked the book from my hands, tossed it across the floor, and said, "Don't read that shit. That shit will make you crazy."

Tenafly had let his sideburns grow, which gave him the look of a lost, road-weary trucker. He was laughing as he looked through an old-fashioned doctor's bag. He said, "Don't worry. In here is the cure to whatever ails ya." He handed two pills to Jamie, who said thank you and dropped the pills into his breast pocket.

It was a relief to get outside. The sun was coming up, and there was a gulf breeze, and the streets were damp and mysterious. Jamie said, "You are free and clear, little brother. There is no duck." It was a twenty-minute walk to the levee. When we got there, we sat on the grass and looked at the river. My mind cast into the future. I saw myself as an old man, writing reminiscences of my youth.

Jamie said, "Where are you right now?"

I said, "I am thinking about much later."

"You are not where I told you to be," he said. "You are somewhere far down the road, which is nowhere, and here I was, looking for you in the five minutes from now. Drugs are the only way I can think of hauling you back into frame."

He handed me a pill.

"What is it?"

"Something better than Ecstasy."

In those days, Ecstasy was still in its first youth, and so it wandered the countryside, raising hell. We all knew of its origins, how it was engineered in a laboratory somewhere overseas where a forward-thinking chemist believed he had at last found the key to the pleasure center—to a fast, carefree place in your otherwise mournful, envious brain. We knew too that for several years the drug had been legal, off the charts of the police, and some spoke of those years as a lost paradise. I told Jamie that I was afraid of the drug, and besides I was already drunk and stoned.

He said, "You have hit a wall. Take the pill. Climb over."

Over the years, there has been a lot made of peer pressure, almost all of it bad. Peer pressure—kids telling other kids how to behave—is said to make people do stupid things, drink too much, run wild, vandalize, shoplift. Mothers, pointing out the logical fallacy of peer pressure, often mention the Brooklyn Bridge and how you shouldn't jump off it. But in my life, peers—and here I am talking mostly of Jamie—have pressured me into doing many things I would certainly not have done on my own, and in almost every case these have turned out to be the great adventures of my life.

Jamie said, "Take the pill."

I chased it down with warm beer.

As we walked to Magazine Street, Jamie told me his theory of life. It was based on the Winnebago. Here is what he said:

"Every kid knows about the Winnebago, right? It's a myth, a dream. I mean, every kid, given a choice, would choose a Winnebago. This is a house we are talking about, but it's on wheels! When you get tired, or bored, or life is just too much, then fuck it; just drive away. But as you get older, you forget about the Winnebago. Or maybe you are made to forget. You come to believe that the Winnebago is just the opposite of a good way to live. You come to see it as stupid, or low-class, or whatever. And so this knowledge you had from the very beginning, like so much of that first pure childhood knowledge, is drummed out of you, and soon they've got you lining up in the ranks of the apartment dwellers! So you see! You have been forged into forgetfulness and brought into society! But some of us, a remnant, a fucking holy remnant—we have never forgotten. We hold on to the dream of the Winnebago."

Somewhere along the way, as Jamie was talking, the drug kicked in. It was like one of those science-fiction movies, where, as the trusty ship shifts into warp speed, the stars—there are always about a million stars out there—turn from stationary points into streaky lines, and then—*wham!*—the ship is catapulted clear to the other side of creation! And that's just how I felt: like I was flying through space, with the stellar wind in my hair, and galaxies and quasars racing by, and far below—isn't it beautiful from this distance?—the twinkling settlements of man. I guess I was smiling a luckiest-man-in-town smile, because Jamie leaned over and looked into my eyes and said, "It kicked in! And it looks good! I'm right behind you, little brother, and I can't wait!"

And then we were both reeling down Calhoun Street, giggling and hugging, and the sun climbing higher. We turned onto St. Charles and made our way to Fat Harry's. It is strange to walk into a bar at seven in the morning and find it still reeling with its nighttime crowd: kids at the jukebox and the pool tables, bartenders pouring drinks and the girls sipping Coronas, Jason and the Scorchers on the stereo, and everyone laughing and waiting for the next parade.

Jamie and I found a place in the corner so we could lean. The morning drifted by in a dazzle; the music poured through me. Sometimes, as I looked at a girl, or out the door at the trees, or at the efforts of the bartender, I would forget that Jamie was even in town and then, moments later, discovering him at my side, I would smile and shout, "Oh, Jamie! Hey! It's you! Wow, it's great to see you!" His pupils were so dilated that his eyes were no color but black, each eye a camera, the lens wide to capture this strange scene. He had his jaw thrust out and he was grinding his teeth. I was doing the same. Looking around, I saw that everyone in Fat's was doing the same: this face, the telephoto eyes and outthrust jaw, was a shared mask. Everyone was on Ecstasy. Everything was booming.

As we listened to the music and talked to girls and raced into the street, where it was morning, and back into the bar, where it was night, I realized that this was turning out to be one of the great days of my life. I felt like I was using up something that had collected inside me over many years; that a pair of hands had lifted my brain from my skull and was squeezing out the juice in one mad rush. And the result was a euphoric, charming me, empathetic as hell. At the bar I talked to Jon Close, a kid I had long considered a fool, a big dumb guy, with a gaggle of drones in his wake.

Jamie said, "I thought you hated that guy."

I said, "Yeah, I do. But you know what? He's got a point of view!"

Sometimes Jamie wandered off, and when he got back it seemed he had been gone for years, had crossed mountains and oceans, had lived lifetimes. We greeted each other like long-lost friends. At one point, he said, "You have more in common with everyone living today, even with those poor emaciated bastards you see starving in

Time magazine, than you do with anyone dead, even your own grandfather or, in my case, my own father, who died tragically young. And it is not just that you have more in common with them in comparison to a dead person; you really have everything in common with them, just by the simple math and great miracle of being alive; and you and me, who grew up in the same town, we are brothers and that is not even our choice. It is no more a choice than it is your choice to have Steven as your real brother, who, as you know, can be moody as hell, except of course, I am your real brother just as much as he is—more, because I fulfill my fucking duties."

We decided that we should make a movie of this day as seen through our eyes and call it *Two Dudes at Mardi Gras.*

We decided we should go downtown to Zulu, one of the great parades of Mardi Gras. Congo's car was still parked behind Fat Harry's. I told Jamie he should drive.

Jamie said, "Do you realize how fucked up I am?"

I said, "So is everyone."

He said, "Yeah, well, here is something I never told you. My father died in a drunk-driving wreck. He just had a couple of beers, but it was enough to send him across two lanes of traffic into a speeding truck. They had to pry him out of the wreckage."

Jamie had tears in his eyes. I started to cry too, and I hugged my friend. I told him I was sorry, to forget it, we would find some other way. After a long moment, he said,

"You know what just happened? Two dudes at Mardi Gras just became two responsible dudes at Mardi Gras."

We congratulated each other and went outside to hitch. The bar had emptied out and there were no cars. We stood out there forever.

Jamie said, "Fuck it, I'll drive."

As he got behind the wheel, he said, "Two responsible dudes at Mardi Gras just realized Mardi Gras is no place to be two responsible dudes at Mardi Gras."

He buckled his seat belt, checked the mirrors, and started the engine. As we pulled out, a car stopped directly in front of us. It was a cab. It was empty. Jamie said, "See what just happened here? Two dudes at Mardi Gras just had responsibility thrust upon them."

The taxi sped us along Magazine Street, the shops twinkling like cheap jewelry. I stuck my head out the window and lapped at the wind like a collie. The cab turned sharply, and for a moment my face seemed to hang over the street like an effect in a Saturday morning cartoon— my eyes bugged out, smoke came from my ears, and then my head snapped back.

Jamie said, "Easy, boy."

We got dropped off on Canal Street, where the few tall buildings of the city gather in conference. At Mardi Gras, the towers look as uncomfortable as men on the beach in business suits. Some of the buildings were covered in mirror glass, and you could see the sky reflected, the clouds as sluggish as wet cotton. I stood under a tree that must have been two hundred years old; the limbs were twisted like rope. I was amazed at the beautifully effortless way it climbed into the sky. The leaves shifted on the breeze, and with each gust they filled up like sails. The leaves were so green and so soft they looked like fur. I said to myself, "Whatever else happens to me, I will always have this tree."

"Here it comes," said Jamie.

In the distance, I could see the tall floats of Zulu. We fought our way to the front of the crowd. The men and women on the floats were dressed like storybook versions of old Africans, in war paint and elaborate headpieces, earrings, and nose bones. They shouted and danced and moaned. The parade began years ago as a put-on, the black community's response to the all-white Crewes of Mardi Gras. In addition to beads, the marchers tossed out spears with rubber tips and coconuts. Every year, a few dozen people were brained by a coconut. In the economy of Mardi Gras, where beads can be traded for goods and services, mostly sexual, there is nothing more valuable than a spear from Zulu.

Midway through the parade, Jamie grabbed a spear. It was like watching him take a bolt of lightning from a stormy sky. The crowd cheered. Across the street, a beautiful girl motioned to him. He said, "I am just going over to see what it is about, and I will be right back." I told him not to go. "It's too hard to cross. You will never find your way back. We have to stay together." But there was so much chaos and noise, I don't even think he heard me. He just said, "I will be right back."

Two feet from the curb, it was as if he were swallowed under the surface of a great river. A cop yelled at him. He vanished and a moment later surfaced on the other side of the street. I saw him talking to the girl, and he turned around and turned around again and then was lost. The sun glittered off the trumpets. The drums pounded. His spear disappeared in the crowd. For the next few days I encountered him only in stories, the battlefield reports of friends, or the friends of friends, who had seen Jamie on the street, in a bar, at a parade. He was moving through the city like a dervish, a step ahead of the crowd, of the cops.

In New Orleans, during Mardi Gras, a black bus with black windows ghosts through the streets. If a cop sees something he doesn't like—maybe it's a fight, or someone pissing on a curb, or someone smoking a joint, or maybe it is nothing at all—he calls for the black bus, which is never beyond the next corner. And so here it comes, bounding through the evening smoke, with a tangle of stunned girl-friends and angry mothers in its wake. And out of the bus come a half dozen officers in riot gear, each face a smear behind its plastic shield, and billy clubs waving. And, just like that, it is over, another sucker loaded on the black bus. When the bus is full, it drives to Central Lockup, the city jail, where holding tanks overflow with the thousands of players who have lost at the game of Mardi Gras. If, after two days, no one comes to claim a prisoner, he is moved to Tent City, a fenced-in field on the outskirts, an echo of the Great Depression, a Hooverville of prisoners sharing cigarettes and telling hard luck stories. "Aw, man, this motherfucker got me coming out of Fat's with a fistful of pills."

Many times that week, with the hours drifting by and no mention of Jamie, I feared he had been taken away by the black bus. But always, just before I went to bail him out, some bright-faced girl would race up and say, "I just saw your friend Jamie. He was over on Rampart Place. He was marching behind a band and shouting *Payday!*" Or "Jamie is over on Freret Street, up on a float, dancing a shimmy." Or "Jamie bought a round of drinks at Frankie and Johnny's and vanished before the bill came. Even the bartender got a kick out of him." When discussing Jamie, people spoke in three tenses: he was so fucked up, he is so fucked up, he is going to get so fucked up. Each time I raced off in search of my friend—to Rampart, to Freret, to Frankie and Johnny's, where I paid the bill—he had always left just a few minutes before. "No, man, he's gone. And too bad. He's wild." At one point, I actually caught sight of Jamie in the distance, on a wrought-iron balcony on the third floor of one of those old French houses on a back street in the Quarter. His eyes were closed, his arms were moving, and the sun cast shadows on his face. I shouted and waved but he didn't hear me. There was a bouncer at the door, and though I pleaded he would not let me in. And then Jamie was gone, on with his batlike flittings across the city.

On Fat Tuesday, I was in the French Quarter, standing amid the strip joints and tacky bars, squeezed by the clown-car crush of the crowd. The street was a tunnel of balconies twisting out of sight. The sky was filled with garbage and ash, and pieces of ash settled on my hands and stained my face. And then, exactly when it seemed there would be no end to this day, it got very quiet—the kind of quiet only a crowd can make. And before I knew it the crowd was being pushed, jostled, driven down the street. Up ahead, I could see a blue wall of cops. Within a few minutes, we had been forced into the drab, empty blocks of the business district. I was suddenly aware of the sun. We had been pushed from nighttime back into the day. In the distance, the police stood around talking. Behind them, municipal employees went to work with hoses and trash cans and brooms. Mardi Gras was over.

I took the streetcar to Napoleon Avenue and walked through the Garden District: boulevards deserted, houses dark, cars snug in their carports. Here and there, a shop owner was sweeping a sidewalk; cabs ghosted by. Otherwise the city was asleep, drifting through its collective dream, each breeze carrying soft snores and *zzzzzz's* rising like smoke from the chimneys. In the dorm, many of the doors were open and I could see the boys tucked into their beds, still wearing souvenir caps and beads. When I opened my door, I saw Jamie in my bed, stripped to the waist. The blinds were down, the slats filled with light. I touched his shoulder. He sat up, rubbed his eyes, and told me, as best he could remember, what he had been doing over the last several hours. And then he hesitated, and stammered, and shut up. It was as if he had suddenly realized that his stories, no matter how well told, would not keep, that their essence would not survive in the everyday world. So instead—and he would do this more and more as he got older—he just stopped talking. I suppose he had decided instead to keep his adventures in his mind, where they would lose none of their strangeness.

I lay down on the other bed and was asleep before I untied my shoes. It was 4 p.m. I slept through the afternoon and the night and did not wake up until the next morning. I could hear voices in the street, and trucks and cars, and I knew that the strange city of the Mardi Gras was already gone. My shoes and clothes had been taken off and were stacked neatly on a chair. I found a note on the desk:

> Gotta get back. See you in Chi.
>
> ——Jamie.

After finals, I packed my bags, went to the airport, and caught a flight home. From the window of the plane,

Chicago, that great smoky town, rose out of the tablelands as clean and colorful as rock candy. Ronnie met me at the airport. He was driving a low rider with tinted windows and Little Feat on the tape deck.

In just one year of college, Ronnie had executed a complete identity change. He went from clean-cut would-be jock and proud member of the hundred-pound club—Ronnie, at two hundred pounds, could safely bench-press three hundred pounds—to groovy drugged-out stoner, aviator glasses to hide his bloodshot eyes. He had begun the year at the University of Iowa, where he was a dashing frat boy; had gone, after a semester of failing grades, to Carl Sandburg College in Galesburg, Illinois, where he was a lost youth; and ended the year at the University of Miami, where he bought a gun, smoked his first joint, and killed targets at a shooting range. As we merged onto the tollway, he said, "If you want to score some dope, I got a man in Kingston. And don't worry 'bout customs. He packs the shit in coffee beans."

In those weeks, I did not know what to do with myself. In many ways, I felt I had left this town behind and was now a man of the world. On occasion, I even called a movie a film or referred to a famous writer by a nickname. "So anyway, I was out in the woods, but of course I took old Doc Percy along." And yet here I was, back in Glencoe, no place better to be. So I just wandered around, amazed at how tame and lifeless and sleepy and bland and empty and small everything seemed to me. Each after-noon, Tom Pistone came by in his GTO. He wore T-shirts and jeans, sat with boots on the lawn, pulled at the grass. Tom had cut his hair short and, as in the story from the Bible, had lost some part of his strength. Once the toughest kid in school, he had now become just another guy on the sidewalk. His friends still treated him with the greatest respect, though, as you will continue to call a president "Mr. President" even after he has been voted out of office.

Jamie had taken a job painting houses. It was his own business, set up with some of the local boys. Kansas was cheap but not free, and Jamie needed the money for rent and tuition. For him, it was truly a summer of hard work. I would see him only at the end of a long day, wiped out but trying, with that deep, rough workingman's tan, his boots dusty and speckled with primer, and his chest swelling from his trips up and down the ladder. He said he dug the view from the scaffolds: the geometry of low houses, porches and shrubs, front yard, pool in back, a girl sunbathing.

If it rained, he would show up at my house in the early afternoon. If my father happened to be home, they would crash side by side in the family room, watching my father's favorite movie, *Gunga Din*. By the second or third scene—Cary Grant fighting off a band of howling fanat-ics, killing for the love of Kali—they were both dead asleep to the classic summertime sound of rifle shots and tribal whoops coming from a beat-up TV. Otherwise, if Jamie got off late, we went down the street to get high with Ronnie and to watch him eat. Jamie said Ronnie had become a stoner because dope heightened his most acute passion—food. When Ronnie was stoned, his eating habits were indiscriminate. He ate jelly beans with ketchup, bananas in pickle juice, dry packs of instant oatmeal. One night, I opened a tub of butter in his refrigerator and saw where he had scooped a hunk, his finger marks as well preserved as prehistoric vertebrae in amber—the remnants of a lost civilization. "No more aesthetic concerns," said Jamie. "Ronnie is now down to the guts of the matter."

I suppose this is the place in the story where I should say something about my father and how we began to fight, calling each other names, and how these fights turned violent because he did not understand me and would not let me grow up, because he was old and I was young. Maybe, for drama, I should say that Jamie, who had no father, moved in to fill the void, becoming closer than I was to my own dad. After all, I spent my first conscious years in the 1970s, when the notion of the generation gap, of sons against fathers, of a necessary patricide, became a social religion. Our after-school specials were full of it, as were our Movies of the Week. But the truth is, there never was anything like that between my father and me. Maybe each of us just believed too strongly in the comedy of everyday life, or maybe we just liked each other too much, or maybe, more realistic and less bothered than my older siblings, I was just not shocked to discover that my parents did not know everything. Don't forget: I grew up after all those wars and hearings and scandals. I knew the world had fallen. If the world has fallen, everyone in the world has fallen too. Even my father. (But still I had *Caddyshack* and Bill Murray to say "Gunga, ga-lunga, gunga.") So instead, in a very natural way, I began to drift beyond the old man's jurisdiction.

My mother was angry at me that summer—for doing nothing, for coming and going, for "using the house like a hotel." At last, for my own protection, I began to look for a job. And that is when my real summer began, what I call the Summer of Bad Jobs. I spent most of June walking in and out of offices, cinder-block buildings, mall restaurants. I was questioned, looked over, filed, and rejected. At the end of the month, I was offered a job at Danny's, a day camp for rich kids out in what my friends and I used to call Comanche Territory, the prairies in southwest McHenry County, where once, at a festival called the Taste of McHenry, I sampled fifteen different kinds of custard. Danny, a pot-bellied, buck-toothed rah-rah-rah suburban dad who often said, "We are about the *we* and not the *I* here at Danny's," fired me just three days into my second week, for, according to him, forming, among the seven-year-olds, a "cult of personality." In his office, he spooked me by saying, "You are not the same Rich Cohen we hired."

Who is this other Rich Cohen, I wondered, and will we ever meet?

A few days later, I was, in essence, picked up from waivers, hired on by Poppa George of Poppa George's Pizzeria. The first night I was put in charge of something called the Beef Bar, where we served spaghetti cooked in what Poppa George called the "North Shore style"—a fistful of noodles held under a lukewarm tap. This was, said Poppa George, "our little secret." At the end of my first shift, Poppa George, who was a foul-tempered old man, ran a finger across a plate I had not rinsed properly and said, "Boy, I'm disappointed in you."

I said, "You've known me for less than five hours, Poppa George. If you are disappointed in me, you're a fool."

Poppa George slapped me and I quit.

Then, in the strangest twist of the summer, I was hired, irresponsibly, as a counselor for mentally and physically handicapped adults. (My first New York résumés still carried this job, a ghost of some forgotten existence, listing my duties as "Supervising field trips, driving the handicapped van, dispensing medication.") My charges were schizophrenics and other crazies. When I got home, my father would say, "Let's hear it," meaning the many surreal things that happened to me every day on that job. An old female mental patient told me she had found a penis in the trash, "a darling little penis." At the bowling alley, a schizo, lip-smacking from a megadose of L-dopa, heaved a ball down the carpet into a Coke machine. A young woman who had no disability other than sheer meanness greeted me by saying, "Good morning, motherfucker. And I bet that's what you do: fuck your mother." On my birthday, she gave me a card that said, *You're my favorite counselor, you little bastard.* There was a tremendously fat patient named Wilbur who told me I looked like a young Jose Ferrer. Another patient, given the wrong pill (by me, by accident), recited a haiku and then passed out. One rainy day, for kicks, I brought Jamie along—the mean lady called him a shithead and Wilbur said he looked like Prince Charming, not in the film but in the illustrated books.

By the beginning of August, having burned out, I was working on a road crew and as a part-time janitor for the Winnetka park district. It was as much responsibility as I could handle. We built playgrounds and cleared dead trees, and after storms we shoveled roadkill into the back of the park district truck. Most of the other members of the crew were drunk drivers sentenced to community service. Our bosses were the same lifetime custodians whose secret world of mop closets and playground cigarette breaks I used to wonder about in grade school. So now here I was, one of the boys, exchanging banter and shirking duties, taking the landscaping truck out on personal business. I spent most of my time with Santiago, a hardworking immigrant who wore overalls and floppy hats and had the dark, handsome face of a figure on a Mexican mural. Sometimes, a few of the convicts and I went off to get stoned—we hid in a scaled-down student-built replica of Abe Lincoln's log cabin—but Santiago always found us. Creeping past the butter churn, he would shout, "You must produce!"

At the end of the summer, Santiago and I stripped and waxed the floors of the Hubbard Woods school. I crossed the room with the mop, spreading solvent. Santiago hummed by with the stripper. When I told him I wanted to run the stripper, he said, "You will lose control, smash up the room, and burn a hole in your foot, and your rich parents will sue poor Santiago."

After much hectoring, Santiago let me run the stripper. Before he had even turned his back, I lost control. The stripper buzzed across the room, knocking everything to pieces. It was headed for my foot when the engine died. Sliding through the solvent, Santiago had yanked out the plug. He said, "You see! I told you. Now you must produce in the old way—with the mop."

Most of the time, I was in the basement with a half dozen janitors who had worked at the school for years, arriving each day, summer or winter, before dawn. One of these men was born in Romania and had fled through the mountains when the Communists came to power. When we screwed around, he said, in a heavy accent, "You dammed kids think you got the world by the ass!" His beloved son, who was my age and worked at the school, was always running off with the truck to get stoned on the beach. The rest of the janitors were just working-class guys. There was a father-son team. The father was in his nineties, waiflike and frail but still smoking a half pack of Marlboros before breakfast. He would sit there grumbling in his ribbed T-shirt, a butt dangling from his thin lips. Too old for anything else, his job had narrowed to just one task: he painted doors. Not walls, not fences, not trim, just doors. There was a tennis day camp behind the school and one of the counselors was a beautiful girl who wore short little skirts and was always flipping her hair. I thought of asking her for a date but chickened out, fearing the social divide (janitor, teacher) was simply too great. One day, this girl went into the ladies' room in the school to change her shirt, and it just so happened the old janitor was in there painting a door. He came back to the basement, saying, "I seen it all, every bit of it, her little boobies too."

By the end of each day, I was as worn out as any other working man in America. Sometimes I would stop at a lonely spot along the shore, cut down the bluffs, strip off my clothes, and jump into the lake. I would then drive to Sloppy Ed's. It was a sad time at the hamburger stand. A few months before, in a divorce settlement, Ed had lost control of the business. His wife, Rachel Carter, had taken over—a slight strung-out woman, in over her head but making a go of it. Ed, who by court order was not allowed inside the stand, stood on the sidewalk, shouting, "You can serve hamburgers! You can put on the mustard and the pickle and even the secret sauce. But you will never be Sloppy Ed."

Ed became a biblical figure in our town, singing out his sorrow. At night, he holed up in a road motel, his hair wild, his cheeks as red as ground beef. I asked if he wanted me to stop going to the stand. He said, "No, I want all the worshipers in the temple. That way, when the false priest is driven from the altar, the services can resume without delay."

Most of the time, Rachel Carter just ignored Sloppy Ed. Now and then, however, she wiped her hands on her apron, stepped into the street, and said, "Why, tell me, why would I want to be Sloppy Ed? I divorced Sloppy Ed!"

This would humble the old man. He would start pacing. "OK, fine, you don't want to be me!" he would shout. "You don't love me! OK. You want to divorce me. Fine! But why steal my birthright?"

Of course, this is just the sort of scandal Jamie and I would have spent hours discussing. "It's a split in the very center of town," Jamie might say. "It is a call to choose up sides, progress or tradition, legal documents or human soul, boys or girls, shirts or skins."

But Jamie was not around. He painted houses from early morning into the sundown. And even when he was around, I did not have time for him. By then, I was giving every moment—that is, every moment not concerned with stripping and waxing floors—to a girl who had climbed quickly through the ranks from stranger to crush to girlfriend. Jamie let it be known that he did not approve of this new girlfriend and that in losing myself to her I was in some way violating his teachings.

I met Sandy at a party in Winnetka, introduced by Haley Seewall, who said, "This is the prettiest girl in Lake Forest." If Haley had not said that, who knows what would have happened? I have always been highly suggestible. In the future, whenever I looked at Sandy, I heard Haley saying, "This is the prettiest girl in Lake Forest." She had long blond hair thrown to one side, and her eyes were big and brown and she was wearing a blue shirt. She always wore blue. Maybe blue was her favorite color, or maybe she just knew she looked good in it. She said, "I am so drunk I am spinning."

Only later did I learn the entire story of that night. Sandy and I spoke over the keg; Sandy went outside and kissed some other guy; Sandy came back inside and talked to me some more; Sandy went back outside and threw up in the bushes; Sandy went to the bathroom and swallowed mouthwash; Sandy went home with me. The night ended with me following a confusing traffic of mumbled signals: Go, Stop, Yes, No, Yes, Stop, Crossing, Yield, No, Yes, Go.

Sandy soon made her first daytime visit to my house. Stepping into the kitchen, she said, "I almost ran over your yard man." A few minutes later, my father, covered in peat moss and fertilizer, came in the back door and said, "I was almost run over by a girl in a fancy car." Of course, Sandy did not know that my father was a fanatical gardener; that he worked in the yard for days at a time; that he was often seen by the neighbors gardening at night; that he had been forbidden, by my mother, from gardening for more than three hours at a stretch; that, so he could evade this edict, he purchased several sets of identical clothing; that when my mother left for the grocery store or the pharmacy, he would race out for a few stolen moments in the garden; that, on my mother's return, he would quickly race into the house and change from a dirty striped shirt and muddy khaki pants into a clean striped shirt and clean khaki pants; that, on one such occasion, he was given away only by his white shoes, which had turned black. Needless to say, my father took an instant dislike to Sandy. He said, "Just being around a girl like that, you sustain a loss in brain tissue."

On weekend mornings, Sandy would drive to my house, sneak past my parents, and climb into my bed. She was a former Miss Teen Great Lakes. No kidding. There was a full-length picture of her in the window of the Glencoe Photo Shop. In it, she was smiling with her hands on her hips, her teeth glossy, and her hair all brushed down one side of her head. It was a kind of symbol in our town, that photo, in that it seemed to stand for something else, though I could never figure out exactly what. It was very uncool, that's for sure; still, in those weeks, I found myself carrying a copy of it around in my wallet.

This was no ordinary girl. Her mother had divorced and remarried, and her stepfather was a practically illiterate multimillionaire, jug-eared and sour and constantly complaining, throwing money at his stepdaughters—three girls standing before him, shouting, "Gimme! Gimme! Gimme!" And him: "Take it! Take it! Take it!" Sandy said she hated him. At fifteen she had run away, stuffing some cosmetics into a bag and calling for a limousine. She charged the getaway car to her stepfather's account, which made it easy for him to track her down; she was at a friend's house in Kenilworth, watching cartoons and getting high. She spent two nights in a guest bedroom and then went home, again by limo.

We were together every night, eating picnic dinners and drinking warm beer. I will never forget how she looked coming out of the lake. Even the silly times leave distinct memories. At that age you are essentially longing in the shape of a body. One afternoon, I borrowed the park district truck for a made-up errand and drove to Lake Forest. It was raining. The streets unwound before me, swinging into focus: the trees, the houses, the glistening yards. When I turned onto the main street, there was Sandy in a yellow slicker, hair stuck down to her face. We went to my house; the yellow slicker was tossed into a corner. Each day, she gave me a gift—hair gel, money clip, cologne—until, piece by piece, she had turned me into a different person. At night, we went to Ravinia, a bandshell in Highland Park, to see the Chicago symphony or modern dance. Or else to a high-falutin' suburban restaurant where they treat you like a sophisticate. Her father said, "If you go to Froggies at your age, what can you possibly look forward to later in life?" But Sandy had it all figured out. We would be married after I graduated from college, and a few years later she would be pregnant, and then we would have three kids and I would be riding to and from the city on the commuter train. One night, as we came out of the Village Smithy, the swankiest restaurant in Glencoe, we stumbled into Jamie. He was walking home from work. He gave me a look that said, You poor bastard.

When my parents were out of town, Sandy lived in my bedroom. We dragged the television upstairs, so we could have sex and still watch David Letterman. What I remember best is not the way her body felt—this I remember not at all—but the way her body made my body feel. One night, I drifted off and awoke many hours later, with the TV showing an ape running full tilt up a rocky slope. When the ape cleared a ridge into a valley, where hundreds of apes, each wearing a leather leisure suit, were gathered, he raised a hairy fist and shouted, "Brothers, the humans are attacking! One ape is injured and another is dead!"

At the time, our housekeeper, Dolmi, a middle-aged woman from Ecuador whom my mother considered a member of the family, was bothered by what was going on between me and Sandy and yet could see no way to stop it. So at last she took a pack of condoms from my room and placed them in my parents' night table. When my mom found the condoms, she was far too embarrassed to say anything to me directly. Instead, she called my sister and engaged in one of those endless late-night conversations that have had such a nefarious effect on my life, leading to big-sisterly talks on drunk driving, bounced checks, and AIDS.

On those nights when my friends came around, looking for a party, Sandy and I would shut off the lights and pretend no one was home. Once I watched Jamie drive up, park his car, and ring the doorbell. After a while, he stepped into the driveway and looked up at the attic window. I moved back, trying to fade into the darkness, like the tiger in the old print. But I know he saw me; it registered on his face. He shook his head, got in his car, and drove away.

Tom Pistone invited Sandy and me over for a party. He lived in a creaky house by the train tracks, a garage in back and a weedy yard. We were met at the door by Tom's father, who, for a father, was so young and so handsome that I always felt he was playing a trick on me. He was wearing a white T-shirt, his body just a cord of muscle. He said, "Get in here, boy! Come to see Tommy? Well, all right. Let's get a look at the girl. She ain't too bad!" As he said this, he walked around Sandy, saying, "No, sir, ain't too bad at all."

Tom was drinking a beer on the back porch, staring at the houses across the alley. At dusk, the lights in those houses came on, one after another, like the break of a wave. Then it was night. Jamie walked in from the yard in faded jeans. He asked if I wanted a drink. He went to the kitchen and came back with something that tasted like a hangover. Tom talked to Sandy. Jamie took my arm and said, "I need to talk to you alone."

"Not now," I said.

I did not want to be alone with Jamie or listen to the lecture I knew was coming. That night, I avoided rooms where he could back me into a corner. After dinner, I went into the garage, where Tom had stashed some beer. As I opened the fridge, light spilled across the concrete floor and I spotted Tom's father in one of the cars. It scared me to death. He rolled down the window and smoke billowed out. He handed me a joint and I took a drag. It was skunk weed picked on the far shores of Lake Michigan. "The hippies used to grow it," he told me. "It's the only true thing they left behind." He coughed a little, then said, "Nice girl you got there."

"Thank you, Mr. Pistone."

"I noticed her the moment you came in," he said. "She has nice hair and a good ass, and good tits too."

I told him I had to get back to the house.

"Now you're thinking smart," he said. "You don't want to leave a girl like that alone. Not for a minute."

I grabbed the beer and headed toward the house, glad to get out of there. I had always figured that, as you got older, you grew out of your boyhood weirdness. To me, Mr. Pistone was a warning that youthful creepiness can just as easily dig in and become your personality. From the porch, I could see the kitchen through the window. Light gleamed off the stoves and countertops. Sandy stood before an open cabinet, reaching for a glass. The shelf was high and she was on her toes. Her skirt rode up, showing her legs. Coming up from behind, Jamie put his hand on her back and reached for the glass. As he did this, he said a few words in her ear, and she turned and smiled. I did not think Jamie would sleep with Sandy. That would have been too simple for him, too simple and too drastic. After all, it was not Sandy he was concerned with, it was me: my friendship, my gaze. No. He was just showing me that for him having Sandy would be no more than a good night's work. After all, he had been with dozens of girls like Sandy, or so he let me believe. So no matter where I turned up, Jamie had been there first, been and gone. It was this aura of mastery, of keekness, that, among other things, had attracted me to him in the first place. It was the light he was giving off. But that summer it began to irritate me. It was an example I could not live up to. As long as Jamie was in my life, nothing I had would be truly my own.

And then it was the Fourth of July, which has always been my favorite holiday. In the afternoon, Sandy and I walked into town. There was a warm breeze and a marble sky. The houses looked festive, and the trees were draped in bunting. Some of the stores had set up sidewalk tables. The Korean guy who owned Ray's Sport Shop was doing a brisk business in whiffle-ball bats. Sloppy Ed was at Harry's Delicatessen, eating corned beef and saying, "I have lost my last appeal. I am cut adrift, no way home." The streets were flooded with faces, the faces that make up a small American town: women in sundresses with bronzed legs, men in hats, straw hats and Panama hats, fathers loping toward middle age, mothers cold in judgment, toddlers and kids dressed up for American Legion baseball, old-timers with hard gray eyes. I went into Little Red Hen and ordered the lunch special, a slice of pizza and a Coke for a buck. The pizza was greasy and delicious.

The parade began at the firehouse and stretched through the afternoon strange as a beach dream. There were kids on tricycles, bigger kids on bicycles, the mayor in striped pants riding one of those old-fashioned contraptions with a giant wheel in front and a small wheel in back; there was a high school jazz band and a junior high school marching band, and the kid on the snare drum got a nose bleed; there was every fire truck and police car in town; there were dozens of other vehicles, including the game warden in his panel truck flashing his lights, and a sleek police boat up on a trailer that got the crowd whispering. Chief Tompkins was a keen fisherman, and some wondered why he needed such a fancy rig if not for his own excursions. Bringing up the rear, on a sit-down lawn mower, was Tall Ted Conner, a retarded man in his forties who could be seen in any season racing his visions through the parks of town. Tall Ted weaved down the road, waving and smiling.

As the parade turned off the main drag, it seemed to take the afternoon with it. The crowd headed toward the beach. In less than an hour, everyone had regathered on blankets and lawn chairs on the bluffs above the lake. In Glencoe, it is the same fireworks show every year. The sun goes down; the crowd gets restless; there are shouts of anticipation. Then the first rocket goes up, trailing sparks. For the next twenty minutes or so, due to the small-town budget, rockets scream by in fits and starts, now and then a splash of color setting the town beneath a strange new streamer-filled sky. Otherwise, the night is dead moments, noisemakers, and duds. As a kid, I had watched these sparklers fade, hoping one would burn long enough to set the woods on fire. In the end, there is of course the finale: a run of consecutive blasts, the people ooohing and ahhhing.

Sandy said, "When will it start?"

And then the whole world went up, dozens of rockets sailing into the sky, bursts of light, sharp concussions echoing up and down the lakeshore. Everyone jumped to their feet. This was the best show ever. There were fiery candles and screamers and flashers. After that first flurry, however, the show settled back into its familiar pattern, with each burst separated by stretches of dead air. And then ten, twenty, thirty minutes went by with nothing at all. Not a burst, not a blast. Someone shouted, "What's going on?" Flashlights, dozens of flashlights, began wandering across the bluffs. Here and there, faces, dumbstruck and angry, were caught in the beams. It was the cops, walking through the blankets and chairs, saying, "All right, everyone, time to go home. Some idiot set off the finale first."

It was a play without a third act, an orgasm without sex, premature eJakeulation. The crowd turned surly. The sidewalks filled with grumbling celebrants. I ducked onto a side street and lost Sandy; she had been carried away in the crowd. Jamie was waiting on the next corner. In his baggy coat, he looked like one of the old men of town. "I was hoping to find you," he said.

I said, "Hey! What's up? What about that finale?"

He did not answer me right away. He paced back and forth, arms folded across his chest. His body language was all about confrontation. He was clearly thinking over what he wanted to tell me. I finally asked him.

"I want you to stop it," he said.

"Stop what?"

"You know, stop it," he said. "Stop all of it. Stop wearing cologne."

"What? What are you talking about? Why?"

"I want you to smell your own stink," he told me. "I want you to tear the pleats from your pants. I want you to stop playing house. I want you to rejoin the land of the living."

OK, I thought, so here it is. "You want me to break up with Sandy."

"Fine. If you want to reduce it to that, fine. I want you to break up with Sandy. Ditch her. Dump her. Get rid of her."

The back of my neck started to itch. It was hard to get any words out.

"What are you doing?" I said. "Are you jealous?"

He stopped pacing, thought for a moment, then said, "Am I jealous? Yeah, I guess I am jealous, but not for Sandy. I don't care about Sandy. There are Sandys enough for everyone."

"What's wrong with Sandy?"

"She is no good," said Jamie. "The girl is a drain. If you are sad, you can weep in your sorrow. If you are happy, you can get drunk on your beer. If you are with Sandy, you cannot be sad or happy. You can only be with Sandy."

.   .   .

I did not talk to Jamie for the rest of the summer. I heard stories about him from Tom and Ronnie, and I saw him at a distance, diving off Ming Lee or walking by himself in town. Of course I missed him and thought about him and wondered if he was thinking about me. I guess I was angry. It was not just about Sandy. Jamie and I had begun to drift apart while I was away at school, and that distance had only increased. Neither of us would ever live at home in quite the same way again. We were now visitors on vacation, just passing through. In those weeks, I realized—probably for the first time—that our friendship was tied to Glencoe and to the beach and that it would not necessarily survive forever. There might even come a time when it had faded, Jamie's name just another entry in my address book, a number dialed so infrequently it actually had to be looked up.

At the end of August, Sloppy Ed's burned down. I heard about it from Ronnie. He drove me uptown in his mom's car. When we got there, a crowd had gathered. Flames shot through the roof; firemen chopped through the walls; the burners popped like grenades; the steel sign, as symbolic to us as the Statue of Liberty, swayed and collapsed. It was the finale the town had been cheated of on the Fourth of July. The fire chief discovered evidence of arson, a crime that remains unsolved, a great mystery. For years, the stand remained as a ruin in the center of town. "I want to go to Sloppy Ed's," Jamie once said, "but the bastards blew it up!"

It was summer, it was winter, it was summer. Three
years drifted by. Each fall, I drove to New Orleans. Each
spring, I drove home. I made the trip with other Tulane
students from the Midwest in sports cars or station wagons or, when I was an upper classman, in a car that, in
hopes of giving me a life lesson, my father helped me
negotiate for and buy in a used-car lot one afternoon in
Lincolnshire. My first choice was a blue Honda Civic.
Stenciled on the hood of that car was the name CHUCK.
The driver-side door read BOBBY. The passenger-side
door read BILLIE. Otherwise the car was in excellent shape.

I said, "It's perfect."

"Yes," said my father. "But did you see all that writing?"

"So what?" I said. "We'll paint over it."

"You're missing the point," he told me. "A schmuck
owned this car."

We bought instead a gray, wheezy, salt-stained Dodge
Daytona. In my mind I see it from above, wandering in
and out of traffic, floating over the causeway across Lake
Pontchartrain, which is drenched by green day storms
that blow up from the Gulf of Mexico. In each flash of
lightning, you see a sudden burst of landscape—weedy
shores and rusty barges, trees straining in the wind. On
these trips, I was usually with two or three friends, singing
along with country music or listening to one of those
overheated backwoods preachers on A.M. radio, laughing,

and then crying—crying for our sins and for the death that awaits us all. The cities flew by like beacons: Mobile, Jackson, Memphis. At night we listened to Top Forty, shouting out the names of the songs, cursing the singers—the great paradox of my age; too cool for our own pleasures.

Or maybe we are heading south, getting into the car in winter-bound Illinois, wearing layers of sweatshirts, the defroster clearing a patch in the icy windshield. The outskirts are endless, factory yards and smokestacks reflected in the oily water. Iron bridges span frozen streams. Gas stations drift by. The broken lines waver. You can vanish into one of these little towns, live someone else's life, the years drifting by—it's the future, it's coming. Below Cairo, the rivers churn to white water. There are leaves on the trees. You stop for gas. The windshield is a cake of dead bugs. You have crossed into a new season.

Senior year I lived a few blocks from campus in a house of gables and overhangs with Kurt Zaminer and Seth Coral, whom I had known since freshman year. Zaminer was big and gentle, liked to be called the Crasher, was often drunk, and managed a local bar called Clover. When I went to Clover, the Crasher would pour me two shots of whiskey, serve me dinner, and give me a handful of bills from the cash register. Coral was short and dark, smart, violent, and stoned, or else just about to get stoned, or looped on some more potent drug. At the beginning of the semester, on a visit to the State Fair, he traded a stack of old Styx records for a pit bull that snapped at my ankles and chewed on my fingers. If I was fresh from the shower, the dog lapped the water off my legs, so that all year I never once felt clean. Now and then, the dog disappeared on what Coral called "a dog spree," running with the wild packs, returning days later, scratched up, in the company of a dozen strays.

The wall of my room was lined with French windows. On moonless nights, I would throw open the doors, sit on my bed, and look over the rooftops. I could see dark clouds and wind-tossed trees and telephone lines, which, running from house to house, seemed to stitch the city together. During my time in college, there was never any sense of the outside world, of newspaper headlines, or the rise and fall of markets. At most, I knew that the Japanese, once beaten, were now back at our throats. Otherwise, I was in a room where nothing happened but tonight and the night after that; these nights were, of course, adding up to weeks and months, but this is something I did not realize until it was too late.

Sometimes I drove by the house where the boys had lived, the house of keekness. It was empty. The stories of the house had been forgotten, the boys wiped out by graduation. Like the ancient dynasties of Europe, each had suffered his own collapse. There was Eli Tenafly, who fell in the course of one long night, at the start of which

he banged on the doors of the closed public library—
shouting "I want to read books!"—and at the end of which,
taken away by the cops, he shouted, "Don't beat me up!"
There was Waxey James, who one day was there and the
next day was gone, or was seen in glimpses, wandering
the streets along the Irish Channel. Congo called him
"another poor weaver who has gotten hold of the wrong
thread." There was Congo himself, whose fall was as
glacially picturesque as that of the Ottomans. After quit-
ting school, he passed through a series of odd jobs, in the
end delivering pizzas, until one night, instead of complet-
ing a large order, he broke into the houses of eight friends
and left a pizza on each kitchen table with a note, *A gift
from the Congo.* I last saw him on the back patio of the Ren-
don Inn. He said he was leaving New Orleans and wanted
to share one last drink, "something truly terrible." I
ordered Mind Erasers. Congo drank his down and walked
out. Years later, a friend told me that Congo was living
with a migrant family in California, traveling with the
harvest, picking grapes.

Of course, there were all those parties that thunder
across senior year, when, facing the same uncertainty, you
become friends with your enemies; parties that began at
sundown and continued until the first flush of dawn. This
was a time of exciting uncertainty, with kids going off to
job interviews in distant cities, waiting rooms in glass
towers. I was engaged in a struggle with my father, who
wanted me to go to law school. It is his belief that a person

with a law degree is a person protected from the ups and downs of life. As a kid, when I told him I wanted to play pro hockey, he had assigned me a favorite player, Ken Dryden of the Montreal Canadiens, because Ken Dryden, before entering the NHL, had first gone to law school and so he "always had something to fall back on."

I took the law school entrance exams but really wanted nothing to do with any of it. I want to be a writer, I told my father. We fought. And fought. In the end, he stopped talking about it. I congratulated myself. I had battled him to a standstill. I had become a man. I wrote up a résumé and sent it out to various national magazines. That spring, in addition to rejections from those various national magazines, I was surprised to receive rejections from schools I had never applied to, law schools my father had applied to in my name. It was like a girl that you have never asked out calling to say that under no circumstances will she date you. There were more than twenty rejection letters. My father said, "You want to be a writer? Good! I am teaching you about rejection."

That spring, Bob Dylan moved into a house not far from campus, a house surrounded by a fence that I imagined myself climbing. Bob Dylan would read my short stories and call me *the kid,* as in *Hey, how is the kid doing?* Each morning at 7 a.m., he ate breakfast at the Bluebird Café on Magazine Street. In a vague way, I planned to show up at the Bluebird, slide into his booth, and say something essential, which in the end I did not do because

I had nothing essential to say. Besides, I was busy with my own life, waiting for the future to unfold, drifting through the Garden District or heading out to the Jazz Festival, which is held in the swampy heat of the fairgrounds, a horse track approached down endless empty streets that unspool like loops of cartoon animation, miles of identical houses beneath a flat blue sky. Jazz Fest runs for two weekends in late April. I was out there every day, wandering the boozy crowds, the faces like flowers, swaying on the sticky wind. We believed, with graduation, our world was coming to an end. Coral said, "If you have any drugs, I suggest you take them while there is still time." We went from stage to stage, Dash Rip Rock to Clarence "Gatemouth" Brown to Beaujolais on his washboard. I ran into my math professor, a big long-haired Australian, who, not wanting to wait on line, traded me an A in his class for a six-pack of Budweiser. Walking behind a family on their way to the Arts and Crafts Center, I marveled at the distance between them and me. Sitting in the gospel tent, I watched as the St. Cloud choir, substantial flaxen-haired black women in pink and white gowns, tantalized me with thoughts of the afterlife, singing, "Heaven! Oh, yeah, Heaven is a place where I will lie around all day and watch TV!"

One afternoon I passed out at the fairgrounds and woke up in a car being driven by Coral, speeding in and out of traffic, saying "All right, all right, all right!" There was sunlight on everything, shining off bumpers, glancing off windows. We turned uptown and the sun was behind us and the stars came out and it was night. I passed out again. I woke up at a restaurant, a table of food in front of me. Mexican food. Crasher said, "Eat up, we've got a lot more distance to cross." And we wandered out into the narrow streets of the French Quarter, in and out of the lamplight.

We stepped into the Napoleon House; smoke hung above the bar. A crowd was gathered around a kid telling a story. People were laughing, buying him drinks. I could not see his face but there was the rise of his voice. The crowd burned off like fog and then the kid was alone—in blue jeans and a red cloth coat, face lean and handsome. I said, "Goddammit! That's Jamie!"

I felt like old Tom Sawyer spotting Huck Finn when, until just that moment, he thought he was dead. I walked around Jamie, touched him, asked a dozen questions. It was as if he had wandered into my dream. He said, "Your mom told me you were going for a job interview in New York, and since she doesn't like the idea of you making such a long drive alone, I volunteered to look after you."

When I asked why he had come to the French Quarter, he said, "I just got off the bus and walked into the first good bar."

I had not seen Jamie in months. His hair was tucked under his collar, his eyes were bright, his lips were chapped, and he looked thin and pure, as if he had shed every excess. For a long moment, he was a stranger to me;

but then, frame by frame, this new Jamie, this strung-out, whispery kid of the road, merged into the old Jamie—all the arguments and distance forgotten—until we were right back where we started, and time could not touch us.

It started to rain the morning of graduation, and by afternoon the streets were fast-flowing rivers and the radio broadcast news of the flash flood. The ceremony was held in an auditorium. Families gathered in the doorway, men in seersucker peering into the rain. My parents flew in from Chicago and my father carried my mother through the current. A man in a straw boater said, "The word for that is chivalry." That night, when Jamie and I got back to the house, Seth Coral was leaning out the living room window, shooting off bottle rockets, which exploded on the roof across the alley.

The waters had receded by morning, and the streets were strewn with debris. Seth Coral and the Crasher had already packed up and gone. So had everyone else. When it ends, it ends fast. Jamie and I walked through the empty campus. The trash cans were filled with notebook pages, some covered with equations, others with the inner meanings of great texts. Jamie read a page out loud: "Gatsby is you and me, and Gatsby is the American dream."

We packed my car and took a farewell drive through the city. The sun had come out and glittered off the storefronts and streets. The city, rundown houses and vines, more than ever looked like a port in the Caribbean. We stopped by Tipitina's on Tchoupitoulas Street, bought T-shirts, and listened to Oingo Boingo run through a sound check. We went to Domalici's, a legendary sandwich shop on Annunciation Street, and got oyster po-boys for the road. Then, for the hell of it, we swung by the Camellia Grill, a whistle-clean lunch counter on St. Charles Avenue, with black waiters in checkered pants, sandwiches naked or dressed, pecan pie, omelets.

We drove along the grassy levee, the overloaded Daytona grinding and bottoming out. The river stretched away to the gulf, its green banks under a blue tropical sky. We saw an abandoned ship in the last stages of dilapidation. It had been one of the great riverboats of polished decks and staterooms, but it was forgotten and rusty, with weeds on deck and vines in the pilothouse.

We reached the Huey Long Bridge at 7 p.m., with the sun dying in the flats. It carried us over the river and into a thicket of smokestacks. And then we were running in the dark, the city far behind.

We drove without saying a word, watching the road unwind, stopping at a Waffle House for pancakes. Jamie stood in the door, smoking a cigarette. We studied maps, followed whims, traveled hundreds of miles out of the way to tour a stupid stalactite cave. By moving we were at last standing still. One night, after not speaking for hours,

Jamie said, "You know, when I was a kid, I used to drive my mom crazy with questions. But my favorite questions were always about dying, and again and again I would ask her if I would ever die."

Jamie was driving. I had no idea where we were.

"So what did she tell you?"

"It bugged the shit out of me, but she always gave me the same answer," said Jamie. "She said, 'Yes, you will die but you will live forever in the hearts of those who love you.' And I smiled like this made perfect sense and like it was very good news but inside I was thinking, That really sucks! I mean, all those kids I ran around with will be at Great America riding the roller coasters and smashing the hell out of each other on the bumper cars, and maybe as they fly down a drop they will think about me, and that is how I live forever? I mean, I'm sorry, but that really sucks."

The Gulf Coast highway took us through Mobile and Pensacola. After a big lunch of oysters in Jacksonville, we followed I-95 into Georgia and then cut over to U.S. 17, a stop-and-go run of sun-baked beach towns. In Parkers Ferry, South Carolina, we sat in a honky-tonk listening to country music and eating grilled cheese sandwiches. In Honey Hill, Jamie got a haircut and stood on the sidewalk afterward, saying, "I'm the one should be having a job interview in New York. Just look at me!" On the way out of town, we passed a Lincoln Continental driven by a black man in a cream white suit, wife at his side, kids in back. "Why can't I be one of those kids?" said Jamie. "Or that daddy? Just for a day, why can't I live that life too?"

By the end of the week, we were blasting through the sweet blue pine forests of North Carolina. We checked into a motor lodge on the Atlantic Ocean, changed into our bathing suits, and stumbled across the highway to the sand. The beach was deserted. There was the strange sea-weedy smell of an incoming tide. Jamie went into the water. He swam out so far I could not see him. I stretched out and fell asleep. When I woke up, Jamie was at my side.

"How is it?" I asked.

"Incredible," he said. "I've never been in the ocean before."

For a moment, I just looked at the waves. Then I asked, "What about Reach the Beach? On that trip, didn't you swim in the Pacific?"

Jamie thought for a moment, then said, "Well, it didn't work out just the way I wanted it to."

"Tell me."

Jamie hugged himself; his eyes were as clear as lake water; he was on the verge of saying something. Then his mood shifted. His voice got high and tight. He said, "You see, on that trip there were all kinds of mix-ups that you absolutely have to plan for on the road and there were contingencies of course and backups that led only to more contingencies and more backups and so my adventures had to be found on the fly and in between the hassles but isn't that the way it always is?"

"So, what? You never made it to the ocean?"

"No."

Back in our room I closed the drapes and turned on the air conditioner. We could have been anywhere in the country. I got into bed and immediately vanished into that strange kind of dreamless hotel sleep that burns off everything that came before. I did not wake up until the middle of the next afternoon. My interview was in just two days. We took showers and got back on the road. Washington, Baltimore, Trenton. On every horizon were those vast brown buildings that signal the approach to cities. "I hate places like this," said Jamie. "Not the city and not the country, not even the suburbs, just nowhere." The closer we got to New York, the faster I drove.

We rolled through the Holland Tunnel into Manhattan—those endless, sweaty, car-tangled avenues. I stopped at Union Square. As I got my bags from the trunk, a cab was honking; otherwise we might have had a better good-bye. As it was, Jamie simply ran around to the driver's seat. He would take my car to Chicago and sell it. He got in, rolled down the window, and said, "If any of those big shots start riding you, just tell them you've got a friend Jamie who does not know or even care that any of them are alive." And just like that I was alone in the city, my bag over my shoulder, a list of phone numbers in my pocket.

Part Three

There were blue afternoons and muggy summer nights, a band playing in the back of a bar, air steaming up from the grates, sidewalks filled with sweet young girls, each the prettiest from her hometown—or else riding a subway down to the East Village, standing in the front car, watching the track unwind out of the dark, screeching into the station—those are my first memories of New York. I had taken a job as a messenger at *The New Yorker*. I had been offered more substantial jobs at lesser magazines but my father, who grew up under the spell of J. D. Salinger and E. B. White, said, "Better to Xerox your ass at *The New Yorker* than write a column for the *Daily News*." When I told him I intended to work at *Regardie's*, a magazine in Washington, D.C., he said, "How did I raise a schmuck for a son?"

The *New Yorker* offices were then on 44th Street between Fifth and Sixth avenues. In those halls it was still the old martini-fueled New York, writers sleeping it off on daybeds. I would deliver mail and packages around the city or lounge around in the messenger room, which was as forlorn as a train station out in the sticks. The messenger department was run by a wispy guy who protected his boys, most just out of college. We argued, competed, complained. Between errands, I ducked into the magazine's library, where I tried to give myself the education I had not gotten at college.

The most revered figure at the magazine was Joseph Mitchell, who, in the 1930s and 1940s, wrote his mystical stories about the lost characters of New York, legendary books of reporting on rats and shad fishermen and eel pots. Joe Mitchell published his last story in 1963, and his books had since gone out of print. You had to hunt for them in secondhand bookstores; there was a kind of underground traffic in his work. By the time I reached the magazine he had become a sainted figure, an elegant man with white hair, often in seersucker, who seemed to reflect a distant world. He came into the office each morning and worked at his typewriter all day and produced nothing. To ask after his writing was considered bad form, so I admired him from afar, his comings and goings, past and present. I knew he had grown up on a tobacco farm in North Carolina, that he began his career during the Depression as a reporter for one of the now defunct New

York dailies. I had been in search of the real world beyond the theme park which has taken the place, or so it seems to me, of every city and town in America. In Joseph Mitchell, I at last found proof of this other world—of the authenticity that Jamie too was after. His writing was modern and exotic, a guide to a city that had ceased to exist, a Constantinople lost under decades of advertising and noise.

One afternoon, though I had been told Joseph Mitchell was a recluse and the last thing he wanted was to be bothered by someone like me, I said, "To hell with it," and went to his office. I was nervous, of course—about the possibility of an icy reception and how the real man might shatter the image. But when I knocked, the door flew open and Mitchell leaned back in his chair and said, "Come in, come in," as if he had been waiting for me. He wore a rumpled suit, the sleeves rolled up, his eyes the same soft blue as the fabric. I explained my admiration for his writing, and he asked about my hometown and told me about his. He got excited as he talked and rubbed his palm along his bald head and stammered, as if the right words eluded him. When he could not explain just what he wanted to say, he showed me photographs of old New York, pier sheds and town houses. Pointing to a sign high on a brick wall, he said, "That is a ghost sign. It advertised a store that had already been gone for eighty years. To me such signs have always been strange and scary."

I told Joe Mitchell my biggest fear—that I had reached

the city too late and that the world itself had become a kind of counterfeit. "I felt just the same when I got to New York," he said. "I was too late. I said it to myself again and again: 'Too late. Too late. Too late.' And then one day, in these offices, way up on the wall, I noticed those same words, 'Too late.' And I began seeing those words everywhere: 'Too late. Too late. Too late.' I found out it was James Thurber, from a world far older than mine, who had been writing them. So you see, even Thurber thought he had come to the city too late. And the people before Thurber? Well, they thought they had come too late too! That's the human condition. Wherever you go, you are by definition too late. You missed the whole show. Which, if you think about it, means that wherever you go, you cannot help but be right on time."

Before I came to New York, I thought I wanted to be a writer, though I was not sure what kind. A fiction writer, I supposed, because it seemed to me that fiction writers get to tell the best stories. The writing of Joseph Mitchell convinced me, however, that there is a shape to the real world and real life that is just as beautiful and strange as anything in the imagination. So I went from delivering packages to delivering packages *and* looking for places and people that I myself might write about: a suite in the Penta Hotel where New Jersey railroad workers, dozens and dozens of them, sleep away the afternoon in a single room; Eli Ganias, who, having caught a foul ball at a Mets game, found his life utterly changed; a mostly forgotten stone crypt in the middle of the city, traffic speeding all around, with the remains of a legendary Civil War general.

It was a great way to see the city, rambling block to block, searching for experiences that could be converted into stories. Or, as a good friend of mine said, "Into writing of some kind!" But really it was the city itself that interested me. Manhattan, squeezed between its two rivers, seamed with avenues and streets, as prickly and mysterious as one of those stalactite caves. I liked the fire escapes and how they looked against the brick walls, how exotic debris collected in the gutters, how Park Avenue wound through the Pan Am building, and Chinatown was another country at night, and the sun looked so good going down between the buildings. At night, I went to the Brigadoon Bar, so called because it appeared only rarely, when I was incredibly fucked up, out of the mists of the East Village. Stepping through the door, seeing again, as if they had never left, that same old cast of characters, I always felt a strange rush of assurance and said to myself, "So here I am again," meaning not just the bar but a peculiar mental state that fused this moment with the last such moment, though it might have been months before, obliterating all the moments between.

I found an apartment in Greenwich Village on one of those narrow streets I had imagined in high school, when

Jamie looked at my brother's photos and said, "New York, how can you beat that!" It was a fifth-floor walk-up on Grove Street with a skylight and a glancing view of Sheridan Square. In the winter, when it snowed, the tall buildings were hidden and the streets so quiet the city seemed to fall back into the nineteenth century. My friend Jim Albrecht hired a cabdriver to drag him (rope, skis) down the desolate storm-bound avenues. In spring, when the snow melted, the runoff seeped through the skylight and flooded my apartment. I got a bucket to catch the water. The super finally showed up. He looked at the ceiling and said, "I think you need a bigger bucket."

When I was not at work, or killing the day, I would sit at my computer, listening to Little Walter and writing about Glencoe. With my eyes closed, I could see the waters of the lake, the bonfires along the beach, the sidewalks freckled with leaf shadows. I wrote about Sloppy Ed's—the glory, the fall. I wrote about Jamie, road trips, double dates. On the page these memories became stories. In this way, they were preserved and destroyed, taken from my mind and fixed in place. Never again would they haunt me in quite the same way.

One of these stories was called "Always Be Closing." It was about Ronnie, who, after graduating from the University of Miami, moved to the Panhandle and took a job selling used cars. The idea of Ronnie Flowers, the most trusting kid I knew, assuming the totemic role of used car salesman was mind boggling. Ronnie described his job to me over the phone. He told me about his training and how he had studied from a manual called "Always Be Closing"; about spotting a mark the moment he or she steps through the door; about the high jinks of the financing shed; about Rodeo Days, during which Ronnie sold used cars (EVERYTHING MUST GO!) dressed as a cowboy, in a hat and chaps. My favorite stories were about the idol of the scene, the slickest stud on the lot, who had written a book of poems to chronicle his exploits:

> I track him like a fly ball, drifting
> back,
> and now I have him,
> fat with money, and
> hopes in the
> highway, so he leaves with a
> Le-
> Baron and
> without his
> cash,
> sucker!

Ronnie worked the job for two years. The week he quit, he came to see me in New York, sleeping on my couch and filling my life with statistics and lot talk. Each night, before we went out, he took a long shower, clouding the mirrors, his beauty products scattered across the shelves. He wore a thigh-length leather coat and a silver watch.

Now and then, he jiggled his wrist to adjust the watch. Or twisted his gold class ring. Or banged the ring on the table—*thunk, thunk, thunk*. He was screening a new image. After a few drinks, he would throw an arm across my back and say something he picked up at the dealership: "So where do you see yourself in three years? Do you have a five-year plan, or are you drifting?" In his voice, there was a corporate seriousness, an executive branch responsibility. Everything about him seemed to scream *I am in control!* In control of my once-runaway body; of my pores, which for years were filled with pus; of my image, which each afternoon, before the bell and after, had been dragged across the playgrounds of Glencoe.

I would stare at Ronnie, searching for the kid who, standing in the foyer of my house, believed my father when he said, "Ronnie, this is the Lord thy God." I could not find that kid anywhere, and it spooked me. I thought to myself, Where is my friend? Can a person vanish so cleanly into adult life? And: If this is not Ronnie, who is it? And: If this *is* Ronnie, who is Ronnie? In remaking the present, had Ronnie remade the past? Had Ronnie ever been Ronnie? And what about me? Have I also lost my childhood self? If so, where? When? Does that mean I am now an adult? And what about Tom Pistone? And what about Rink Anderson? And what about Tyler White? And what about Drew-licious?

Part Four

Jamie was at the University of Kansas for six years. Between semesters, to earn money for tuition, he painted houses or worked construction. When he graduated, his friends were gone. He packed a bag and went traveling. He passed through bus stations, small cities, and early morning landscapes. He returned to Glencoe in the fall of 1992. The trees were bare, the roads strewn with leaves. He moved in with his mother and grandmother. He went for walks—a soldier home from the wars. He had grown into a kind of hard elegance that never goes out of style; he was gifted. He recognized the joke even in sad stories. He was never fooled by hype. He carried a heightened sense of the real world. His presence alone changed a situation. In a sense, though no one was around to see it, he had fulfilled his promise. On Friday nights he got drunk downtown and went home with college girls. To them he was older, experienced, on the edge of a meaningful existence. He took a job with a road crew. In the evenings, he could be seen in town in work clothes. There were no cars on the streets; the stores were empty. His friends had gone off to law school, to girlfriends, to jobs in the city. He felt left behind, forgotten—a sketch of his former self, an outline, detail and color drained away.

Years went by. Young couples moved to town to raise young families. Old couples, having sent their children out into the world, moved away. My parents took their bow-out, my father making a final inspection of his garden, the vines and flower beds, the trees he had planted. As the house had yet to find a buyer, my parents asked Jamie to move in as caretaker. "You will at least get out of your mother's house and have a place to think," said my father. In the winter of 1995, with my parents settled in Washington, D.C., Jamie moved into my house, starting first in the attic and then making a steady progression from bed to bed until he unpacked in the master bedroom and started his new life, giving out the address and phone number that had once identified me as surely as my name or hair color.

It was as if Jamie was the last inhabitant of a lost city. He would wander from room to room, looking into drawers and closets. He stared at the clothes my father had left behind, signature garments, the shirts and suits of his younger days. To Jamie, these clothes represented a lost legacy, what his own life was missing, the lush smell of a father. Jamie ran his fingers over these clothes and tried them on for the mirror, shirts and ties, boots and loafers. As my father was heavier than Jamie, the shoulders of the shirts sagged. Jamie rolled the sleeves and cuffed the pants. He wore the clothes to town, a ragged ghost, a reflection. So good as a kid, he did not have the patience or stamina to be an adult. His mad energy had dwindled. He was twenty-seven.

Jamie bought a 1974 Plymouth Road Runner, which he drove to the beach. It had a blue velvet interior. He had become an infamous figure in town. Cruising the streets, brimming with desperation, he would share sultry looks with the sweet young mothers of suburbia and bring them back to the house and take them to my parents' bed. Afterward, he lay in the dark, hoping his life would take shape. He prayed for a catastrophe—an earthquake, a war, anything that might shake the world free and put his life back in play. I would get calls from friends: "Have you heard about Jamie? It's all my mother talks about. He's being passed around by the women of the village." When I asked Jamie, he sighed and said, "Well, little brother, there is just no one else here to play with."

In 1996, my father at last closed a deal on the house, which had been on the market for over four years. On occasion, my father had used Jamie as a negotiating ploy, dismissing an unacceptable offer by saying, "Sell? For that price? Why should I sell? Why should I make a homeless man of Jamie?" Of course, that is just what the sale did do to Jamie—the loss of a home, the end of an idyll. The prospect of moving back in with his mother and grandmother was ominous. It seemed like a failure. For some time, Jamie had been aware of his symbolic place in my life and in the life of kids up and down the shore. His every hesitation, his every misstep registered, to us, as a generational failure—another lesson delivered. In the house on the Bluffs, he had been able to escape such expectations and vanish into a parallel existence. On the phone, he told me, "I have been living the life of old Glencoe, as one of the chosen, and now I must go back into the world. But I have nothing to give the world. And so what will the world make of me?"

I told him I would be home to box up my possessions. We would have a few days in the house before my parents flew in to ship the furniture. He picked me up at the airport, and we went bouncing off down the highway. Jamie was wearing a silk shirt covered with birds. He was the same as ever, smiling, slapping at the wheel, looking at the green fields fattening with summer. And still, there had been a change—some hardening of his features. When you are a kid and you make a face, your mother says, "Your face will freeze like that." Of course, this is only to scare you, but that really is what happens—your face *does* freeze like that! Depending on luck and experience, in your twenties or thirties or forties, your face settles into a distillation of all the faces you ever made.

We drove into Glencoe. There were trendy stores and tremendous new houses that filled the modest lots property line to property line. The town looked as if it had been torn down and redrawn from memory, refashioned for a new race of men, which, I suppose, it had. "And now," said Jamie. "I will take you to the saddest place I know."

In the center of town, on the former site of Sloppy Ed's, there was a food court, a collection of restaurants with phony, regionless, market-tested names: Godfather's Pizza, because mobsters are Italian and Italians love pizza; Wall Street Deli, because Wall Street is in New York and New Yorkers love deli; Wok & Roll—Oh, those punny Chinese!—Einstein's Bagels, because bagels are Jewish, and who is the smartest Jew the world has ever known? As we ordered, women at the tables, surrounded by families, watched Jamie, some smiling, some frowning. Jamie told me he came here several times a week—because he hated it, because he wanted to remember what he lost, because he was teaching himself there is beauty even here. "It's like a brand-new kitchen table made to look a hundred years old," he explained. "Or like people in the city writing in cafés, or like the McRib sandwich at McDonald's. It's fake as hell but it's all we got, and it tastes pretty good, so eat up!"

For the next several days, Jamie and I went through the house, running up and down stairs, digging through drawers, packing up, throwing out. On a closet in my parents' room Jamie taped a note that read *Everything inside here belongs to Jamie.* One afternoon, when he was in town getting us lunch, I opened the door. Jamie's clothes were lined in neat rows, linen pants and silk shirts I remembered from high school, but also clothes that belonged to my father—suits, shoes, jackets. Seeing those things, I felt a rush of anger in every way disproportionate to the crime. It was as if, by claiming my father's clothes, Jamie was taking something from me. By the time he got back with the food, I had weeded out my father's clothes and thrown them across the bed.

When Jamie saw the clothes, he flushed. "Why are you going through my things?"

"That's just it," I said. "These are not your things. I want to know why they were in your closet."

"Those things were left behind," said Jamie. "I was here and no one was wearing them, and so I took care of them and now they are my things."

I was as angry at Jamie as I have ever been at anyone. I had my fists at my sides.

"You know what?" he said. "You're a greedy sonofabitch."

He turned and left the house. He did not come back and I did not care that he did not come back. A few days later my parents came home and settled into their bedroom. I slept in the attic. It was as if the clock had been pushed back and everything was as it had been. My father asked why he had not seen Jamie. When I told him, he said, "Oh, Richard, what's wrong with you? Jamie can have those clothes. Jamie can have whatever he wants."

I went to Jamie's house the next afternoon. His mother said he was at work and asked me inside for lunch. The windows were open, and a breeze blew from the lake. Jamie's mother moved from sink to refrigerator. In the way that parents never seem to age but, instead, track against the distance like a landmark, she looked the same as ever: sandy blond hair, sharp green eyes. She said she was worried about Jamie. "What will he do?"

I asked about Jamie's life in Glencoe, at work, at school. Then I said, "Do you know what happened to Jamie after high school?"

"What do you mean?"

"Well, after graduation he went off to swim in the Pacific Ocean," I said. "But I never heard from him, and when he got back he was in such a gloomy mood and he never did tell me if he made it out to California."

She looked out the window and made clucking noises that told me she was trying to remember. "Well, yes, Jamie did take a trip, but it was not to California," she said. "He went to Wyoming. In fact, he went out there to see his father."

"His father?"

For a moment I was dazed.

Then I said, "It had been my understanding that Jamie's father died when Jamie was very young."

"Oh, no," said Mrs. Drew. "He builds houses in Casper."

"Why does Jamie talk as if his father were dead?"

Mrs. Drew considered the question. "Well, his father is not a very pleasant man," she said. "Jamie went out there unannounced, and his father—he has his new life and his new family, after all, so how can he be bothered with Jamie?—put him on the first bus back early the next morning. He just couldn't wait to get rid of him."

Over the next few days, working at the house, I thought about this new information. It was like a splash of color that changes the entire picture. It explained the longing that made up so much of Jamie's personality. His relationship with his father, a relationship that was expressed, like man's relationship with God, mostly by its absence, was, after all, the great sunless center of his being. His father even spoke in the voice of God—that is, in silence. I imagined Jamie heading toward that distant encounter, down empty highways, with hopes vague and thrilling. Those hopes were with him in lonely hotel rooms, crickets in the grass, a vacancy sign in the window; he carried them into the foothills. And at last he saw his father for the first time in years, a slim-hipped hero of the snowy west—a man of that American generation that somehow let it all slip away. Jamie slept on the couch and in the morning was on his way home, flat-land wilderness wandering past the windows of the bus.

The day before I was to return to New York, Jamie showed up at the house. He did not say anything about our fight or about my discussion with his mother. Did he know that I knew? I did not ask. I have always found it difficult to bring up any subject that might make anyone, especially a friend, uncomfortable. And Jamie was more than my friend. He was what, for years, looking in a mirror, I had hoped to see looking back at me.

When Jamie realized I would not question him, he said, "I have something to show you."

In the attic, he removed a panel that covered our favorite high school hiding place. Against the wall, glazed with dust, was a six of Mickey's big mouth. "It must have been up here for ten years," said Jamie.

We opened a bottle out in the yard. It fizzed like crazy. We each took a sip. It was warm and skunky.

Jamie said, "Let's go to the city."

I made some calls, and a few friends from New York who happened to be visiting Chicago agreed to meet us, and so did Ronnie, who was living downtown. We met at a bar in Lincoln Park. Ronnie was wearing a dark Italian suit and talking interest rates. He had taken a job at some kind of mutual fund. Each time I saw him, he looked more sure of himself, more prosperous. That night I realized Ronnie would surely be the most successful of my friends. He was protected by a strange confidence— the confidence of someone who, as a boy, had spoken to God.

At some point, we started drinking. We drank in the bars, in the streets, in the back of an underground club. The liquor got us talking and joking and racing from discussion to discussion. In the club, which was in a basement on the West Side, there were girls in bell-bottoms and belly shirts. Jamie said he was appalled by the retrocraze. "It's regressive," he explained. "It means you are out of ideas, have surrendered to the past, have convinced yourself time has stopped." Wearing such clothes, he explained, requires an industrial-strength irony, a joke so finely tuned it forgets it's a joke. "So you see, these people are not actually living in the world but in a muddy reflection of the world." That led him to the subject of multitasking, wherein people, in one moment, perform two tasks: talk to the bank, fold the laundry. "The age of the multitask is a bankrupt age," said Jamie. "It's an age in which, by trying to have two experiences simultaneously, you ruin both and so have no experience at all."

At some point, as we leaned over a bar, I remember thinking, Why can't we go on like this forever? Why can't we be free? If we had no parents, I decided, we could be free. If we had no one to answer to, if we were truly adults, if we were autonomous, if we could make our way free of role models and lessons and expectations, free of grandparents and photo albums, free of heredity—but we can never be that free.

The night ended at Ronnie's apartment, what you

would call a closer, the sun rising at the end of the street. As Jamie and I talked, Ronnie stretched and yawned. One of my friends from New York said, "I think Ronnie wants us to leave."

"We've wanted Ronnie to leave for twenty-five years," I said. "We're staying."

Much later, riding the train with Jamie, I said, "When my parents go to Washington, you should get out of Glencoe too. Just take off."

When I got back to New York, there was a message on my machine. It was from Jamie. I could hear the highway at his back. He shouted, "Hey, little brother! I'm standing on a corner in Winslow, Arizona. I'm heading out to Los Angeles. I'm gonna reach that beach."

Over the last few years, most of my old friends have gotten married and settled down. Some have even moved back to Glencoe. It rises from the suburbs, and so it returns. At first these friends went in bunches, two or three a season. I would speak of them the way people once spoke of wild Indians who at last settled on the reservation as having "come in." Or as Missouri lawmen spoke of Frank James, upon his surrender, as having come in. "It is for the best that old Frank James has come in." Or as we spoke of those kids who, after dinner on a summer night, had been told to come in, leaving just a few of us on the street.

Sometimes, if I cannot sleep, I look at pictures of those friends. Tom Pistone, married with two kids, his once-beloved Pontiac GTO rotting in the grass behind his house. Ronnie at his wedding, wearing a bow tie because he always had a Frank Sinatra image of himself at his wedding with his bow tie undone. Rink Anderson in a church out west, a mountain rising steeply in the door.

Or I look at pictures of the Glencoe beach or downtown Chicago, or at a picture that Jamie snapped at a Cubs game—infielders moving with the pitch, the batter stepping into the swing, the catcher on his toes, the ball hanging ten feet off the plate.

If I still cannot sleep, I think of all the years I have already put behind me. To give a face to these years, I think of all the girls I ever slept with, all the girls I ever kissed, starting with Paige Morrison in a field behind North School, her skirt riding up—or was it that girl from Deerfield, who put me down like a prison riot?—and then of every person I have ever known. Or I think of my signature, which my father helped me invent on a couch in Skokie, Illinois, in the house of my grandmother's second husband, Izzy Blustein, a stooped little man who had lied about his age and died less than a year after the wedding, causing my brother to say, "Izzy come, Izzy go." That signature is looped and curled, and my father said, "Now you can be famous." I think of all the times I have scribbled that signature and of all the places I have left it—at gas stations and bars and hotel lobbies—a ghostly image of my passing.

About a year ago, I saw Jamie in New York. For a thousand dollars, he had driven a truck from Los Angeles, dropped it off in midtown, come to my apartment, told me about some of the things he had seen on the road, including London Bridge in Lake Havasu City, Arizona, and then stretched out on my bed and gone to sleep. By this time, I myself was married. When I got married, I felt that my relationship with my old friends had somehow changed. Even when we went out, the night was no longer open to us in quite the same way. Getting married had not caused this change, but it did seem to acknowledge it. It was like signing a treaty for a war that ended long ago. When Jessica came home from work, I brought her in to see my famous friend Jamie. He was face up on the bed, skin dark and smooth. In high school, I explained, Jamie's most memorable antics were talked about and told and analyzed and commented on and retold, until they became legends. I said, "This is what my friend looks like sleeping."

When Jamie woke up, we went out for a drink at a neighborhood bar. Jamie ordered Jack Daniel's and talked about his life in Los Angeles. He said he was working as a carpenter, designing and building the sets of B-movies. He said this life might sound boring to us, but that he was in fact living it fully and with great passion. "I have tremendous respect for ordinary lives, like the one I'm now living," he explained. "Such a life is like a song that, in high school, you were too cool for, like 'The Devil Went Down to Georgia,' but that, if you really listen to it, you have to admit it really is a pretty good song. It is sweet and funny and you can dance to it, and really, what more do you want from a song?"

We headed to the Port Authority, where Jamie had to catch a bus back to L.A. A job was waiting. It was one of those strange summer nights in the city when the sky rides high and everyone on the street looks famous. This is just the kind of thing Jamie would have once noticed, but he did not seem to care. This is the problem with writing about people—people change, as cities change, as families change, as even the past changes, forever weaving itself into a new pattern. At best you can hope to capture a single moment, like a lightning bug in an overturned glass.

Jamie tossed his bag over his shoulder and climbed onto the bus and waved in the window as it drove away.

Acknowledgments

Writing this book was really fun and I want to thank all the people who helped me with it. My sister Sharon and my brother Steven, who is in the process of raising that long hoped for messiah, the Jewish Bobby Orr. I want to thank Bill Levin, Lisa Melmed and Robert Blumenthal, and also my friends Jim Albrecht, Ian Frazier, Alec Wilkinson, David Lipsky and C. S. Ledbetter III, a colossus of American letters; my agent, Andrew Wylie, and Jeff Posternak, also at the Wylie agency; all the people at Knopf but especially Jordan Pavlin, my editor, who really should visit the great city of Chicago. And, while I'm at it, I might as well thank Chicago too! Thanks for everything, Chicago, but especially for the redhots and the Cubs! I also want to thank my mother, who, whenever I demanded a birthday present, used to say, "Your whole life is a gift." I was stupid then, but now I know that she was right. My father, for his yellow legal pads and his red pens, for his never-ending belief that there is still time for law school. I

Acknowledgments

also want to thank every kid I grew up with, even the ones I was mean to and even the ones who were mean to me. Thanks for not turning me in to the principal, for coming over on a weeknight, for letting me see your test, for letting me date your sister, for lending me your car, for buying me beer. Some of these friends I still talk to but most are scattered. Where are you, Vooch? And what about you, Todd? You were my best friend. And Jenny and Becky, I've got some really funny stuff to tell you. Spitzer is still around, but what ever happened to Rocket? Of course, I also want to thank my wife, Jessica, who stood on the other side of this story like the prize in the Cracker Jack box. It has been more fun than a day at Coney Island.

KEEP MY SECRET

Also by the same author:
Murder Stalks A Mansion: A Newport Mystery
Gilded Death: A Newport Mystery

KEEP MY SECRET

A Newport Mystery

ANNE-MARIE SUTTON

authorHOUSE®

AuthorHouse™
1663 Liberty Drive
Bloomington, IN 47403
www.authorhouse.com
Phone: 1-800-839-8640

Published by AuthorHouse   04/15/2013

ISBN: 978-1-4817-3729-6 (sc)
ISBN: 978-1-4817-3730-2 (e)

For Samantha and Madeline,
who inspire me to keep writing

CHAPTER I

———◦◦◦———

"There's nothing ill can dwell in such a temple. If the ill spirit have so fair a house, good things will strive to dwell with't."

"That sounds familiar, but I can't say I know exactly where it comes from. Is it Shakespeare?"

"Yes. It's not one of the important speeches, and the temple really refers to a man, but it so suits this place, that it came back to me. I played the woman's part, you know."

Caroline Kent studied the profile of her companion. Meredith Hackett was looking through the window of the gazebo and gazing contentedly at the ocean below. The water was calm in the late afternoon, the tide gone quietly out. The face of the woman opposite Caroline was fair. And handsome despite a sharp nose and a long neck. The auburn hair was pulled off the actress's forehead to show a distinctive hairline and a face which while no longer in its first youth, retained the vigor of youthfulness. Theater audiences could always be counted on to respond to Meredith Hackett's strong looks and her rich, textured voice. Not yet forty, she had an uncommon power beyond her years to take on heavy, dramatic roles.

"Let me guess," Caroline said. Although she and Meredith had acted together on several occasions, they had never played Shakespeare together. Caroline tried to remember her classical training. "I suppose it couldn't be Juliet talking about Romeo." Meredith shook her head. She seemed to be enjoying the game. Caroline hadn't seen her this relaxed since she had arrived at Kenwood Court three days ago. "But, it is a woman." The affirmative nod. "A woman in love?"

"You could say that."

"Where did you play it?"

"In a Godawful theater in the center of New Jersey. Before anyone had ever heard of me." Meredith was smiling as she turned to look straight at Caroline. "It's from *The Tempest*. Now do you know?"

"Of course. Miranda. You would play Miranda."

"As you could, Caroline. You're just as talented as I."

Caroline found herself blushing. Unlike Meredith, her career on the stage had not led to the leading roles and critical acclaim which had come so easily to Meredith Hackett.

"But, you think the house," Caroline answered, looking up at the broad white shape of Kenwood Court, sitting majestically on the hill above the gazebo, is a temple. What was it? *So fair a house . . .*"

"Nothing ill can dwell . . . with't."

"Nothing ill," Caroline repeated. "It would be nice to think so."

"Newport is so lovely, a fantasy of place." Meredith was being dramatic now, turning away from the house to allow her arms to take in the Atlantic Ocean, the green lawns, the grand old beechwood trees, and even the sky over Rhode Island. "You're so lucky to be able to live here, Caroline."

"Lucky," Caroline murmured. The events which had brought her to this place were in fact not charmed at all.

"Oh, no." Meredith's hand flew to her face. It was as exaggerated as a stage gesture on the platform in that long ago New Jersey playhouse. "I didn't mean that. Honestly, Caroline. I don't know what's come over me. It's the air. It's intoxicating."

She was out of the wicker chair and at Caroline's feet. Again, the stage gesture. Caroline allowed her hands to be enfolded in the long, tapering fingers of the other woman. Up close, in the harsh daylight, Meredith's hazel eyes looked tired and the lines around them unexpectedly deep. "Can you ever forgive me, Caroline? I didn't meant to be so damned asinine."

"I understand."

Meredith let out a sigh, continuing to hold her friend's hands tightly. For an instant, Caroline wondered who was comforting whom. It had been an interesting several days. First the phone call on Monday night. Meredith's voice intimate and lilting, as if it hadn't been over two years since they had last spoken. Now this rush at closeness and understanding.

"I'm sorry I didn't come to Reed's funeral," Meredith said, breaking into Caroline's thoughts. "I was in Chicago, performing. I always thought the show must go on and all that, and I would go on despite my grief." She paused, looking straight into Caroline's own eyes and added, "I was doing Strindberg, you know."

"How did you learn about his death?" Caroline thought she saw a flicker of disappointment when she didn't ask which Strindberg play.

"Tom called." Tom Benton was a fellow actor during the years Meredith and Caroline had known each other in New York City, three of many aspiring actors looking for work on Broadway and other stages where real drama was still put on. "A car crash. It was awful to hear about."

Caroline flinched. Her husband Reed had been killed instantly in a late night car accident, the blue black rainy November night providing the scene which at that moment was as fresh in her mind's eye as if it had happened yesterday. Caroline had also gotten a telephone call. Unlike Meredith, she had once imagined she couldn't go on.

"But you've done things so well, Caroline," Meredith said, loosening her grip and rising to her feet. She looked tall and fit. "I've watched the way you work so hard around here. Coming back to Reed's old home to re-build your life. And bringing his mother with you. I don't know if I could have done it."

"I had no choice," Caroline said. "Looking back, I see that after Reed died I had to will myself to go on living in whatever way I could manage it. Once I didn't think I could, but, time . . . well it will soon be two years."

"Time," Meredith said. She repeated the word in a whisper.

"Time heals," Caroline said. She had learned to believe it was so. She had learned to live without Reed.

"Does it?" Meredith asked. "I never thought so."

The Newport Police Department was located on the opposite side of the city from the Gilded Age mansions the tourists came to see. The unassuming low brick building was ignored by the tour buses which daily trudged the streets from the colonial houses and the harbor around Narragansett Bay to the high cliffs and mighty houses on the coast of the Atlantic Ocean.

September was generally a quiet month for the department, the calm after the storm. The house loads of single, summer visitors packed up and went home on Labor Day. The bars were less crowded, the calls from the regular residents complaining about noisy parties stopped, and street fights and public urinating were down to a minimum. People still visited Newport, but the tourist trade was conventional in the fall. The cruise ships and the fall foliage bus tours arrived. There were weekend visitors in town for weddings and day trippers who wanted to take the mansion tours and hit the shops. Restaurants did a good lunch business, and Newport went into a recess which could be counted to last until later in the fall when the local university students had settled in and were ready to begin testing everyone's patience.

The faded paper desk blotter in front of Lt. Hank Nightingale was bare, revealing the rings of coffee stains and blotches of grease spots. Hank ran his fingers through his curly black hair and wondered if it was possible that he was beginning to experience boredom. It was only three weeks past Labor Day, and already the afternoons were looking long and tiresome. He stood up and stretched his arms, looking at his watch. There was no reason why he couldn't leave now and have time to catch a jog on the beach. He would enjoy the quiet there.

"Lieutenant," the young female voice interrupted his thoughts.

Hank looked up to see one of the sergeants standing in the doorway. "Yes, Sgt. McAndrews?" Keisha McAndrews's face always gave away when something interesting had happened. She was a tall black woman with short cropped dark hair. Her brown eyes were twinkling, and the muscles around her mouth were upturned.

"We brought in a guy last night. A bar fight. We kept him overnight." Hank's eyebrows rose. "He wouldn't call his mother until this morning to post bond."

"Yes," Hank said impatiently. He was a detective. He didn't investigate bar fights.

"He says he knows you."

"So?"

"He wants to see you, sir," she said.

"I've been here since seven. I'm knocking off, Sergeant. I can't be bothered—"

Hank heard the voice and saw the trap he was in, cornered as he was in the small office. He hadn't heard it in years, but there was no mistaking the high-pitched cackle.

"Hey, Hank, it's me." Hank stared as the thin, disheveled body in the dirty jeans and mud-streaked white T-shirt pushed past Keisha to enter the room. The figure's brush cut pale yellow hair was almost white.

A ragged days' old beard of soft blond hair covered his cheeks. "Don't you recognize me? It's your old buddy, Spider."

Hank saw Spider Shipley's lopsided smile in the same frame as Keisha's wide eyes.

"I almost forgot you was a policeman these days. I just got here last week from L.A., you know, and I guess I was making rather merry last night with some of the guys we knew in high school. Remember Billy Hanigan? We called him the Sundance Kid." Spider turned and grabbed Keisha by her arm, a motion which froze her to the floor. "We used call this guy Butch Cassidy," he squealed, waving his other arm toward Hank. "I bet you can't guess why."

Keisha was staring at Hank. There was a beginning of a grin, which she was fighting hard to suppress. With all his heart, Lt. Nightingale entreated any nearby angel to use all its power to make sure that he didn't look as foolish as he felt.

Unlike many people who live in a mansion, Caroline Kent had a day job. It could even be said that she had a night one, too. While Kenwood provided a home for Caroline and Reed's mother, Louise Kent, the house also gave them their income as the two women had opened the big house to paying guests. The old stone pillar on the entrance gate still said KENWOOD in deeply-etched Roman letters, but in the glossy brochures available in the entrance foyer, the house had become The Inn at Kenwood Court. It was an upscale guest house, with rates to match the grand surroundings. It was life as it was lived in the Gilded Age for the price of a night's lodging in one of the spacious old bedrooms.

Kenwood had been the Kents' family home since before the turn of the last century. At the beginning of the 21st century, there were no natural born Kents left, only the two women who had married into the family. And there was no money left. Caroline's husband Reed had been the last of the family, and when she had inherited the house on his death two years ago, she had faced two choices. The first was to sell the property for whatever it would fetch on the open market. Despite the public's endless fascination for Newport real estate, she chose the second of her options.

Leaving Manhattan and the theater, Caroline had moved into the house and began the enterprise of running it as an inn. Her mother-in-law had joined her to help with the business, partly out of loyalty, but mostly out of loneliness. Her own husband Frederick had been dead for almost twenty years, and Reed had been their only child.

Meredith Hackett had surprised her old friend Caroline by telephoning earlier in the week to request a room at the inn. Although they had lost touch with one another, Caroline had followed Meredith's career during the past two years and had noted her increased success in New York stage productions. Caroline admired her old colleague's devotion to the theater and her apparent indifference to the more lucrative parts she must have been offered in films and television.

"A rest is what I need," Meredith had said on the telephone. "A good, long rest, away from New York City." She explained that she had run into Tom Benton, who had related the story of Caroline's Newport venture, and Meredith had decided, "I must see this place for myself."

The period after Labor Day being slow, Caroline had several vacancies and Meredith arrived in a hired car on the following day.

"I want to be left alone," Meredith told her when they met at the door. "I want to vegetate."

It had been a dramatic declaration, and Caroline had indulged it. She was happy to have the actress as a paying guest. Meredith had chosen the most expensive suite.

And now after four days in her company, Caroline had to admit that despite Meredith's penchant for theatrical moments, Caroline was enjoying the long conversations about the old days in New York and the happy memories talking to Meredith could bring back.

CHAPTER II

⸺⸺⸺⸺

"You look like you could use some help, Mrs. Kent."

"Thank you, Meredith. And, please. I've asked you to call me Louise."

"I know, I know. Louise. Shall I set these out?"

Crystal for the six place settings needed for the guests' dinner was resting on a tray at the end of the long dining room table at Kenwood Court. Without waiting for an answer, Meredith Hackett lifted the tray and began putting a grouping of stemmed goblets above each china plate. Louise watched the actress's movements, precise and particular.

"Six people are lost in this room," Louise said, looking up at the high ceilings and glittering chandeliers. She was a tiny woman and had always felt dwarfed by the more formal rooms of the mansion. "Caroline has considered replacing the long table with several small ones, but she's afraid the guests wouldn't like that as well."

Meredith studied the room thoughtfully. "No," she said, "I can see her point. The set would be wrong. In a house like this, one would expect to dine at exactly this table. Rather like those English movies where the lord and his heir eat in silence, one at the head of the table, the other to his right. And, of course, the old butler and the footmen standing behind each chair." She laughed as though she had made a huge joke.

"Yes. Well," Louise began. She made no further comment, as Meredith went back to straightening the table settings. What was it about this woman that Louise couldn't say she liked her?

"This sixth place is for me, isn't it?"

"Yes."

"I wonder . . . would you think me rude to ask to eat with you and Caroline this evening? These other guests, the Campbells and Mr. and Mrs. Rayburn. I find them so tedious." She sighed. That was it, thought Louise. Does she never lose the melodramatic movements? Always acting. What was real?

"I'm sure Caroline would like that, Meredith." Despite her own dislike, which she was too polite to acknowledge, Louise saw clearly that Caroline enjoyed Meredith's company.

"Good. I'll take away my place."

Louise followed the younger woman through the passageway, past the pantry and into the spacious kitchen. Mattie Logan, the elderly cook, was busy at the old stove, her thin face close to the pot of soup she was stirring. Caroline was across the room, putting the finishing touches to the large bowl of green salad on the old wooden table in front of her. From experience, Louise knew the heavy silence meant she had just missed some disagreement between her daughter-in-law and the old cook.

"My, things smell good in here, Mattie," Louise said. Without looking up, Mattie made a sound which was her familiar grunt of acknowledgment that a comment had been directed toward her.

The cook, who had been employed by the Kent family for over forty years, was a reluctant participant in the inn business. Only her loyalty to Louise caused her to temper her innate snobbery over having the family summer home turned into a hotel. That her former mistress was now her co-worker was a fact which she found to be virtually inexplicable.

9

"Mattie has the most gorgeous pastry in the oven," Caroline said. She brushed a handful of her long hair back over her ears. It was a light brown shade, near to the color of pecan shells, and blended nicely with the emerald green in her eyes. "It's going to be a fabulous dessert."

"I'll gain ten pounds before I leave here," Meredith laughed. "I won't be able to get into the costumes for my next play." She put the tray on the table next to the salad. "I brought my things in here, Caroline, to eat with the family. I'm tired of you treating me like a guest. I don't want to be waited on anymore."

"That's fine, but you know you'll have to wait until the dining room guests are served."

"I might don an apron and do the serving myself," Meredith said, offering Caroline an elaborate curtsy.

Louise was struck by the dissimilarity between her daughter-in-law's congenial face and the other woman's contrived one.

"I'll lose business if it's ever found out that the paying guests have to work for their supper," Caroline said lightly.

"My lips are sealed," Meredith said, unbending her waist and looking pleased with herself. "I'll tell you something else."

"What?" Caroline asked.

"I've finished with being cooped up in my room each night with my book. I want to go out and see the town. How about it? It's Friday after all. Let me see what night life the city of Newport has to offer."

"Oh, I don't know," Caroline said, looking surprised. "It will be late by the time we clean up and—"

"I won't take *no* for an answer. It's the week-end. And Louise, too. What about it? Come out with us." Meredith's face was flushed with excitement. Standing at the stove, Mattie was surveying the scene with disapproval.

"Oh, no," Louise was quick to respond. "But, Caroline, dear, why don't you call Hank to see if he'll join you?"

"Hank? Who's Hank?" Meredith asked.

"A policeman," Mattie said unexpectedly.

"A policeman?" Meredith looked surprised.

"You know he'd love for you to call him, dear," Louise said. No snob, she was pleased with the blossoming relationship between her daughter-in-law and the handsome detective from the Newport Police Department. It was Caroline's first attempt to begin a relationship since Reed's death, and Louise approved of her choice.

"He's just a very good friend," Caroline said to Meredith, not ready to disclose that Hank Nightingale had definitely become more than a friend to her in the last several months. It had taken much patience on Hank's part, but Caroline was finally at ease with thinking of them as a couple.

"And when were you going to tell me about this? Why, this is wonderful. A man."

Meredith sounded reckless as she took Caroline by the arm and propelled her toward the telephone. "And a policeman. Call him. You must. We'll definitely need a man to take us out on the town tonight."

"I'll call him from my office. I have the number in there."

Louise thought Caroline must know the number by heart, but she didn't bother to mention the fact.

Newport at night can always be depended on to be a vibrant place. The lights shimmering around the harbor brighten the wharves and alleyways, welcoming pedestrian traffic. The doors of the restaurants and bars open and close with frequency, letting the friendly noise from inside radiate out into the cool sea air.

Caroline led Meredith down the cobblestones of Banister's Wharf and pushed open the old door of The Black Pearl. The bar was one of the city's most popular attractions, a good starting point for a Newport pub crawl.

"Hank ought to be here ahead of us," Caroline explained as Meredith's eyes moved around the crowded room. It was dark, nautical inside, and the air was filled with the sweet aroma of spent clam shells.

Caroline felt a quick flutter in her stomach as she picked out the broad form of Hank Nightingale sitting at the bar. She was still getting used to this shape, so different from the fair, slender body of her late husband. Hank was dark, with black hair and olive skin that easily tanned. She hoped wherever Reed was he was happy for her.

Caroline called out his name, and Hank turned. She felt the pleasure of his deep blue eyes focusing on her.

"Hello," he said, jumping off the bar stool. He came close to her, his hand touching hers.

"I've brought Meredith Hackett, my friend from New York. Meredith, meet Hank Nightingale."

"Hello, Hank," Meredith said, her eyes openly appraising him.

"Hello," he answered, conscious of the stare. "Welcome to Newport. Caroline says you're up here for a little R&R."

"That's right."

"Well, you've come at the right time of year. Fall's the best time in Newport." He turned toward the man at the bar, who had been watching their introductions. "And I have a friend, too."

"Hiya," the man said in a high-pitched voice. He was off the stool in quick, rabbit-like movements. "Spider Shipley, an old friend of the officer's here. I just come back in town, and we are catching up on old times."

"This is Caroline Kent, Spider. She owns the Inn at Kenwood Court. And this is her friend who's visiting her, Meredith Hackett."

The small, effervescent man shook Caroline's hand heartily.

"Pleased to meet you both," Spider said. He grabbed for Meredith's hand next, but she drew back and took a seat at the bar.

The bartender came toward them, and Hank asked, "What are you drinking, Meredith?"

"Dewar's on the rocks," she said. "No twist."

"Caroline? Gin and tonic?" She nodded, and Hank pointed to his own empty glass. "Another vodka and tonic here. Spider? Ready for another beer?"

"Yes, sir, and let me buy this round for these lovely ladies and yourself, sir." With a grand motion, he took out a roll of bills and peeled off two twenties. Caroline saw a brief look of concern pass over Hank's face.

"Thank you, Spider," she said.

Meredith was staring ahead, suddenly very interested in watching the bartender mixing their drinks.

"So, Meredith," Hank said. "How long are you staying in Newport?"

"I'm not sure," she said, taking a swallow from the Scotch now in front of her.

"Meredith's starting a new play in New York later this fall," Caroline explained. "She's an actress, Spider."

"Like on TV?"

"Not usually. Isn't that right, Meredith?" When Meredith didn't answer, Caroline added, "She prefers acting in a theater."

If Meredith was disappointed in sharing her evening out in Newport with Spider, Caroline could understand that. But she ought to try to hide it a little better. She was an actress after all.

"I just got back from L. A. myself," Spider said. He was standing, beer bottle in his right hand and his left hand on the bar. His eyes were bright, and Caroline wondered how many beers he'd already had this evening. "Now there's a place where you see a lot of movie stars. Ever been in a movie yourself, Meredith? Besides that dinner theater stuff."

Caroline winced and stopped herself from answering the question which Meredith was so clearly ignoring. There was a silence, which Hank wasn't helping to fill. Smiling gamely, Caroline asked Spider what he had been doing out in Los Angeles. Meredith looked at her watch.

"I stayed with some guys I knew out there. One of them did some work as an extra in the movies. Took me with him to the set once, but they wasn't hiring that day. I never went back, but who knows? Maybe I could have got myself in a movie." He looked pointedly at Meredith who was draining her Scotch. When she was finished she put the empty glass on the bar and glanced at her watch again.

"Nobody was going to put you in any movie," Meredith said, turning around on the stool and looking directly at Spider. "Let me give you that piece of important news." Caroline stared at the sudden change in the actress. Her eyes were blazing and her voice had the sound of spit.

Caroline spoke quickly. "Why don't we move on to another place, Hank? I did promise Meredith a tour of the city nightlife."

"Wait a minute here," Spider said. "I think this lady, if I may call her such, owes me an apology for the way she just spoke to me."

Meredith scowled her reply.

"You say you're some kind of actress but I ain't never heard of you," he said as his speech began to slur. "I never seen you in the movies or on television."

Now it was Spider's words which bit the air. Hank started to get up as the little man took a step toward Meredith. In an instant his feet were entangled in the bottom of her bar stool, and he had fallen on to her. She pushed him back with a fierceness that caused Caroline to grab for Spider.

"Get that drunk off of me," Meredith said. "He stinks."

Before Caroline could think of something to say, Meredith was standing and brushing the front of her leather jacket as if it were dusty.

"I'm going now, Caroline," she said.

"I'll come with you."

"No, I wish you wouldn't. Give me your car keys, will you? I'm sure Hank will give you a lift home."

Caroline handed over the keys as Hank shook his head and tightened a grip on Spider. His face was red, and his nose twitched as he glared at Meredith. Caroline thought Spider looked like some small rodent.

"Good night, Meredith," Hank said. She nodded and left the bar without speaking again. Caroline watched the closing black door. Her instinct was to go after her, but she saw Meredith was showing a temperament, and she wasn't in the mood to feel the brunt of it tonight.

"What she needs is somebody to teach her some manners," Spider said.

"Sure, Spider," Hank said. "Some other time."

"I hate women like that. Cold as an ice cube."

Hank was looking like a police officer now, and his frowning expression had its effect.

"Yeah, well, three's a crowd now. You don't have to hit old Spider Shipley on the head with a two by four. I'm going, too, and you don't have to tell me twice." He tipped them an imaginary hat and began to walk uncertainly toward the door. "I'm going down Thames Street. Drinks are cheaper there."

"Do you think he's had too much to drink, Hank?"

Hank shrugged. "It's hard to tell with Spider whether he's drunk or sober. Anyway, he's walking home."

Caroline picked up her drink from the bar. The ice had melted, but she drank a large gulp from it. The lime tasted bitter.

"How about a fresh one?" Hank asked. She nodded, and he signaled to the bartender for another round.

"I thought you'd enjoy meeting Meredith," she said.

"And I thought you'd get a kick out of Spider."

"No you didn't." His eyes were big and warm, and she liked to think of being lost inside their pull.

"I can't believe he's even one of your friends," she added, then smiled.

"He spent last night in jail. That's how we met up again. We did go to high school together, and nothing would do that we shouldn't go out and have a drink together to talk about old times. I tried to blow him off, but he wouldn't take no for an answer."

"You have a soft heart."

"Yeah? You really think so?"

"I like that about you," Caroline said.

He looked pleased. "I'm glad to hear that, but I have to say I hope that's the last I'll see of Spider Shipley for a long, long time."

CHAPTER III

Hank Nightingale always kept the windows of his bedroom wide open while he slept, and the following morning as he felt himself waking, his senses were greeted by the familiar damp, cool Newport air. Still keeping his eyes shut, he hunched down under the blanket and turned on his side toward the empty middle of the bed. His hands wandered over the soft, smooth sheets, as gradually his eyes opened. The place where she had been was cold now. He stretched across and grabbed the pillow where Caroline's head had so momentarily rested and pulled it toward him, his nostrils searching vainly for the scent of her existence.

"Damn," he allowed himself to say. He pushed the pillow away and rolled onto his back, his eyes staring up at the ceiling. The pleasure he felt was his due after last night's lovemaking was gone. Instead, he felt the anger of her going, the sorriness of being alone.

"Why don't you stay the night?" he had asked as they lingered in bed, the sensation of the night's cold keeping them wrapped in each other's arms.

"I can't," she had said. "I've got to be up so early at the inn. It's better if I leave tonight."

"I like to wake up and see you next to me. Wouldn't you like that, too?"

"Nothing would make me happier, Hank. But I can't ask Louise to be up at six to help get things started in the kitchen. Mattie would never allow it, for one thing." She stroked his chest and he didn't say any more. He knew how long it had taken Caroline to accept his attentions after they had first met, and he had learned not to press her to be entirely his.

Caroline had stayed until almost two a.m. before he drove her home. And so he was alone now, when he wanted so much to have her presence with him to share the smell of the sea air and drink coffee and sit across from one another at his kitchen table and make plans for the day.

But, of course, she had the inn to run and today, Saturday, would be especially busy for her. The financial strains, which he had recognized were heavy on the two Kent women, forced Caroline to assume a large physical burden in the day-to-day managing of the inn. He admired her tenacity. It was so much a part of who she was and why he had begun to love her. This morning he knew he was only looking for excuses to feel sorry for himself.

He had never been married, at the age of thirty-eight never even coming close, and he felt it was an unfair advantage she had over him to have once had a spouse herself. It was as if Caroline understood some mystique, and he did not. He wished, perversely, that he had known Reed Kent when he was alive. There were photographs of Louise's son at Kenwood, and Hank had studied them closely for some clue to the man and why Caroline had come to love him. Patience, he had reminded himself on more than this occasion, was key to the winning of the heart and mind of Caroline Kent.

Now he needed to get up, make his coffee, sit at the table, read the newspaper and think about his own plans for the day. Later he would call her. He knew she would like that. Women did. He would ask if Meredith Hackett, whom he was sure was the type of woman who would enjoy rehashing the entire scene, had gotten over her pique of the previous evening at The Black Pearl. He would make some positive remark about the actress and blame Spider entirely for causing her to storm out of the bar. Hank would suggest a time for him and Caroline to see one another in the near future, perhaps a quiet mid-week dinner, hopefully when Meredith had returned to New York.

Armed with his plan, he threw the blankets back and got out of bed. His bathrobe was hanging on the closet door and he was on the other side of the room, retrieving it, when the telephone rang. His first thought was that it was Caroline, calling him to see what he was doing, how he was doing. He hurried to pick up the receiver.

"Hello," he said softly.

"Lieutenant? Is that you?" Keisha McAndrew's voice seemed unnecessarily loud at the other end.

"Yes," he answered, making his own voice stronger. "What is it, Sergeant? It's my day off." He was trying to put his right arm into the robe while holding the phone against his left ear. "I might try to do some sailing. It looks like a good wind today."

"We've got a dead body, sir," Keisha broke in, "and it looks suspicious."

He switched the receiver and pulled the robe over his left shoulder. "What did you say?"

"I said it's a woman. She was found in a car in a parking lot on Freebody Street near the back of the Tennis Hall of Fame. First look is that she was strangled."

"Yeah? So it's my case?"

"The chief thought we ought to call you—"

"All right." Now he interrupted her. As much as he needed a new case, he was already determining how much it would interfere with his free time and Caroline. "I've got to get dressed." He wanted coffee. "I can be at Freebody Street in ten minutes." His apartment, located in one of the old Victorian villas behind the Redwood Library on lower Bellevue Avenue, was close to the crime scene.

"The thing is, Lieutenant, about the car the body was found in. It's registered to Mrs. Kent."

He thought he had stopped breathing.

But it wasn't possible. He had driven her back to Kenwood early this morning in his own car. The room was dark. He had shut his eyes to the worst. "Caroline . . . was . . . she?" was all he could manage.

"No, sir. No. It's not Mrs. Kent. We know it's not her."

He started coughing to release the tension in his chest.

"The dead woman had a handbag in the car with her," Keisha said, and he tried to concentrate on her words to recover his balance. "The driver's license makes it that she's a woman from New York City named Meredith Hackett."

"Damn it," Hank said as he remembered the confrontation between the dead woman and Spider the night before at The Black Pearl.

"What, sir?"

"Oh, just thinking of someone we'll have to question if this turns out to be a crime." He sighed. "I'm on my way."

The sight of Caroline's familiar old BMW convertible surrounded by the trappings of the crime scene was an unnerving sight to Hank as he pulled his own unmarked blue car behind the cluster of the department's black and whites assembled on Freebody Street. Even though he knew that Caroline was not the corpse inside the waiting grey vehicle, he still waited several seconds before exiting his own car. The crowd of curiosity seekers had gathered, and he now moved quickly past them, never taking his own eyes from the BMW. He had to see inside for himself.

Sgt. Ben Davies was standing next to the BMW, whose beige convertible top was up. He stepped aside so that his superior could peer into the interior of the car. The sergeant was a short, freckled middle-aged officer with whom Hank often worked. Ben waited while the lieutenant's eyes roamed the interior.

Finally Hank spoke to him. "How long has she been here? Do we know yet?"

"A guy going into the 7-Eleven," Ben said, pointing to the building which housed the convenience store and gas station across the street, "parked here about 7:10 a.m. to go pick up coffee. The 7-Eleven lot's small and it's pretty full then, and he figured it was easiest to run across the street. When he came back, he happened to look through the windshield."

Hank looked over at the store. He could use some coffee.

"Do we have the guy?" he asked.

"He's over there with Officer Edwards. She's getting his statement, name, where he works. I don't think he had anything to do with this." Ben motioned to the BMW. "She's been dead for hours. That's clear. She's cold. Real cold. And stiff."

Hank looked into the car again. The body was sitting in the driver's seat. Its head lay back, lodged in the space between the seat and the driver's window. He looked hard at the face of the actress. He realized he hadn't done that on his first inspection. Now he saw the bulging eyes, which had looked at him with such interest only the night before, dull and clouded by death. Meredith Hackett's mouth, which only a short time ago had been able to represent all her passions, now was ugly and distorted with swelling. The tongue protruded out in a asymmetrical flop. He was reminded of a pantomime scene, a tableau of repulsive death, with the actress at its center.

"Is there anything in the car which could have been used on her neck?" The thin marks of the strangulation were deep, but the skin was not bloody. Not sharp wire, but something strong.

"No. Nothing in the car but the body and the purse." At Hank's raised eyebrows, Ben added, "Wallet's there. Money, credit cards still inside. That's how we made the I.D . . . Photo on the driver's license matches."

"That's Meredith Hackett for sure," Hank said. His mind replayed the movement of the retreating figure of Spider Shipley, walking away from The Black Pearl's bar. Hank would have to question him as soon as possible. "I met her last night."

"Oh," Ben said. "Of course. Through Mrs. Kent. We wondered how the car came into it."

"We were all out for the evening. Maybe you ought to be writing this down, Sergeant."

Ben frowned and shifted his weight. His pink face, framed in unruly greying red hair, was flushed. Hank saw the discomfort his disclosure caused in the man at his side.

"It may be that I'm one of the last people to see the victim alive. She was staying at the inn. One of Mrs. Kent's guests. And she's also a friend. Damn! We haven't notified her yet, have we?"

"No, sir. I thought we'd leave that for the time being. Mrs. Kent hasn't reported the car missing or anything."

"No, she gave Ms. Hackett the car last night so she could drive herself back to the inn." He looked at his watch. It was twenty minutes to nine. "I expect Mrs. Kent hasn't realized yet that her guest is missing." He pictured Caroline moving about with the breakfast service, assuming Meredith's empty place at the table meant the actress was still asleep in the bed upstairs. "I'll have to call Mrs. Kent shortly. We'll have to interview her, also, and see if Ms. Hackett returned to Kenwood last night. We need to determine why she came to be here. Is that 7-Eleven open all night? We'll have to see if she went in there for coffee or whatever."

"Nothing's in the car to indicate she made a purchase. No bag, cup. Nothing."

"Check anyway. Maybe she missed the turn on to Bellevue and wanted directions back to Kenwood."

"Why wouldn't she park in their lot? It wouldn't have been crowded that time of night."

"Good question, Ben." Even though he often found himself relying on Keisha's youth and energy these days, Hank had great affection for his old colleague who could always offer perceptive insights during an investigation.

As she listened with a feigned, but practiced interest to Lisa Rayburn's lengthy commentary on her five days in Newport, Caroline understood why Meredith found the couple boring meal companions. Lisa and her husband Rich were ending their stay this morning. They had lingered at the breakfast table, blithely holding Caroline captive while she waited patiently to clear the table. She continued to smile, as if each revelation about the city was new and entertaining to her. The thirty-something Rayburns owned their own tech consulting business in Boston, and throughout their visit had never failed to impress upon her that their supply of money was limitless. Without question Caroline hoped to see them return often to The Inn at Kenwood Court, and she had gently dropped hints that their friends would be more than welcome as well.

"Marble House I prefer over The Breakers," Lisa was saying now. "And Belcourt Castle is such a funny old pile. Some of the mansions I could live in. Couldn't you, Rich?" Rich nodded. Caroline smiled inwardly. The wealthy inhabitants of the Gilded Age in Newport never referred to their summer cottages as *mansions*.

"Alva," Lisa' continued with an intimation of familiarity to the woman she called by her first name, "had such taste." She looked at her husband for confirmation of the fact, and Rich nodded again.

Alva Smith, who had been first married in the nineteenth century to William K. Vanderbilt, the grandson of the Commodore Cornelius Vanderbilt, had been dead since 1933. She had planned the building of Marble House, widely accepted as the most ostentatious of the Newport cottages. Her husband's brother Cornelius Vanderbilt II and his family had lived nearby in the magnificent house called The Breakers.

"How Alva could have gone from Marble House to Belcourt Castle is just amazing to me," Lisa said, shaking her head in disappointment at her newfound friend's conduct. Alva had divorced William in 1895 to marry another neighbor, Oliver Hazard Perry Belmont, the owner of Belcourt Castle. "You've been inside, Caroline. What do you think?"

Before Caroline could answer, Lisa gave her own view.

"I don't like the way it's decorated," Lisa pronounced. She continued offering her opinions and Caroline nodded agreeably, thanking the very practical way in which her acting training still served her. Being nice to the guests was imperative and she often thought of it as being on stage as she recited her dialog. Continuing to nod and smile like a bit part player at stage right, she was able to begin mentally to list her household chores for the day. The Campbell family was also leaving this morning, and she was expecting three new couples to arrive. Karen Moore, a local college student who worked week-ends at the inn, was already upstairs stripping beds and running the vacuum cleaner in the bedrooms. Mattie was preparing the lunch menu in the kitchen, along with Louise who would later help Caroline with the tidying of the downstairs rooms. Somebody needed to do some food shopping, and Caroline debated on whether she or her mother-in-law should go on that errand. She looked at her watch. It was almost ten o'clock. Perhaps she could fit that in herself while Louise served lunch to the early arrivals.

"And I certainly want to see that again," Lisa was saying. "We didn't have enough time for the grounds, did we, Rich?"

Caroline, unaware of which site was to be revisited, glanced at Rich, who was thankfully looking at his own watch. Caroline was tired. The aching of her stiff muscles reminded her of her abbreviated sleep time. She wished she could swim or run, or move in any direction freely and without purpose. She was tired of lifting and bending around the house. A day off would be nice, Caroline thought. And for several seconds she allowed herself to construct the most pleasant of days, sailing in the bay with Hank on a warm, sunny day without a clock to watch or a telephone to answer or a dish to carry.

"We'd better get going," Rich said when his wife took a breather from describing her joy at "seeing all those tennis legends at the Hall of Fame, I mean just everybody you ever heard about growing up." Lisa looked momentarily deflated to have to halt her narrative, but her husband reminded her that they had to get back to Boston to work on "that project" for the coming week. The prospect of the fee they would earn must have been compelling because Lisa Rayburn immediately put her napkin on the table and stood up. She turned from Caroline in a brisk motion, Rich close behind.

Caroline called good-by as they strode from the room, offering them wishes for a safe trip home. Their bill, as all the guests were expected to do, was paid in advance. They could leave without her seeing them again. Quickly Caroline began collecting the rest of the dishes from the table. She glanced at her watch again. Meredith had not been down to breakfast yet, but she was sure something could be sent up on a tray later in the morning to accommodate her sleepy friend.

25

CHAPTER IV

———— ∞∞∞ ————

The house in which Spider Shipley lived with his mother Irene was an unpretentious one story white-shingled house in the northern part of the city, far away from the gilded houses and estates. The grimy porch in need of a coat of paint and the two cheap folding chairs, which were its only furnishings, revealed the limit of Irene Shipley's ability to care for her home. Hank studied the peeling paint of the window frames as Keisha tapped smartly on the front door.

The lieutenant had left Freebody Street fifteen minutes earlier, and his mind was full of the scene he had observed. The medical examiner would confirm it shortly, but there seemed little reason to doubt that Meredith Hackett had been garroted from behind with some sort of cord or wire. If she had struggled with her attacker, he would also know this in a matter of time. Perhaps her assailant would provide them with some visible mark or wound to make their job easier.

Caroline's car had yielded nothing yet in the way of clues, but they were just beginning. Fingerprints would be collected, and the BMW would be carefully gone over for hairs and fibers and any other traces of its last occupants. Hank had left Ben Davies with the car and the body, giving him the rapid instructions for what he would want to know, a list Ben could make on his own.

"Someone's coming," Keisha said. She looked eager, thrilled to be selected to accompany him for this questioning. On the way over, in his car, he had filled her in on why Spider needed to be seen immediately.

"I've known the guy since the eighth grade. He was drinking a lot last night. And they did argue. He's got to be considered as a possible suspect until we can rule him out."

The door was opening and a short, sturdy woman, about sixty now he guessed, with a rough face and dry complexion peered out at them. She had dark eyes, almost black, and her coarse, wavy hair was a mix of iron grey and white. Hank hadn't seen Irene Shipley in probably twenty years, but he saw the woman he remembered. She was older and more tired-looking, but the face was there. He smiled at her, but she didn't appear to know who he was.

"Mrs. Shipley?" Keisha asked. She held out her identification. The woman squinted at it. She would need her glasses to read it. "Newport Police Department. Is your son Neil Shipley?" she asked, using Spider's given name. "Is he at home?"

At the questions, Irene Shipley puckered her mouth into an irritated scowl. She stood immobile, as if she was deciding her next step very carefully. Hank was impatient.

"Where's your son, Mrs. Shipley," he asked. "Is Spider inside? This is official police business. We want to see him."

"What's he done now?" his mother asked.

"Right now we want to ask him some questions," Hank said. "Do you know where he is? Is he inside?" He said the last three words slowly, definitely, and finally she nodded.

"Come in," Irene said flatly.

They followed her into the small living room. It was clean, but worn. Several thick glass vases of plastic flowers provided the only spots of color.

"I got to go to work," she said. "I have to be there in half an hour. I'm just leaving. Why do you want Neil?"

"Where do you work, Mrs. Shipley?" Keisha asked. She was ready to note the information in her book.

"Out on the Drive at Windward." Hank knew the estate. It was a rugged, desolate house perched on an isolated cropping of rocks overlooking the Atlantic Ocean. "It's Gen. Patterson's place."

"What do you do there?" Keisha asked.

"The cooking. Some house cleaning I only work half a day on Saturday."

"We'll want some information from you, Mrs. Shipley. We won't try to keep you," Hank said, looking back through the open door to the kitchen. "But, first would you get Spider? Neil. Is he asleep?" He was surprised that their entrance into the small house had not brought out any other occupants to see who had arrived.

"Yeah, he came in late last night. Sleeping it off now. Was he in another fight? Can't keep his hands to himself," she said wearily. "Ever since he was a kid. Never accepted he was a runt like his father. This time you can keep him in jail. I'm not putting up any more bail money."

She shuffled toward a hallway off the living room, calling as she went. "Neil, get yourself out of bed. You got to get up. Cops are here." Keisha followed a few steps behind her. And then the groggy figure of Spider Shipley came out. He was clad in grey underpants that had once been white, and his feet were bare.

In the small space, his bare white flesh was close enough to touch. He was sleepy, unfazed by their presence and certainly not embarrassed to be half-naked in front of a strange woman. Keisha was looking hard at his face. There were no scratches or other marks which might indicate a recent struggle.

"Hi, Hank." Spider seemed happy to see them. "Ma, this is Hank Nightingale. Remember him? He's a cop now in Newport."

His mother didn't answer.

"I need to ask you some questions, Spider. This is an official visit. Do you want to put some clothes on?" Hank looked inquiringly at Irene. "Mrs. Shipley, can you get his pants?"

Irene didn't seem inclined to do so, but something in her head must have told her this was not the occasion to be disagreeable.

"And I'd like to see the clothes he was wearing last night."

"They're on the floor, Ma. By the bed," Spider offered helpfully.

Once again Irene Shipley shuffled down the hallway. Hank motioned for Keisha to accompany her.

"What's official, Hank? What does that mean?" Spider smoothed down his hair, which was so short that the gesture made no difference to its appearance.

"It's official because it's part of my job to ask you some questions."

Keisha came back with a crumpled white T-shirt and blue jeans. Irene handed Spider a second outfit of the same set of clothes, which he slid into in several quick motions.

"Sit down, Hank, why don't you? You too, Miss."

"Sergeant McAndrews," Keisha said.

"Sergeant? That's nice. A lady sergeant."

"Are you ready?" Hank asked. He sat down on the threadbare sofa.

"Ask away," Spider said, sitting on a shabby brown upholstered chair opposite. Keisha sat down with Hank on the sofa, but Irene stood in the doorway to the kitchen.

"What did you do after you left us at The Black Pearl last night? I think the time was about quarter after ten."

"I guess I went up to Thames Street."

"Were you alone?" Hank asked.

"What do you mean?"

"Did you go to Thames Street alone?"

"Yeah. I must have."

"And you hit the bars?" Spider nodded. "Which ones did you go to?"

"Well," Spider said, touching the top of his head again, this time rubbing it, "I can't honestly say I remember. I was drinking pretty good last night, and I can't say for sure." He laughed self-consciously, looking in his mother's direction.

Hank mentioned the names of several of the drinking establishments along Thames Street, but Spider only frowned and shook his head. Keisha added two more, but the response was the same.

"Did you meet anyone you knew?" Hank asked.

"No, but I made some friends."

"Did you see Meredith Hackett?"

"Who?" Spider squinted at him, and Hank saw some resemblance to Irene in the hard stare.

"The woman who was with us in The Black Pearl last night."

"Oh, *her*. The ice lady. Nah. I never saw her no more."

"She left just ahead of you," Hank said. "You must have seen her when you went out into Bannister's Wharf."

"It was pretty crowded and to tell you the truth, Hank, I was a little wasted by then."

Hank sighed. He turned to Irene and asked her what time Spider had come in. She shook her head.

"It was late, I know that. Way after I went in to bed. I go to bed around eleven as I got to get up early." She looked in her son's direction. "Neil hasn't got a job yet."

"I told you I'd get something, Ma. I—"

"Did you go into more than one bar?" Hank interrupted, and Spider looked blank. The slow, plodding questioning of all the bars on Thames Street to retrace Spider's steps the previous night would have to begin.

"How did you get home, Mr. Shipley?" Keisha asked. "Do you remember, Mr. Shipley?"

"I sure don't know." Spider seemed to be thinking hard. "I think somebody put me in a cab, now that I think about it."

"Who put you in a cab?"

Spider looked apologetic. "I told you. I don't know."

They'd have to check that, too, Hank thought. Well, Keisha would do a good job with it. Get some others of the uniformed officers to help with the spade work. It would take some time. He'd have to get a photograph of Meredith Hackett to show around town. He didn't suppose Caroline would have one, but the Hackett woman had been a professional actress. It wouldn't be hard to get one of her publicity stills. Caroline said she was starting a new production, and a photograph of her could probably be found online. She could even have her own web site.

"Can I go now?" Irene asked. "The general doesn't like me to be late."

"Don't forget, Ma, that you said you'd talk to him about having me do some work about the place. I'm a good handyman."

"Like you are around here?" Spider lowered his eyes, and his mother shook her head. "I'll see. The general hasn't been feeling too good lately." She turned to Hank. "He's got a real weak heart."

Hank stood up. "I'm going to have to ask you to come down to the station, Spider, to take your statement about your movements last night, and anything else you can tell me about Meredith Hackett."

"Why?" his mother asked. "Why does he have to give a statement?"

"Meredith Hackett was found dead this morning."

"Dead?" Spider's high voice was strained. "You didn't say anything about her being dead."

"We need his statement," Hank said, as Irene moved toward her son.

"And you think I killed her?" Now Spider's voice was panicked.

"No one is accusing you of anything, Spider. But I saw you leave The Black Pearl shortly after she left, and I need to get your account of what you did last night after you went out onto Bannister's Wharf around quarter after ten."

"Don't talk any more," Irene said in a hard voice. She turned to Hank. "He didn't do it. I know he didn't do it. You got to find somebody else, Lieutenant. Neil didn't do anything like that."

"You don't know that, Mrs. Shipley," Hank said. "You don't know anything about it. Or do you?"

"I never heard of that woman, but I know Neil wouldn't kill anybody." She paused. "Does he need a lawyer?"

"He can call somebody if he wants." He knew she would be thinking of the cost after having to cover his bail the day before.

"You go to work, Ma. Don't upset the General," Spider said. "I'll call you when I'm finished. O.K.?" He gave her an awkward pat on her dry, chapped hands, and she nodded her head slowly. "Hank and me been friends a long time. He ain't gonna do nothing he doesn't have to do."

"Let's go, Spider," Hank said evenly. "Let's get this over with."

"I got to get some shoes," Spider said. He gave his mother a brave grin, but Irene Shipley didn't smile back. Hank watched his old friend pad back down the hall, followed by Keisha, toward his bedroom.

"Should I come with him to the station?" Irene asked.

For his part, Hank thought that Irene was right that his old friend couldn't kill anybody. Garroting a victim was a brutal means of killing. But he couldn't rule Spider out as a suspect until the clothes were tested and his fingerprints matched against any found in Caroline's car.

"No," Hank said. "He'll call you like he said."

CHAPTER V

When Kenwood was built in 1882, it was not conceived on the grand scale of the two Vanderbilt houses in Newport, The Breakers and Marble House. But the Kents' regal house with its grey facade and arched Palladian windows trimmed in white had been planned much like all the rest of the resort's Gilded Age estates. It was to be a summer plaything for its wealthy owners. Designed and built by the celebrated architect of the period, Stanford White, for Frederick Kent and his family, the property had served this function for twelve weeks each season for a span of over a hundred years. As a young bride, Louise had been brought to the estate where she was to spend many leisurely summer days and nights filled with the pleasures of society.

But the Kents were not good conservators of the family trust given to them after the first Frederick Kent made his fortune in the China trade. Each succeeding generation whittled down the fortune until it was a twig. The ultimate blow came when Reed's father, also named Frederick, entered into a series of disastrous business deals, each believed to be the savior of the last and became, for all practical purposes, broke. At his death in 1993, the only Kent asset left was Kenwood itself, and that had been mortgaged heavily. Reluctant to part with the old family home, Louise and Reed had put the estate up for rent to a series of tenants eager for admittance into Newport society. That goal had proved difficult, if not impossible, for most of the anxious newcomers, but the Kents had made a respectable return off their lodgers' aspirations.

Caroline's decision to move into Kenwood after Reed's death brought her home to an estate which had become neglected over the years of the tenancy. She had invested what money she had into restoring the house, but there was so much yet to be done, especially to the grounds. After The Inn at Kenwood Court was up and running, she continued to save costs by doing much of the work herself. Caroline had not been sure of how much her mother-in-law could contribute to the venture, but Louise did more than her share of the work. Although the two women's financial existence was still day to day, business at the inn improved steadily. Some months were showing a modest profit.

Caroline had made her office for the managing of the inn out of the old smoking room at the back of the east wing. It was located off the back stairs and near to the kitchen. Above, on the second floor, was the small suite of rooms which provided the living quarters for Caroline and her mother-in-law.

Caroline's routine was set. She was up early and generally worked seven days a week. Several maids and a cleaning service did the heavy work, but the task of keeping things going was disproportionally hers. In the months after Reed's death, work was exactly what she had needed to bear her grieving. Now, almost two years later, she was beginning to envision some relief from the burden she had once so willingly assumed.

On the desk in front of her lay the estimates for the repairs to the roof over the main part of the house. Water had come into two of the guest bedrooms during the last heavy rain storm. At the beginning of the summer, as the bookings were increasing, Caroline had begun considering if she could afford the luxury of hiring a part-time manager to give her some free time. But, if the roof needed major repair, that extravagance would be put off. She would have to use the bulk of her revenues from the summer's guests to fix the roof. The one early lesson she had learned after becoming a new businesswoman was of being practical.

A knock at the door interrupted her thinking, and she looked up to see Karen opening the heavy old oak door.

"Excuse me, Caroline," Karen said, "but Lt. Nightingale is here." Hank had become a regular visitor to the house, and Karen smiled as she stepped aside and allowed Hank to enter the room.

"Thank you, Karen," Caroline said as the young woman left them alone. Caroline got up and moved toward Hank as he closed the door. She was surprised that he didn't embrace her. She looked at his face. "What's wrong?" she asked. She knew his moods, and this one was black.

"I need to talk to you," he said. He was looking at her face, and she tried to think what might have happened since they had parted early that morning to displease him. He told her. Quickly and efficiently, he explained that Meredith Hackett was dead and that she had most probably died in Caroline's car.

"Where is she?" she asked softly.

"They'll be doing the autopsy," Hank answered. He was watching her eyes filling with tears. She looked at one of the photographs of Reed hanging among the old family pictures in the room. She had lived through someone's telling her that her own husband was dead, and now the news of this death would bring back the old feelings of grief she had known so well.

Several seconds passed before she spoke again. "Do you know who did it?"

"We have one suspect."

"Who?"

"Spider Shipley."

"Oh, no, Hank. He couldn't have, could he? Did he confess?"

"No, he claims to know nothing about it, but he was drunk last night and can't remember where he was or what he did. Because of the scene with Meredith in the bar, we have to consider him. We're checking the fingerprints in your car for a match. We'll have to take yours, of course. I'm sorry. And Louise's and anyone else you can think of who has been in the car."

"You."

"What?"

"You. I picked you up at the station the week before last. Remember? We were going to the upholsterer's in Portsmouth to pick up that chair, and you were going to help me put it in the back seat."

"Of course, I'd forgotten that. Well, I'll add my name to the list."

Suddenly she began to cry. "I thought she was sleeping late, you know. All this morning, and even a few minutes ago, I was sure she was upstairs."

"Damn," he said, putting his arms around her and pulling her against his chest. Caroline was sobbing, loud, graceless sobs of anguish.

She was grateful for his broad chest and the feel of his large hands on her back. He was massaging his fingers into her shoulders now, soothing her. She coughed a few times and stopped crying. "I'm all right. It's just the shock." She sat down and he stood beside her, still holding her shoulders. She blew her nose. "I wasn't expecting anything like this to happen."

"I know," he said gently. "Can we talk about Meredith? Do you feel up to it? I'd like to ask you some questions about her."

"Yes," she said, sniffing and making an effort to recover her composure. "What do you want to know?"

"We need to determine where she went after she left The Black Pearl. Where did you leave the car?"

"We found a space on Thames Street near the post office, right across from Bannister's Wharf. All she had to do was walk across America's Cup Boulevard and the car was right there. It would have taken a few minutes at the most."

"Would she have walked around before she went to the car?"

"Why? She said she wanted to go back to Kenwood. You heard her. She was upset."

"That's just it. She was upset. Would she have gone into another bar to have a drink to settle herself down?" Caroline looked perplexed. "How about driving back here? She would have passed a few bars on her way up Memorial Boulevard to Bellevue Avenue."

"I don't know, Hank. I can't think."

"Somebody killed her, Caroline. Somebody she met after she left us. Where did she meet this person?"

"You think a bar?"

"Would she have let someone pick her up?"

Caroline shook her head. "I don't think so. It doesn't seem like her. She was very . . . you met her . . . she was, well, discriminating."

"And you don't see her talking to strangers in a bar."

"No," Caroline said, "but I can see that it makes it all the more important that she did know Spider. But why would she have gone off with him? Not to one of the bars on lower Thames where he said he was going." She shook her head. "No, none of it makes any sense."

"Right," Hank said. "What about Meredith's family. We'll have to notify them . . . the next of kin. Do you know how to get in touch with anyone?"

"I'm not sure. She was always on her own in New York. I never knew anyone. I'm sorry."

"Do you know where she's from? Is she originally from New York City?"

"I don't think so." Her mind was groping for memories. Who talked about their childhoods when the New York stage was their life? "I'm pretty sure not. Everyone came from somewhere else. I mean, most of the actors and theater people I knew." She thought hard. "I'm not sure. Nothing's coming back to me." Caroline had spent her college years at Yale in the drama program there, and several of her colleagues from New Haven had come down to the city together, but Meredith had not gone to Yale. Had she gone to NYU? Tom Benton had, but no, Caroline didn't think Tom and Meredith had known one another as far back as college. "I can't think of anything," she said, surprised that she couldn't put one fact before him. "It seems I really don't know anything about her." She thought. "I know I certainly never met anyone else from Meredith's family. She never mentioned them now that I think about it."

"Do you know who her manager is?"

"No, she didn't say while she was here. But I think Tom Benton would know. He's another actor. I'll give you his phone number."

"Do you have any photographs of her?" Caroline shook her head. "Keisha's checking the Internet for a publicity shot. She was surprised Meredith didn't have a web site. You'd think an actress would want her name out there."

Caroline shuddered. "You've got to find out who did this, Hank."

"We will. But we've got to establish what she did after she left The Black Pearl. Did she come back here at any time?"

"That's going to be hard for me to ascertain, Hank. I didn't get in until—"

"Yes, I know when you got home." He paused. "No one's been in her room to make the bed?" She shook her head. "You did think she was still asleep?" She nodded. "Let's go upstairs now. I want to see the room." He went to the door. "Who was in the house besides you and Louise last night?"

"Mattie. But she sleeps up on the third floor. I doubt she heard or saw anything. She keeps her door locked up there."

"What about the other guests?"

"Five people. But they've all just left today. They couldn't have had anything to do with this, could they?"

"I'll have to take their names and addresses and check that out. We can't eliminate anything or anybody."

Caroline thought of Lisa and Rich Rayburn, with their laptops and BlackBerrys. And the Campbells, a middle-aged couple from New Hampshire, who had brought her mother along with them to see the city. It couldn't be possible that one of them had murdered Meredith. Guests strangling guests? It was monstrous to consider any of them as killers.

"Louise hasn't mentioned anything to you this morning about Meredith?" Hank asked. She was relieved to be interrupted.

"No, we've been very busy." She looked at her watch. "She's doing the lunch service now. I was about ready to run some errands." She stopped and looked at him. "My car. What about my car? Where is it?"

"I'm afraid you can't have that back for a while. We'll have to make some arrangements to get you something else to drive in the meantime."

"That's all right. I can use Louise's car. That's not important. Come on upstairs."

As Caroline started through the door she turned back to Hank. "Oh, Hank, did she suffer? I didn't even ask."

"It doesn't look that way," he said quickly. It was too early to know, but it was what he wanted her to hear. "I think it went pretty quick. She couldn't have been conscious long."

"My God," Caroline said, and he wrapped his arms around her shaking body again. "I can't believe it. She was so alive. I thought she was so beautiful, and so talented. Why?" She repeated herself. "Why? It's awful that she was all alone up here when she died."

"We'll find who did it," he said reassuringly. "I won't let you down."

"I was really happy to see her." And Caroline had been. It had been good to let the old days come back without feeling sorrow. And now another death marked her existence.

They opened the door and entered Meredith's room slowly. Caroline looked straight at the bed, her brain telling her that there was still a chance that the sleeping actress would move about, stir as they arrived to disturb her lie-in.

Hank went to the empty bed, but Caroline remained near the door. She knew that civilians were unwelcome during murder investigations. She watched as he looked down at the creamy white lace bed covering and the high mound of feather pillows. Hank was staring, thinking. His eyes next went to the bedside table. There was a small travel clock and a box of tissues.

"The room is very neat," he remarked, looking at the rest of the furniture. "The bed hasn't been slept in."

The room was part of a suite. A three-quarter wall partitioned the bedroom from a sitting room. Hank walked around the wall and entered the other room where there was a sofa and two chairs grouped in front of a marble-framed fireplace. Caroline waited, and Hank returned shortly and now entered the bathroom, which was on this side of the suite. She heard him moving about.

"When did she arrive?" he asked from inside the bathroom. She finally let herself move further into the room so she could answer without raising her voice.

"Tuesday. After lunch."

"You knew she was coming?" He came back into the bedroom and stood close to her.

"She called on Monday evening. I hadn't heard from her in ages. We'd lost touch after I stopped working in the theater. I was very surprised."

"Didn't it seem odd that she came the very next day? How did she explain why she wanted to come immediately?"

"Oh, people like Meredith are often unpredictable. She said she needed a rest and wanted to get away from the city."

"She wasn't in a play?"

"Oh, no. She had finished a run, and she had an offer to start something next month. She said she had a script with her." She looked around the room. It was exceptionally tidy, with no stray article of clothing or papers visible in the room. Suddenly Caroline had a thought. "She said she was reading a book every night. I wonder where it is. It's not on the table next to the bed. Did you see it in the other room?" Hank shook his head.

"I'll do a thorough search of the room later. Ben is coming to help me. Did she spend much time in other parts of the house?"

"She liked to go outside and sit in the gazebo down by the ocean. And she liked going into the conservatory in the morning. She used to take her coffee and the newspapers in there."

The conservatory was at the back of the west wing, across from the library, and on the opposite side of the house from the dining room where Meredith had tried to avoid the other guests as often as possible.

"And you both talked a lot?"

"Mostly late, after dinner when I wasn't busy otherwise. Twice we sat in the gazebo and talked in the afternoon."

"What did you talk about?"

"My life. Her life, too, I guess." She didn't want to share their conversations about Caroline's adjustment to life after Reed's death.

"Did she mention any names of people? Someone she might have been involved with romantically? Or any other associates in the theater? Friends in New York?"

"We caught up on where everyone was whom I knew from when I was still working in New York. Nobody we talked about seemed anyone especially important to her, if that's what you're looking for."

"At this stage, I'm not looking *for* anything. I'm gathering." She didn't answer, and he frowned. "Did she talk about anything that surprised you? Anything out of the ordinary that sticks in your mind that—"

"—that doesn't fit," Caroline finished the sentence for him. He nodded. "She was tired. I definitely noticed that. Lethargic some days. She always had so much energy, but not this week. That's why I wasn't surprised when she didn't come down for breakfast this morning."

"Did you think that outburst last night, the one against Spider, was typical of her?"

"Yes and no. She was a snob, which I suppose is understandable, and she wouldn't have time for your friend Spider. Of course she had an ego, but she was talented, Hank. Believe me. She had a real gift for acting and she knew it. But, I never thought she was mean. And I thought Meredith sounded mean last night. I would have easily characterized her as self-absorbed, possibly she could be thoughtless . . . but never mean."

"She was angry," Hank said. "I'm wondering if it was anger which she meant to be directed at Spider, or whether it was something else. Someone else."

"Who?" Caroline asked.

"She could have had some break-up with a boyfriend. Or even a serious argument which would have made her want to put distance between them."

"It's the kind of drama she would have liked," Caroline said and found herself smiling. "But I honestly didn't get any clue that there was a man in her life. In fact, I never knew Meredith to have a serious relationship. Escorts for parties, if you know what I mean." He nodded. "Louise didn't take to her, you know." She saw the fact didn't surprise him.

"Louise wouldn't say it to me, of course, but I could see it in her expression. I was used to Meredith. She was always on stage, even when she was doing something ordinary, like putting the soup in bowls." She was remembering the actress's elaborate actions of the previous evening, as she had insisted on helping with the meal preparation. Every movement so artful. "She couldn't have been thinking of giving up her career, either," she added. "She loved it so. It was her life."

Her life. Caroline shuddered. Acting was her friend's life. But it would be a life no more.

CHAPTER VI

—∞∞∞—

The Sunday newspapers carried articles on the death of Meredith Hackett. The story was too late for the city's paper, the *Newport Daily News* which published a combined Saturday-Sunday edition, but the Boston and Providence papers all featured the story on page one the day after the actress's murder was discovered.

Television stations also had the story. The city had no station of its own, but its local news was carried on several outlets in both Rhode Island and Massachusetts. Almost every medium had a photograph of the dead woman, a professional stage portrait which showed her heavily made up and looking her best.

On Sunday, as she stooped to pick up the stack of newspapers lying near the front door of the inn, she saw the page one photograph of Meredith's face immediately. She unwrapped the plastic covering and stood on the steps and read the entire story in *The Boston Globe*. Next she read the Providence *Journal-Enquirer* and saw that its account was similar to the Boston paper's article.

Caroline also had two copies of *The New York Times* delivered each day. Meredith's death was not important enough for the front page, but in the metro section, nudged between an article about a new E.P.A. clean-up plan for New Jersey and the sighting of a black bear in downtown Peekskill, she found a small Associated Press story giving

44

only the barest details of the murder of stage actress Meredith Hackett in Newport, Rhode Island. Returning to the kitchen with the armful of papers, she met Louise in the passageway. Her mother-in-law looked grimly at the bundle. Caroline nodded, and Louise shook her head.

"It's dreadful," Louise said, "and it's just beginning. What do the papers say?"

Caroline dropped the stack onto the wooden table and offered one to Louise.

"I almost don't want to read it," she said. She took a paper, then held it in her hands as if it were contagious.

"The details of the murder mostly." Caroline took the paper back from her grasp. "You don't need to read it. The Newport police are asking for anyone who saw Meredith in the city on Friday evening to come forward. There's a long quote from Hank."

"Is there anything about where she was staying?"

"Not by name. Only that she was traveling and stopped in Newport. I think Hank may have downplayed the name of the inn for our benefit."

"It's bound to come out. But, I don't know that fact will be especially interesting to anyone. My guess is the news people want something more sensational."

"The police don't have much at this point."

Caroline and Louise had talked about the death of Meredith Hackett on the night before after the guests had retired. The two women had sat up in their sitting room, and Caroline had explained to Louise what she knew about the case and Hank's early suspicions that Meredith had been killed by a man she had met in one of the bars.

"I don't see her being careless," Louise had said. "I don't think that's the explanation."

"I agree with you. I told Hank that I don't think she was after a one-night stand."

"What about this Spider Shipley? Could he have followed her and killed her out of spite? You told me she wasn't very nice to him."

"You don't kill a perfect stranger because they're rude. No," Caroline had said. "It doesn't make any sense. My impression of Spider is that he is a harmless hanger-on. He was delighted to be out with Hank. Hank's a policeman. If Spider was some kind of maniac who killed women, he wouldn't have wanted to hang out with a cop."

"Hank is sure Meredith didn't come back here on Friday evening, after she left you?"

"There's no evidence. Hank's been in contact with the Rayburns and the Campbells. They said they didn't see her that night."

"Their rooms were in the west wing. Meredith's suite is on the corner of the east. Next to your bedroom, Caroline."

"I didn't hear anything. And the bed wasn't slept in."

"Oh, dear. I'm sorry, Caroline. I know how genuinely happy you were to see her again."

"We talked about things I hadn't talked about in several years," Caroline had said in response and added, more to herself than to Louise, "I must be getting old, to enjoy going down memory lane like that." Louise had let the conversation end at that point, and they had both gone into their bedrooms to get ready for sleep. For Caroline, the night had been fitful, and the realization of what had happened caused her to wake that morning with a dull headache.

"Meredith Hackett didn't strike me as a very happy person."

"Why do you say that, Louise?" Caroline asked, coming back to the present. Louise was staring at the newspaper photograph lying on the kitchen table.

"The way she looked so faraway," the older woman answered. "I noticed her quite often, looking preoccupied."

"I thought she had been overworking and couldn't begin to relax. But you think that was because she was unhappy?"

"Or worried about something," Louise suggested. "Did Meredith mention anything that was bothering her?"

"No, not particularly."

"I wondered if she might be ill."

"Oh." Caroline became distressed. "She did look tired, but she had said she just needed a rest. You think she might have been seriously ill? That she had just gotten some diagnosis that was life-threatening. Like cancer or something?"

"The autopsy will tell that, I expect. And I'm sure the police will find her doctor in New York."

Caroline had put her hands to her throat. "Is that why she came up here? Why didn't she tell me? I would have tried to help."

"Perhaps she was planning to," Louise said gently.

Caroline expelled a deep breath and picked up the *Globe* again. Meredith's shining face stared back at her.

"It's so senseless that she was killed, Louise. I feel responsible."

"What nonsense. You're upset, but I don't want you to talk so foolishly."

Caroline was recalling that last afternoon when she and Meredith were in the gazebo. Caroline had said that she had learned that time heals, and now she remembered how Meredith's face had grown grave. She hadn't thought so, the actress had said. Was that her fear? That she had no time left to her for healing.

"I should have gone with her when she left The Black Pearl. It makes sense, Louise. Don't you see? If she was ill . . . that's why she became so angry that night."

"She was a grown woman," Louise said firmly, "who had a mind of her own. I'm sorry she was attacked, but you need to understand that you couldn't have prevented that."

47

"I'm not sure. I could have driven her home right then and there, and she'd still be alive today."

Spider Shipley left his mother's old Ford Taurus station wagon parked on the road and took the shortcut over the hill to reach the overgrown path which led to the secluded Newport estate called Windward. After spending several hours of the previous day at the police station, Spider relished the sense of freedom that came from walking alone on this desolate crest above the ocean. When he had gone with Hank to the police station, Spider had been disappointed to have been handed over to the black lady sergeant. She spent some time with him in a tiny, windowless interview room where she asked him questions about what she called "his movements" on Friday evening after he had left The Black Pearl. Spider had grown tired of repeating that his memory was hazy, that he couldn't remember. He had been drunk after all.

"It's no good you hounding me, miss," he had said after Sgt. McAndrews had asked him for the third time to recollect the scene outside The Black Pearl and whether he had seen "in which direction Ms. Hackett had walked."

"Sergeant," she had corrected him.

"Sergeant," Spider had said. "But, I was still drinking, sergeant, and I can't tell you what I did, but I know I didn't kill no one. Sergeant." She had looked at him suspiciously, and Spider wished Hank had been the one to question him. Hank was an old friend, and he wouldn't have stared at Spider liked that. He half-expected to be held in a cell after the interrogation was finished, but instead he had been allowed to go home where his mother berated him for getting involved with the police for a second time. To placate Irene, and to get her to fix his supper, he had promised to begin looking for a job immediately. Windward was the first, and he had a notion that it might be the last stop on his list.

Spider remembered the estate from when he was a teenager, and he and his buddies used to look for secluded places to park along Ocean Drive. There they would drink, smoke, and on lucky occasions, bring some girls along. Windward's grounds were dark, and the house was far off the main road, so that parking at the beginning of its long driveway provided dependable privacy for the clandestine pursuits of the younger generation of Newport.

None of his friends had ever ventured anywhere near to the house, and now Spider stared up at the looming structure, seeing it up close for the first time. It was impressive in the Sunday afternoon sunlight. The house was broad with two diagonal wings which branched out to face the ocean. The massive brown walls were made of cocoa-colored stone. Huge red brick chimneys rose in clumps from several locations in the dark slate roof. The windows were high and narrow, like those in a medieval castle.

The path under his feet was rocky, and Spider had to push aside the wild branches of shrubbery as he walked. The house's layout puzzled him. He couldn't make sure which side was the front and where the front door was to be found. His mother wasn't working today. Sundays were her day off. Despite his reliance on her, Gen. Patterson managed to get on without her providing his meals on this one day of the week. Spider hadn't paid much attention to Irene's description of her household duties at Windward. All he knew was that there was a chauffeur who drove the old man around and who lived in the house with him. Slept in the next room in fact, he had remembered his mother explaining. She always said that the general was sick and he couldn't be left alone.

Spider thought a man who was rich and dependent on others to live ought to need more help than a housekeeper and a chauffeur, especially when he lived in such a large house. Spider could see by the state of the grounds that there was definitely a want for gardening help. In L.A., he had cleaned swimming pools for a maintenance company, and, despite his slight frame, he was used to outdoor work. Gaining a job on this Newport estate ought to be simple for a man with his background. He couldn't see why he shouldn't present himself at the general's door and put his proposition for work before him. His mother's faithful employment at Windward ought to be reference enough for her son.

"Hello there," a man's voice called. It had a friendly tone and Spider turned toward it. Looking for the main entrance which he supposed faced the ocean, he had come around the side of the mansion and found himself in a courtyard with a surprising complex of structures protruding off the three wings of the main building. A young man, dressed in jeans and a dark T-shirt, was standing next to a rusted black van parked in front of a corner of the main house which jutted asymmetrically out into the courtyard. The singular structure had high, wide leaded-glass windows and elaborate wood gingerbread on the eaves.

"Hi," Spider said. "I'm looking for Gen. Patterson. Are you his chauffeur?" His mother had doubtless said the driver's name, but Spider couldn't recall it.

"Oh, no," the man said, laughing. He was about Spider's height, boyish looking, with lemon-colored hair and grey eyes. "I'm Will Patterson. Charles Patterson is my father."

"Yeah, sure. Pleased to meet you. Spider Shipley's the name."

"Any relation to Mrs. Shipley?"

"That's my mother."

"Are you looking for her? I don't think she's here today."

"Ah, actually . . . no. It's your father I thought I could speak to."

"I'm not sure he's up at the moment, Spider. He doesn't sleep well at night. He ends up napping during the day. Evening's the best time to catch him."

"Geez, I didn't know that. Mom should have told me." Spider looked in the open door of the van and saw that it was cluttered with numerous cardboard boxes and half a dozen crammed black plastic garbage bags. Will followed his eyes.

"I'm moving into the studio," he said, pointing to the timbered appendage to the house.

"Yeah? I just got in from L.A. myself. Been out there for about four years. Where you been living?"

"Montana," Will answered. Spider waited for an explanation of what was in Montana. He could understand anyone's knowing the lure of California, but Montana was where they had moose and elk.

"You been a cowboy or something?"

"No, other reasons took me away from home."

"Well, I got to get some work now that I'm back." Spider wondered if this Will was in the same predicament or did his father support him. "I kind of thought your father could use a handyman about the place. Ma said there's a lot of work that ought to be done around here." He looked around as if to indicate the validity of his claim. In truth, the courtyard was neat, and the house walls looked in good repair. "The grounds I could start with. I saw the path as I was coming up was pretty overgrown."

"I think my father prefers things that way. He's pretty much of a recluse these days."

"Yeah. I know Ma said he's sick. That's too bad. But do you think I could try to see him, though? To ask about the job?"

Will ignored the question. He was surveying the inside of his van.

"That all your stuff?" Spider asked, and Will nodded. His face suddenly looked serious, and Spider knew he was bothering him by hanging around. He did want Will to take him into the house to talk to the general so he gestured to the bags in the van. "Want me to help you carry some of this stuff inside?" He indicated the studio. "Is that where you want it?"

"I'm staying in there while I'm here." Will Patterson turned back and studied Spider for several seconds. The scrutiny made Spider uncomfortable, but he smiled bravely. "It's my mother's old studio," Will said. "She used to paint." Spider nodded his interest. "Yeah, why don't you help me carry some stuff up? I hauled a lot of this crap inside yesterday, and I got tired of doing it. I've been driving around with it in the van, and I'm afraid someone might break in to it while I've got it parked somewhere."

"Sure," Spider said. He reached in to pull out one of the biggest cardboard boxes. From its resistance to his tug, he realized the box contained books. He struggled and hoisted it up on his shoulders. "Lead the way," he said, as Will took two of the garbage bags. "I'm right behind you."

They walked up a flight of steps to reach the studio's interior. Spider saw that the inside had once been elegant, but that the room had been neglected for a long time. Will had not appeared to have done much unpacking. More boxes and plastic bags were piled against one of the walls. There was a camp bed set up in one corner next to a low table with an old stereo system with a turntable for playing records. On the floor next to the bed were boxes of vinyl records along with some dirty dishes and three empty beer bottles.

Opposite to the bed were the remains of what must have been part of the room's original furnishings, an artist's easel and a multi-colored paint spattered wooden table. Two plain wooden chairs and a floor lamp stood abandoned in a far corner. There were no paintings in the room, nor other artwork. Spider put the books on the floor next to the record boxes and looked appreciatively around the room.

"Nice up here," he said. He looked up and saw the ceiling contained skylights. "Must be nice when the sun comes up in the mornings." He went to one of the side windows and looked out. "You can see the water, too." He thought Will must be lucky to have this place all to himself. Was the general's son planning on a long stay, or was he only visiting? Spider's mind was already musing on the possibility of his living in this studio once he became Windward's handyman-in-residence.

"Maybe I ought to take you over and see if my father is able to see you now? Isn't that what you said you wanted, Spider?"

"Yeah, no time like the present," Spider answered. "Like I said. I got to earn my living, so you'd better let me get on with it."

CHAPTER VII

During his tenure with the Newport Police Department, Hank Nightingale had handled several capital crimes, and his enjoyment of a job which sometimes dealt with violent death was something he couldn't fully explain. But he realized now, reading the results of the autopsy done on the body of Meredith Hackett, that until this case he had never had to contend with the investigation of the death of someone he had known. This corpse had once looked at him with an appraising eye and spoke to him. He had seen the muscles of the face move and heard its voice. As a result he was finding it unexpectedly difficult to concentrate on the black and white pages full of clinical facts and details in front of him.

The actress had unquestionably been murdered, strangled with a length of cord or coated wire. Death had resulted when her larynx had been crushed. According to the report, there were deep bruises and contusions on her neck, as well as several large bruises on her thighs and arms. Meredith had struggled, but the killer had used strength, and most probably the element of surprise, to overcome his or her victim.

Death would have come quickly.

Hank tried not to picture the victim's face turning dark red as the noose tightened. The compression of the cord would make the lips swell and the tongue protrude. He remembered the dead woman's clouded eyes. All the life had been squeezed from them. A sudden feeling of nausea came over him. He looked up to see Ben Davies and Keisha McAndrews standing in the doorway. He motioned for them to come in and sit down.

"I'm reading the report of the autopsy. The medical examiner puts the death sometime after midnight," Hank said, "based on how far the rigor had spread."

"What time did she leave you and Mrs. Kent?" Ben and Keisha sat down on the chairs near to the desk.

"I put it around quarter past ten. I didn't look at my watch, though."

"That's about two hours we've got to account for."

"Yeah," Hank said, "and listen to this part. The body was moved after she was dead. She wasn't killed sitting in that position in the driver's seat."

"Wow," Keisha said. "That opens up some major possibilities."

"I think the first one." Hank said, "is that she wasn't killed while the car was parked on Freebody Street."

"The killer drove her there?" Keisha asked.

"Away from where they might have been seen together."

"It's possible," Ben said, scratching his ear. "So the killer . . . let's call him a *him* . . . strangles her, in the car . . . out of the car?"

"Perhaps in his car," Keisha suggested. "If she struggled to get away, it could account for the bruises on her body."

"O.K,." Ben agreed, "maybe his car. But her car is nearby, so he puts her in the passenger seat, drives her to Freebody Street, places her where we found her in the driver's seat."

"That whole action must have started from someplace nearby," Hank said. "If the killer waited too long, rigor would start to set in and he couldn't have done all this seat switching."

"It fits that they could have met in one of the bars," Ben said. "We've already eliminated that she stopped in the 7-Eleven.

On Freebody, you're not far off Memorial Boulevard. America's Cup Boulevard and Thames Street are right down the hill by the harbor. All within quick driving distance. We've got that missing two hours. She had started to drink at The Black Pearl, right?"

"Scotch. Dewar's on the rocks."

"Somebody'll turn up who saw the Hackett woman in one of the bars," Ben said. "You've got to remember a woman like that, don't you think, Lieutenant?"

"Mrs. Kent is skeptical that Hackett was bar hopping on her own, but I can't be sure myself. What information did we get checking the wait staff at the bars?" Hank was looking at Keisha.

"I've got Officer Edwards and Officer Lopez doing the rounds. It's slow going. So far nobody has recognized the photograph of Meredith Hackett. We showed Shipley's photo around and did come up with a bartender who remembered seeing him around eleven. He knew Shipley. That's the only one. But Shipley did come home in a cab that night like he said. At 2:15 somebody put him in a cab in front of O'Brien's Pub on Thames Street. The driver confirms that. But nobody who works in O'Brien's says they saw him or called the cab. Could be somebody he was drinking with him down there. He must have been in a pretty bad state."

"Still out at two a.m.," Ben said. "So Shipley's still in the frame. We don't know where he was from around eleven until two."

"The fingerprint report on Mrs. Kent's car didn't have any prints that matched Shipley's," Hank said. "We can identify every one of them - Caroline and Louise Kent, Meredith Hackett and me."

"What about the body?" Ben asked. "Was there evidence of sexual activity?" Hank shook his head. "The DNA would sure help us. What about fibers and hairs?"

"I don't have the report back yet," Hank said. "Who did she meet?" he wondered out loud.

Ben shrugged. "Your friend Shipley."

"We have to be open to other possibilities."

"And what was the motive?" Keisha asked. "Robbery seems out."

"Her watch and two rings were still on the body. I didn't notice she had anything flashy in the way of jewelry that night."

"So she meets a guy in a bar, he suggests they go somewhere private . . . he gets amorous, and she changes her mind . . ." Keisha's voice trailed off.

"The strangulation from behind makes it odd," Hank said. "If she didn't want to have sex with him and he got angry, I think he would have just put his hands around her neck and started choking her. She fought back. She's got the bruises to prove it. So how did he get behind her?"

"She turned away . . . she was trying to get out of his car." Ben started speaking quickly. His eyes were squinting as if he could see the scene he was describing. "He had one of those phone chargers. You know, the kind you can plug into the cigarette lighter."

Hank nodded, beginning to see the action happening himself. "He would grab it, loop it around her neck."

"She struggles."

"But she can't escape." Once again he saw the face reddening, the eyes bulging. Why couldn't he stop seeing that image? He wondered if it was because of seeing Caroline's BMW at the crime scene.

"We've got to keep on the house-to-house in the neighborhood of the crime scene. Somebody could have seen something that night. And there's one other thing. The front seat of the BMW had sand on the mats."

"A walk on the beach?" Keisha suggested.

"I'll have to check with Caroline Kent to see if it was there before Friday night. It could be nothing."

"O.K. What else?" Ben asked.

"We still need a next of kin."

"I tried that Tom Benton, the one Mrs. Kent said to call. I left a message and he hasn't returned the call."

"Keep trying." Ben nodded. "What about the manager? Been able to reach him?"

"No, I can't get a name," the sergeant answered.

"We should get her cell phone records soon." The chief had requested the court order for them, and they were waiting for the judge's ruling. "Try finding some names from the cast of her last play. We've got to find somebody to tell us about her. This is frustrating."

"Right." Ben was looking up at the ceiling. Hank waited for the observation he knew was imminent.

"You don't think the crime's more complicated?" Ben asked after several seconds had passed. His lips were puckered and his forehead was creased in a frown.

"In what way?" Hank asked. He enjoyed Ben's musings about cases. He had an active imagination, almost the mind of a storyteller.

"Well, that it just isn't an act of random violence. Somebody really wanted to kill her in particular?"

"What's the motive?" Keisha asked.

"She was in the theater. I thought that was a place full of jealousies and hatreds. Who got the best parts? Other actors steal your scenes. That kind of thing."

"But that most likely would have put the killing in New York, not here," Hank said. To his mind, the case revolved around the Newport bar scene and the actress's prickly temperament. A simple explanation was usually the right one. The melodrama of the back stage wouldn't come into the death at all.

But, just to be sure, he would talk to Caroline. Hank needed to have some better understanding of Meredith Hackett beyond the unflattering impression she had made on the night she died. He hadn't liked her, but she was a murder victim. The life of a human being was inviolate, and society put people like Hank Nightingale in charge of upholding that code.

"Uh oh, there's Igor."

Spider Shipley and Will Patterson were walking across the courtyard of Windward toward the far wing of the main house when Will spoke. Ahead of them, standing in front of a set of French doors at the far end of the house was a tall, formidable-looking man wearing loose black pants and a grey long-sleeve shirt. Spider slowed his pace, looking at the man who was standing, his hands across his chest, watching the approach of the other two.

"Who is he?" Spider asked, catching up to Will.

"My father's chauffeur and all-around henchman."

"Is his name really Igor?"

"No," Will laughed. "It's Jason Forman. But he looks like an Igor, right?"

"He's a big guy," Spider said. "I'd call him *Arnold* for Schwarzenegger. Does your father need a bodyguard or something?" He remembered Will's saying that his father was reclusive. A chauffeur ought not to have much work driving a recluse. What were his other duties?

"Even though he lives like a hermit out here, he doesn't like to be alone, especially at night."

They had reached the French doors, and Spider studied Jason Forman up close. He was dark, totally bald with a protruding forehead and black eyes, probably around forty. His overdeveloped muscles were outlined under the grey silk shirt, and he looked like the bouncers Spider had seen in the clubs around L.A..

"Hello, Jason," Will said. His voice had an exaggerated pleasantry about it. "Is my father awake? I'd like to see him."

Jason was looking straight at Spider, and Spider met his eyes and stared back. If he had hopes of working for the general, he would have to make sure he started out on an even footing with *Igor*, whose bullying type he recognized.

"Who is this?" the chauffeur asked, nodding at Spider.

"A friend of mine," Spider was surprised to hear Will respond.

Jason seemed to give the explanation a great deal of thought before he turned and opened the door. Spider and Will followed the other man into the house.

The big room which they entered was dark. Despite the fact that it was a sunny day, the interior received little light from the outdoors. The walls were paneled in a deep brown wood, and heavy patterned draperies hung from the windows. Spider strained to see. He picked out the shape of a man, sitting in the shadows. As he stared at it, he realized that the figure was in a wheelchair.

"Hello, Father," Will said. "How are you feeling today?"

The voice which answered was unexpectedly strong. "I don't care to discuss my health today, William. Who is that with you?"

"This is Mrs. Shipley's son, Father."

"Come over here, Mr. Shipley," the general instructed.

Spider stepped toward the man in the wheelchair, who was looking at him with frank curiosity. Up close Charles Patterson didn't appear to be the elderly man Spider had expected him to be. The general's face was square and rigid, and the lines around his mouth were hard. His stubble of grey hair was trimmed in a military haircut, and his probing brown eyes were empty of feeling. There was a heavy green blanket over his legs, and Gen. Patterson's large, muscular hands rested on top if it.

"What's your first name?"

"Neil."

"Irene didn't tell me you were coming."

"Actually, sir, she doesn't know."

"Is there anything the matter with your mother?"

"No, sir. The fact is, that I . . ." He paused and glanced back at Jason Forman, who was standing near the fireplace, and then at Will, who was nodding encouragement. "I was hoping you might have some work for me."

"Work?" Charles Patterson's voice sounded puzzled.

"Around the estate, Father," Will said. He came and stood beside Spider in a comradely fashion. "Spider here is a handyman. He can fix anything."

The general looked at Spider. "Is your name Spider?"

"That's just what my friends call me. My real name is Neil. My Ma calls me Neil." He laughed nervously. "You don't have to call me Spider."

"I see," Gen. Patterson said. His voice had become dull, disinterested. "Well, Jason, can we use William's friend as a handyman? That's your department, more than mine."

There was silence in the room, and Spider saw that the general's eyes were closing. Spider realized that Gen. Patterson hadn't moved any parts of his body except for those he used to see and speak.

"You're getting tired, General," Jason said. He moved away from the fireplace and made a show of straightening the blanket.

"I could do work on the grounds," Spider said evenly to Jason. "I saw you could use some pruning and trimming done. Maybe some clean-up."

"The fencing and stonework around the edge of the cliff need working on," Jason said to the man in the wheelchair. "You had said you wanted them repaired, General."

"I could do that," Spider said quickly. He had no idea if he could, but he figured he could fake it. The task didn't sound complicated.

The general, his eyes still closed, was quiet.

"Come back tomorrow," Jason said to Spider.

"I'll come in the afternoon, if that's all right." Jason nodded indifferently. "I've got an appointment in the morning," Spider added importantly. He'd have to be sure to tell his mother not to let on that he had his court appearance for Thursday's night bar fight the next morning.

"The railings on the second floor balcony are loose," Will said. "And there are some loose slates on the roof over the studio."

"I thought you weren't planning to stay long," Jason said.

"I'm sure my father still wants the studio kept in good repair, Jason. It did belong to my mother, you know."

"I was aware of that, William," Jason answered in a superior tone.

"I guess I'd better get going, Will," Spider said. "I don't want to bother your father here any more."

"Sure. Good-by, Father. I'll see you at dinner."

"Sunday is a cold supper, William," Jason said. "We eat what Mrs. Shipley has left in the kitchen for us."

"I'm sure it's good," Will said. He walked rapidly to the French door, with Spider following behind him.

Spider hurried through the exit, the sun blinding him as he stepped out into the courtyard.

"I don't like that Igor," Spider said as they walked away from the house. "I wouldn't trust him as far as I could throw him."

"You couldn't throw him, Spider," Will said, laughing. "You wouldn't stand a chance against him. I don't know who the hell could."

CHAPTER VIII

"Sand?" Caroline frowned. "I don't know how sand got in my car. I can't remember the last time I drove to the beach." She looked at Hank, who was sitting across from her desk in the smoking room. "You and I took some walks there this summer, but we always went in your car." He nodded. She was watching him with a feeling of pleasure. Hank was deep into his case now, stimulated by the new problem. He looked tough and determined, and she found looking at him to be stirring her desires.

Caroline turned away. It was the middle of a busy Monday, no time to be imagining anything in that quarter.

"Has anyone else used the car in the last several weeks?" Hank asked, oblivious to the direction of her thoughts. "When was the last time you had it washed and vacuumed out?"

"I never get that car washed, as you know," she laughed. He often berated her for not taking better care of the old car, which was what collectors called vintage.

"As far as anyone else's driving it, well, no. Nobody else does. Louise has her own car."

"You didn't lend it to Meredith while she was here? I mean before Friday night." Caroline shook her head. "Could she have borrowed it without your knowing it?"

"I don't think so. I keep the keys in the desk drawer." She pointed to the side drawer of the massive mahogany desk, which had been in the Kent family for a century or so. "She wouldn't have known that, I don't think."

"So if you can't account for the sand, it was probably introduced the night of the murder. You said you thought that she had stayed in the house or on the grounds for the entire time she was here?"

"It seemed to me that she did," Caroline answered. "I saw her about fairly frequently." She was bewildered by the idea that Meredith might have gone sneaking out of the house without mentioning where she was going. The four days she had spent at Kenwood Court had seemed so innocent, so simple. Meredith had come for a rest, and indeed she had appeared to spend her days relaxing in the inn. Except for Caroline's office, all the downstairs' rooms were open to the guests. Frequently the actress had gone down to the gazebo or, on a few occasions, lounged out on the veranda which caught the afternoon sun and had a pleasant view of the ocean.

"What did she do?" Hank asked. "How did she occupy herself?"

Caroline frowned. It seemed strange now to think of it, but Meredith often didn't appear to be doing anything. "I've already told you that she liked to read the newspapers in the conservatory each morning," she said. "She mentioned she was reading a book at night, in bed. I might have seen her with a book." She thought hard. "She was carrying a book one day. Let me think. She was going upstairs with it. Before lunch one day."

"Did she know anyone in Newport besides you?"

"I don't think so. She would have mentioned that, I think."

"Maybe somebody who retired from the theater? Can you think of anyone?" Caroline shook her head. "Did she talk on her cell phone? Text?"

Caroline thought for a minute. "I can't say I saw her. Is it important?"

"There was no cell phone in her purse. It seemed strange."

"Did she leave it in her room?"

"No," Hank said. "We searched the suite. It wasn't there."

"Could she have left it in the house somewhere?"

"We need to check. We're waiting for her cell phone records."

"Did the killer take the phone?"

"If he did, he probably threw it away. It would tie him to the murder. You could drop it off one of the wharves into the bay."

"But if she called the murderer in advance, Hank," Caroline began, brightening with an idea, "then the phone would be a clue."

"Yes," he said, "you're right. But that means she knew her killer."

And he told her of Ben's idea that Meredith had been followed to Newport by someone she knew, a rival in the theater.

Caroline looked surprised.

"You could ask Tom Benton, I guess. He knows more about her recent jobs than I do. But it seems far-fetched. Meredith specialized in off-Broadway dramatic roles. There's no real money there, or even much fame for that matter."

"Ben is going to talk to him."

"Have you got any leads on what Meredith did after she left us that night at The Black Pearl?" Caroline asked.

"So far we haven't come up with any one in town who remembers seeing her. We're looking at the time frame from 10:15 on. Midnight, more or less, is when the report says she was killed."

"Killed. What an awful word."

"Yes, well, that's the word, unfortunately." He was looking at her with eyes full of worry, and she knew that she wasn't helping the investigation by sidetracking him with fretting over her.

"So Spider isn't a suspect after all?"

"We can't eliminate him yet. We found the cab that took him home that night around two. Somebody put him in a cab outside O'Brien's."

"And no one saw him and Meredith together after they left us?"

"We haven't found anyone, but right now he's got no alibi for the murder time."

"She went to the beach." Caroline returned to the sand.

"Why?"

"It fits in with that introspective demeanor she had while she was here. She wanted to think."

"I'll buy that."

"Hank?"

"Yeah?"

"Was it possible that Meredith had a serious illness?"

"What makes you ask that?"

"It's something Louise suggested. To explain her behavior. Meredith really came up here to Newport to get away because she had gotten some bad news about her health."

"There was nothing in the autopsy to indicate she had any medical conditions like that. According to the medical examiner, her health was excellent. The most serious thing was the beginnings of arthritis in an ankle, which she had probably sprained very badly at some point earlier in her life."

"Everything would show up in the autopsy? Cancer?"

"I suppose. I'm not an expert."

"Will you contact her doctor?"

"When we find one."

"All right. Let's get back to the sand. Let's say she could have driven out to the beach after she left us . . . to be by herself. She said that when she said she was leaving. Remember?" He nodded. "That she wanted to go alone, she wanted to drive herself home." Caroline tried not to think of what might have happened if she had insisted on going with her friend. It came into her mind that they both could have gone to the beach, if Meredith had insisted on it, and then what might have happened to them both?

"And she went to one of the beaches," Hank said, unaware of the churning going on in Caroline's head. "Let's start with Easton's." It was the beach familiarly referred to as First Beach, located at the eastern end of the city of Newport at the entrance to the Cliff Walk on the border of Middletown. "She got there, parked your car, and walked around for a while."

"She might have sat on the wall, or by the pavilion. And then somebody came along . . . and she wasn't alone anymore." Caroline shuddered, and Hank got up from the chair and pulled her up to hold her close to him. "Did she meet her killer there?"

"Sand was on both sides of the front floor of the BMW. It fits that she was driven from the beach in the passenger seat after she was killed. Then we believe the killer moved her into the driver's seat after the car was parked at Freebody Street. It would have been dark down there at that time of night."

Hank moved his hands to her shoulders and leveled his eyes at hers. "Freebody Street is not far from the beach," he said in a slow, patient voice. She knew he was making her concentrate on the narrative. "You could walk back to the beach from there in ten or fifteen minutes. No more than that. That's assuming the killer came in a car, which he had to retrieve after the murder. Or it could be somebody from the neighborhood who's taken to midnight walks on the beach. Maybe he didn't have a car at all."

"Hank," Caroline said slowly. "Have you checked out the restaurants there, next to the beach?"

"Damn," he said, amazed that she had thought of it first.

"There's the ABC and that fancy place that used to be the Cliff Walk Manor. And past the beach there are a bunch of places in Middletown—"

"We've been concentrating on downtown."

"Does it seem possible that Spider could have gotten to First Beach without a car? That's a pretty far walk from downtown, even when you're sober."

"Well, he got into a cab once that night. I suppose he could have gotten into another. Or perhaps he met up with a group who had a car. And did he meet Meredith at the beach? When?" He shook his head when he couldn't answer his own questions.

Caroline frowned "I can't see Spider driving a dead body around Newport."

"I think I have to agree with you. He'd want to get the hell away from a dead body."

"So it does seem there is definitely an unknown person. And they were at the beach."

"Yes," he agreed. "It would seem that we have got to look for Mr. X. The question is whether he and Meredith met in a bar down there or met on the beach."

"You're sure it's a man?"

"I'm not sure of anything," Hank said. Mr. X . . . or Ms. X."

The sunny September Monday had been seasonable when Louise had first set out to do her gardening tasks the next day. She had been working, planting flowers, around the front entrance to Kenwood, but now the beads of sweat were beginning to make her feel warm and flushed. The old boxwood shrubbery had grown high and thick in front of the two wings which flanked the center portico and the front door to the house. Louise thought visitors to the house ought to be greeted by the bright, distinctive colors of fall chrysanthemums, not the dark massive boxwood bushes.

During her years as mistress of Kenwood, Louise had always taken a particular interest in the grounds, working with the staff of gardeners employed by the Kent family on the design and cultivation of the estate's landscape. She often went out to cut the flowers she wanted and took great pleasure in arranging them for the bouquets to be used indoors. Frequently she had longed to take pruners in her hand and do real work, but in those days that sort of action on her part would have brought instant criticism from her husband. The servants did the work, Frederick would have reminded her. "That's what we pay them for."

Now his widow did not only pruning, but digging, cultivating and weeding. Caroline did currently employ a part-time gardener, George Anderson, who had actually worked at Kenwood in the old days. But the two short days a week George worked were not enough to do all the outdoor tasks, especially after Kenwood's grounds had been so neglected during the years the estate had been leased to tenants. Louise was impatient to restore the land and spent as many afternoons in the gardens as she could, after her indoor chores were completed. The bottle of ibuprofen, for which she always reached after a busy day of gardening, was a valued item kept handy on her bedside table.

First thing that morning Louise had gone to one of the local supermarkets where she had filled her car with the pots of the chrysanthemums on display at the store's entrance. The plants had been on sale, three pots for $10, and she had carefully used all of this month's gardening budget on the purchase. From experience she knew that the house would dwarf anything but a big display of flowers, and she had methodically loaded her cart four times to buy as many as she wanted. Recalling the stares of the other shoppers made her smile. She had practically cleaned out the entire stock. What would have been the thoughts of those other customers if they had known that she was buying the flowers for one of the Newport mansions? They would have been more than a little surprised to realize that her need for economy was as great as theirs.

Almost half of the flowers had been planted, and Louise found she was ready to stop working. Her muscles and bones were telling her that she had done enough for the day, and that the remainder of the planting should be saved for another day. The mind is always willing, she thought, but the knees and back are weak. She stepped back from the front of the house and surveyed her efforts from the vantage point of the drive. A mass of gold, purple, rust and burgundy flowers greeted her eyes. For an instant she forgot they were supermarket blooms and not from the best greenhouses. Louise sighed with the tired pleasure of a job which could be measured in visible results.

"They look really lovely," a woman's voice said from behind her, and Louise, startled out of her self congratulations, turned. A tall, blond woman was walking toward her from around the corner of the east wing.

"Thank you," Louise said, wiping her forehead with her sleeve. She must look a mess, and here undoubtedly was one of the new guests to greet. Louise took off her gardening gloves, rubbed her right hand on her shirt and extended it. "Hello. I'm Louise Kent. Welcome to Kenwood Court."

"Oh," the woman said with a look of surprise. Louise realized she must have been mistaken for some of the hired help. "How do you do?" The two women shook hands lightly. "I'm Sarah Ryder."

"Well," Louise said, still sensing some awkwardness, "it's a fine afternoon. Have you been walking around the grounds?"

"Yes, I've just been down to see the view from the cliffs."

"Your first time in Newport?" Sarah nodded. She had sharp, pale features, and her hazel eyes looked wary. Louise wondered if she should make some excuse to get back to her work. "Well, I hope you enjoy your stay. How long will you be with us?"

"I just checked in this morning. I don't know for how long."

"There's plenty to do and see in Newport," Louise offered. She looked pointedly at the wheelbarrow filled with the chrysanthemums left to be put in the ground. She was about to begin picking up her gardening tools when Sarah spoke in an excited voice.

"The actress who was murdered was staying here, wasn't she?"

"Oh, dear," Louise said. She and Caroline had been worried about the inn's losing customers once it was known that a murder victim had been their guest, but neither of them had anticipated that the connection to the crime might actually attract patrons.

"You must have spoken to her. What was she like?"

Louise frowned. She hoped she looked properly offended. But Sarah was looking at her, waiting eagerly for a reply.

"I'm sorry, Ms. Ryder, but I don't think it's appropriate—"

"The maid, Molly, told me she had been here for four days and never left the house until the night of the murder."

Louise would have to speak to Molly.

"She stayed in the house?" Sarah pressed, the question hanging in the air. "Did she go out to that little house down there at the back of the property?"

"The gazebo," Louise murmured.

"Yes. The gazebo. Molly said she wasn't that friendly."

Molly Casey was a middle-aged woman, one of the first of the maids whom Caroline had hired when they opened the inn. Molly was hard-working and reliable. But she would have to learn not to discuss the habits of the guests with other visitors.

"Molly said she read the newspapers mostly. But, I wonder. Did she read any books while she was here?"

"Now why would that be of interest to you, Ms. Ryder?" Louise demanded. This young woman was bold.

"Oh, please, call me Sarah. And, as far as that actress, well, I think it's interesting what she might have been reading just before she died. The last thoughts on her mind. That kind of thing."

It suddenly occurred to Louise that Sarah Ryder might have a professional interest in the story of Meredith Hackett's murder.

"Are you a reporter?" Louise demanded.

"No," Sarah said, shaking her head vigorously. "I'm not a reporter."

Louise was unconvinced and said so, but the other woman denied vehemently that she had any connection to television or the newspapers. Louise shook her head and abruptly stopped the conversation, rude as it might seem. She was tired and needed to gather up her tools and put them away in the old gardener's shed opposite the kitchen. She left Sarah Ryder standing in front of the house, staring up at the facade. As Louise slowly pushed the heavy wheelbarrow around the corner of the dining room windows, she glanced back at the woman's figure. There was something familiar about the profile, Louise thought. Where had she seen that face before?

CHAPTER IX

As the rattling noise made by the opening of the back door began, Mattie swung around like a cat and watched the handle spin with dark, fascinated eyes. She had been standing at the stove, busy with her cooking, but Caroline realized that all the while she had been waiting, alert for the sound of the knob's turning. When the door opened, Louise, looking flushed and tired, stood resignedly in the doorway, surveying the scene in the kitchen. Louise had expected to find Mattie there, and Caroline had a feeling she was prepared for the reception she would receive. Her mother-in-law was waiting for her lecture. Caroline considered leaving the room. The scenes between the cook and Louise over her working too hard were becoming tiresome.

"How does your planting look?" Caroline asked brightly. Perhaps she could run end around Mattie's pique by introducing a neutral topic. "I'll go out and see what you've done as soon as I've finished with the vegetables." Louise moved slowly into the kitchen, her bright blue eyes riveted on Mattie. Poor thing, Caroline thought. She's exhausted and wants to clean up.

"It's after six," Mattie announced in a brisk voice. "I'll have to leave the stove now, Missus, to run your bath. I don't know who'll watch this sauce. Mrs. Caroline's busy with the vegetables, and the salad yet to make."

"I can stir the—" Caroline began as Louise simultaneously said, "I'm going to take a shower." Mattie looked from one to the other. Both Kent women stared back at her. Stalemate.

"I'm going to take a shower," Louise repeated, "and then I'll be back to set the table in the dining room." Caroline inched toward her side. Emboldened by her daughter-in-law's proximity, Louise added, "That's what I always do, Mattie, to help with the dinner service."

"Molly's still here," Mattie said, the expression on her face hard as rock. "Don't know why Mrs. Caroline can't have her do it before she goes home."

"Yes," Caroline said. "I could ask her to do that." She worked hard not to smile. She could see that Mattie's face couldn't hold its rigidity for long. Already it was softening with feeling for her beloved employer.

"Whatever you wish, Caroline," Louise said in a light, noncommittal tone, as she walked toward the door to the back hallway. "I'll be dressed and back down in twenty minutes, I'm sure."

"If you're tired after your shower, you should lie down to rest," Mattie called after her. "I'll bring your dinner up on a tray."

"I'll get Molly," Caroline said, following her mother-in-law out of the room. "I believe she's in the billiard room. No one ever seems to go in there these days, but it still needs to be kept tidy."

When they reached the back stairs, Caroline was surprised to see Louise pause and touch her arm.

"Caroline, wait, I need to talk to you." Her voice was low, almost a whisper.

"What is it? Has anything happened, Louise?"

"I'm not sure. There are several things. First, who is that young woman who checked in this morning?"

"Ms. Ryder?"

"Yes, what do you know about her?"

"Nothing, I suppose. What is this all about?"

"Did she call ahead for a reservation?"

"Yesterday. She said she was in Mystic, Connecticut, driving through New England on a leisurely vacation and looking for accommodation in Newport for several days."

"Nothing else?" Caroline shook her head. "Did she ask you about Meredith?"

"No. No, of course not. Why should she?"

"Apparently she questioned Molly closely on the details of the murder."

"Did Molly tell you that?"

"No. Sarah Ryder did. I spoke to her a few minutes ago while I was outside working in the front of the house. She wanted information from me."

Caroline couldn't see the problem. The facts of the murder were becoming well known after two days of news coverage, and you couldn't expect people not to show their curiosity to learn more. She said as much to Louise, who greeted her comments with skepticism.

"I think the woman might be a reporter."

"It is possible," Caroline agreed. "We were surprised not to have the press on our doorstep."

"You ought to tell the staff. I wasn't pleased that Molly gossiped about Meredith, Caroline."

"I'm sure she didn't mean any harm."

"It's inappropriate."

"I'll speak to her now, when I ask her to help with the table."

Caroline started to go in the direction of the billiard room, but Louise lingered at the bottom of the steps.

"Caroline?" There was an anxious look in Louise's eyes. "Did you notice anything familiar about Sarah Ryder?"

"No, I don't think I did. But I didn't talk to her that long. I was busy when she arrived. After the usual welcome formalities, I turned her over to Molly to take her upstairs to show her to the room. Molly is quite good at interacting with the guests, and it gives me time to do something else."

"I think she looks familiar. I had the odd feeling just now that I've seen her before."

"I don't know. Nothing struck me. Where did you think you had seen her?"

"That's just it. My feeling was vague, just something that reminded me of seeing her previous to today. I looked at her while she was staring up at the house, and the sensation came to my mind."

"Maybe you ought to have a good soak in a tub after all," Caroline said, smiling "You can relax, let your mind go. See if the image of where you saw her comes back to you."

"I am tired," Louise confessed "I love working outdoors, but I don't have the stamina I once did. If only I could admit to it instead of putting up such a strong front for Mattie. It would be so nice to come through that kitchen door once and complain good and hard. Then after I had my shower, I could put my feet up and have a drink."

"Poor Louise," Caroline said, rubbing the older woman's arm. "I've put you in such a spot by bringing you here, haven't I?"

"Oh, no, my dear," Louise responded, taking the younger woman's hands, "don't ever think that. I didn't mean it in that way. If anybody's to blame, it was Frederick. We had so many expenses, and there was never enough income." She looked around the hallway where they were standing and shrugged. "Finally, it all crashed around us. You're not to blame for that. And neither was Reed, you know."

"I know," Caroline said.

"You're doing the best you can with the inn, and I wouldn't be anyplace else but at your side." Louise hugged her daughter-in-law affectionately. "I'm tired because we're so busy these days. And that's good, you know."

"Thank you, Louise. It means a lot to me to have you say that."

"It's just once in a while, and maybe that day will come soon . . . I'd like to come down before dinner to an ice cold pitcher of martinis."

The funny thing of it was that Louise's final remark stayed with Caroline for the rest of the evening. She smiled through dinner at the various guests who were dining in. Sarah Ryder, pleading a headache, had asked for a tray in her room, and Molly, who had agreed to work overtime to help with serving, had taken it up to her. Louise, as both Caroline and the cook had encouraged her to do, accepted her own dinner on the tray which Mattie had happily brought upstairs to the private quarters. It had been another full day of moving about, bending and carrying, for Caroline, and it was long after ten o'clock when she decided to call it a day. The idea of a soothing drink had been waiting on the sidelines of her brain all evening, and now she let it come out in the open.

Too late for a cocktail, she decided, but brandy might do nicely. A bar was kept stocked for the guests in the library, and an excellent cognac was to be found there. It was something of a splurge for the inn to provide the best brands, but Caroline had found that there were times in the impressing of the guests when certain higher expenditures were definitely warranted.

The house was quiet as Caroline left the kitchen. She took one last look to make sure that the room was orderly and ready for the next morning's bustle of activity before walking through the grand hall at the center of the downstairs and into the salon. The glittering room was elegant, but too ornate by today's standards. Chubby cherubs hanging from chandeliers and gilt paneling dominated the huge room.

Fortunately few of the guests found the salon comfortable, and Caroline was spared the regular, vigorous cleaning of the rococo furnishings.

Beyond the salon, a hallway led to the library in the west wing. It was dark in the passageway, and she switched on a light. A timer regulated the house lights so that guests could always see properly. Night was coming earlier these days, and she would have to adjust the settings to allow for more light inside.

The library was as quiet as the rest of the house. Caroline was grateful that no guests were lingering in here. She had thought she had accounted for everyone's either being out of the house or in their rooms. Although it was her cognac, she would have been embarrassed to be found by one of her visitors in the act of raiding her own liquor cabinet.

The deep amber liquid was a welcoming sight as it swirled into the snifter. Caroline inhaled its heavy, deep bouquet and looked at the sparks of light which reflected in the crystal glass. Kenwood was a comfortable home, and she felt the sensation of what Louise had suggested earlier when she spoke of wanting to enjoy their surroundings and be soothed by the pleasures to be found there. Caroline took her glass to a club chair in a nook by the window. She switched off the small table lamp to enjoy the anonymity of the darkness

The moon was bright this evening. Sipping her cognac, she stared contentedly out of the window at the expanse of the lawn. Because of its sunny western exposure, Louise and George Anderson had made a priority of reestablishing the two large flower beds which lay beyond the library window. From her comfortable chair, Caroline studied the dark shapes in the bed, picking out silhouettes of the tall spikes of iris and the large blooms of the last of the dahlias. Louise took such pride in her work. The front of the house, with its mounds of evenly spaced chrysanthemums, was spectacular. No professional gardener could have placed them as perfectly as her mother-in-law had done. The drink was having its effect. Caroline felt pleasantly and thankfully mellow. She closed her eyes and took another swallow of the silken cognac.

Had she merely shut her eyes for a few seconds or dozed longer than several minutes? It was impossible to tell, but as Caroline opened her eyes, still snug in her corner chair, she was conscious of a quiet movement outside in the hallway. She steadied her eyes, getting accustomed again to the darkness in the room. Slowly she rose from the chair. Passing the fireplace she considered snatching up the poker. Why had that thought come to her? The inn had several guests, and any one of them might be walking about. Yet there was something furtive about the footsteps, artificially slow and cautious. Caroline tiptoed to the doorway of the library in time to see a tall figure disappear into the conservatory. There was something peculiar about the action, and Caroline decided to investigate.

CHAPTER X

—⎯∞⎯—

The outline of the figure who had entered the conservatory had its back to Caroline as she cautiously entered the room. The conservatory justified its name. It was filled with lush plants of all shapes and sizes. Caroline slid behind one of the Ficus trees near the doorway. Thus concealed, she watched in fascination as the person at the far end of the long, rectangular room tried to push a heavy stone potted plant. An angry sound came from the mouth. A woman. Caroline was sure it was a woman who was her mysterious intruder. The pot began to make a scraping noise as it shifted on the old stone floor. Caroline peeked through the leaves of the tree. Moonlight came into the conservatory from the tall glass windows, and as she squinted at the woman, she began to see something familiar in the body.

"Can I help you?" she called in a loud voice as she stepped out from behind the Ficus. The figure turned sharply and sucked in a loud breath.

"What? Who?" Sarah Ryder was flustered. She drew her hands to her face and dropped a small black flashlight. It crashed loudly on the hard floor and bounced a few times before rolling to a stop in front of one of the Bentwood chairs.

"Oh, Mrs. Kent," she said, recovering her composure quickly. "It's you." She paused and studied Caroline for several seconds. "You frightened me."

"I didn't mean to," Caroline answered, wondering what on earth was going on here. "Did you drop something?" She turned on a table lamp.

"Oh," Sarah said. "Well, as a matter of fact, when I was in here earlier, I might have." She smiled an innocent smile. "An earring."

"An earring," Caroline repeated. "Did you find it?"

"No, no," the other woman said quickly. "It could be anywhere. I'm so careless."

Sarah unquestionably had her eye on the doorway now, but Caroline decided that she was not having that move made on her. She sat down on the chair next to the lamp and looked up at her guest's face. Caroline's eyes were on the nose in particular. It had a straight bridge and came to a definite point. Her long gold hair framed the face, but the long neck was evident. Hazel eyes with that same searching movement about them. How had she missed it this morning when they had first met?

"You're Meredith's sister, aren't you? My mother-in-law thought you might be a reporter. I don't suppose you're that, too."

"No. I'm not a reporter."

"But you are Meredith's sister. Is your name really Sarah?"

"I am Sarah Ryder. I can show you my driver's license if you don't believe me."

"Why did you come? And, more importantly, what were you looking for in here?"

Caroline knew that Sarah had every reason to come to the last place where her sister had been alive, but there was more to this visit than that. Otherwise Sarah Ryder would not have presented herself as some idle tourist passing through New England. She would have notified the Newport Police of her arrival and demanded to help with their investigation.

Why hadn't she done that? Caroline looked at Sarah and invited her to sit down. When she hesitated, Caroline smiled encouragement. "We need to talk," she said.

"You were a friend of hers?" Sarah half-asked, half-stated the question.

"We were in the theater together, and yes, we were friends. But I didn't know she had a sister. So I didn't know how to get in touch with you when . . . it happened."

"I saw it in the newspaper on Sunday. I live in New York, and there was a small item in the *Times*. I thought I would die when I read it. I decided I ought to come."

The statement still didn't explain why she hadn't gone to the police straightway, and didn't tell Caroline why Sarah hadn't come to Kenwood Court until the following day.

"The police don't have much to work on at this point," Caroline said. "You must know something which would help them."

"I don't understand," Sarah said. There was an uneasy note in her voice. It came to Caroline that this woman could be connected to the crime herself.

"I hadn't seen your sister in almost two years," Caroline explained. "We'd lost touch. I don't know all of her friends now. And what . . . well, what situations . . . that might have existed."

"You mean, do I know anyone who wanted to kill her?"

"Yes," Caroline said, "I guess I do. Was there someone who hated her so much that they could have, would have . . . killed her? I know it's awful to contemplate, but someone did strangle her."

Sarah drew her hands together in front of her face. She shrugged in a way which did suggest a movement Caroline had seen Meredith make.

"I don't know why anyone would have hated Meredith," Sarah finally said. "She wasn't a person you hated."

"But there's another reason she was in danger?"

Sarah bit her bottom lip.

"Don't you want to have the police find the person who did this to Meredith?"

"Meredith was a very private individual," Sarah began slowly. "I don't know all the details. I don't even know his name."

"A man?"

"Yes, did she mention anyone to you, whom she was seeing?" Caroline shook her head. "I didn't think so. I know he was married, but that wasn't the real reason they were secretive about their relationship."

Caroline was growing impatient. It was late, and she was tired. Couldn't Sarah speed up her story?

Sarah lowered her eyes and chewed on her lip again. "I don't even know his first name. Meredith was quite an actress and could always control what she wanted to say. He was always *he*." She raised her two first fingers as if to put the pronoun in quotes. "Apparently he got mixed up in one of those fraudulent stock things on Wall Street. You know, inflating the price of some worthless stock the way some brokers do. They get their customers to buy large blocks, the price goes up, and then the shady brokerage sells its own position for a big profit."

"I've heard of that being done."

"Then you know that when the price drops, all the pigeons are left holding worthless shares."

"Did Meredith own some of the stock herself?"

"That's a good question. But I don't know. She never offered it to me."

"Did this stockbroker get caught?"

"Not exactly." Here Sarah's face darkened "He did something stupid. He let some mob guy in on the scheme. I think Meredith's boyfriend owed him money. For drugs, if I had to guess. He probably figured this was a good way to pay off the debt. I know he used to spend a lot of money on Meredith. Jewelry, expensive dinners, jet away week-ends."

"So this mob guy would come after Meredith? I don't understand. That doesn't make any sense."

"It's more complicated than that. The mob guy didn't buy the stock at the right time. He got in too high and then got stuck when the price bottomed. You know he had to be really pissed right?" Caroline nodded. She still didn't get Meredith's connection in this and said so.

"Well, he wanted to get even with the boyfriend, leak information to the authorities. I don't know exactly what she had, but Meredith had some papers. She was keeping them safe. I guess the mobster could hold them over the boyfriend. Do you follow?"

"What kind of papers?"

"Oh, I don't know. I told you that Meredith was private. She could keep a secret. You didn't get a hint of anything, did you? I mean, while she was here last week. She was carrying a big secret around with her."

"No, we talked about old times mostly. Now that I think about it, she said very little of her current life, only the play she was going into."

"It was a dangerous game. She shouldn't have helped this man. I think it got her killed."

"For these papers?" Sarah nodded. "But you apparently are still looking for them." Caroline pointed at the plant which Sarah had been trying to move "Did you think the material was buried?"

"I didn't know what to think. Your maid said Meredith spent a lot of time in here. I wanted to check it out."

"And the gazebo, also?"

"I was down there this afternoon. I couldn't find anything. I don't suppose you know of any great hiding places in this house? Like those old English houses with the secret wall compartments and hidden staircases."

"I don't think so," Caroline said, shaking her head. "I think Meredith would have carried these papers on her, if she had them. In her handbag probably. That way they would be safe."

"The police didn't find them, though. If they had, they would be investigating things in a different way."

"That's true," Caroline said.

"Don't you see? If someone could threaten her to get them, she wouldn't want to have the papers on her. They're hidden. I'm sure they are," she insisted, looking around the conservatory, the frustration lining her face.

Caroline tasted the feeling of frustration, also. When Meredith had been killed, no such papers were found with her. Caroline was sure that Hank would have shared that information. It would have been an important clue which would have implicated this mysterious boyfriend and a mob figure, as well. The mob? It seemed unreal that Meredith was involved with organized crime in some way. Her mind called up the recent memories of the time they had spent together, the afternoon chats in the gazebo. Meredith had looked tired. Was it worry? Or fear? Caroline knew if she herself was being pursued by the mob she would have been terrified.

She reminded herself that Meredith was a good actor. Was she able to control her fears that well? Caroline went back to that last night in The Black Pearl. Meredith looking at her watch. She remembered that motion, thinking at the time how it was rude of the actress to appear so bored with her companions. It must have been around ten o'clock. When did Hank say she was killed? After midnight, she thought she remembered his saying. Had Meredith been checking her watch for another reason? Did she have an appointment with someone?

Sarah's knowledge suggested there were two men who might have been waiting for her sister somewhere in Newport. Did Meredith knowingly meet one of them, meet him to discuss these documents which incriminated one, or maybe even both of them? And what happened when Meredith got to her appointment? To Caroline, it seemed simple. One of them killed her and took the incriminating evidence away with him.

Caroline looked at her own watch. It was just past 11:30.

"I think we'd both better go to bed," Caroline said. "I want to sleep on what you've told me. Perhaps something will come back. Now that my brain knows what to look for, I might be able to think of something Meredith said which didn't seem important then but will now."

Caroline looked at Sarah's face closely. The woman looked suddenly pleased herself. The resemblance to her sister was strong now, and Caroline wondered why it should be so definite at this particular time.

What were both of the sisters so keen on hiding from her? First Meredith, who was killed for the secret, and now Sarah, who surely knew more than she was telling Caroline.

Sarah was holding back. Caroline was sure of that.

CHAPTER XI

Hank Nightingale was proud of his city, pleased to call it his home. Driving through the streets of Newport, he never complained about the cramped colonial lanes where cars were frequently forced to travel only a few miles per hour. Unless it was an emergency, he would often go out of his way to drive past the old houses and shops on Spring Street and around Queen Anne Square with their quaint exteriors suggesting candle light and pewter plates.

And Hank seldom griped about the cars of rubbernecking tourists who held up traffic on Bellevue Avenue, the splendid avenue of the Newport mansions, which was the most famous street in Newport if not in the entire state of Rhode Island. The grand homes which lined the Avenue were almost all visible from the road. The Newport summer cottages of the rich had never required much land around them. Their owners wanted their friends and neighbors to see what they had lavished their fortunes on.

The following morning, however, as Hank turned left on Bellevue Avenue and toward the mansion area, his mind was on other matters. He had taken an early telephone call at home from Caroline with a request to come out to Kenwood as soon as he could.

When she had called, she had tried to explain why she wanted to see him, but her side of the conversation had been disjointed and hard to follow. She had a guest, she had said, a woman whom she had found prowling around the inn late the previous night. And then Caroline had started talking about the mob and secret papers and drug money.

"Did I say that she is Meredith Hackett's sister?"

No, she hadn't, and this final bit of information had caused him to hurry his shave and shower.

Caroline was waiting for him in her office.

"Hello," Caroline said, as she came from around her desk and gave him a light kiss on the cheek. "Want some coffee? Molly just brought in a fresh carafe for me." Without waiting for his answer, she poured him a cup, black the way he liked it.

The kiss took him by surprise, and he stood for a second or two, savoring the sensation left by her touch on his face.

"Her name is Sarah Ryder. She is Meredith's sister," Caroline said, her green eyes bright with the prospect of telling him her news. "And she told me all about why Meredith came up to Newport. She was running away from the mob."

"The mob," he repeated in an incredulous tone.

Ignoring his skeptical look, Caroline explained about the boyfriend with no name, the shady stock transactions, and the papers which incriminated somebody.

"She brought these papers up here with her, don't you see? You didn't find them, Hank. I mean, you didn't say anything to me, and I think you would have. Wouldn't you?" The last was said with modest hope that he would have kept nothing about the investigation from her.

"No, we didn't find anything like that on the body or in her purse."

"How about in my car?" He shook his head. They had done a thorough search of the BMW and would be returning it to Caroline in the near future.

"And you have no idea," he asked, "what was the exact nature of these so-called papers?"

"No," she admitted.

"But they have something to do with duping people in the stock market?"

"I think so."

"And the Mafia is behind this?"

She blushed.

"It sounds fantastic," he said in as neutral a voice as he could muster.

"You see this kind of thing all the time on TV."

"That's the point, Caroline. You do."

"Oh," she said. Her face looked like a child's who is going to be left behind while the grown-ups go out.

"What you've told me doesn't add up. This woman Sarah Ryder says that Meredith brought these papers to Kenwood. Carried them on her person. Or better yet, buried them in your garden."

Caroline looked away, suddenly interested in the wall over his head. "Why not leave them in a safe deposit box in New York?" he continued. "And for that matter, why didn't the boyfriend put them someplace safe himself?"

"All right," she said, staring at him stubbornly. "You'd better talk to her, Hank. I've apparently made a mess of my conversation with her."

"No, no, you didn't. I'm sorry."

"Don't be upset with me. I was trying to help."

"I'm not upset with you, Caroline."

"You are. I can see it on your face. You think I've been led down the garden path with a story concocted out of old TV plots."

He couldn't help himself. "Down the conservatory path, you should have said."

Caroline began to smile and shake her head. "I did think of one thing," she said.

"What was that, Miss Marple?"

"If you make fun of me, I'm not going to tell you."

"O.K., Mrs. Kent, what did you think of?"

"I remembered something I think might be important from that night at The Black Pearl." Hank stopped smiling and gave her his full attention. "Not long before Meredith got angry with your friend Spider and stormed out of the bar, she looked at her watch to check the time." He nodded. "I think she may have been planning to meet someone after she left us."

"You might be right," he said. "Sgt. McAndrews is checking the bars by First Beach, showing Meredith's photo."

"But this has got to rule out Spider Shipley. Meredith had already met him, and we know how that turned out. No, Sarah said her sister was being followed. That part I believe has truth to it. Maybe it isn't anything like that story she told me, but there's something wrong. I know it because Sarah Ryder *was* looking for something last night. Maybe it's not incriminating papers, but she came to Kenwood to search for something Meredith had. If you haven't found it, well, it might still be here."

"Or the killer took it," Hank suggested.

"Again, that can't be Spider. Why would he have taken something from her that she brought all the way up here from New York? Something that her sister knows about and rushes up here to find before we can. Don't forget, Hank. Sarah Ryder checked in here on the pretense of being a tourist, not the grieving sister. Oh, what was Meredith up to?"

"The sister's a suspicious woman all right. But remember that this secret whatever that Sarah is searching for could all be a coincidence to the murder."

Caroline shook her head. "You policemen don't believe in coincidences. If whatever Sarah is looking for can't be found, then some unknown person has it."

"Our Mr. or Ms. X."

"Yes. But who is X, Hank?"

"Ms. Ryder may know. They could be working together."

Caroline nodded slowly, and Hank continued with his theory. "Let's say that X kills Meredith, but doesn't find what he's looking for. He gets the sister to come here. She casually checks in, then begins searching the inn."

"It's very possible."

"Otherwise, you know, I think you might have had a break-in."

"Oh, no, Hank."

By thinking out loud, he had frightened her, and he was immediately sorry.

"The Mafia could have gotten one of their operatives to do it," he said gravely.

"Are you trying to be funny again?"

"No," he fibbed. "Just trying to make sense of it, that's all." His joking had calmed her down.

"But you're worried."

"Yes. If Meredith did leave a secret something here at Kenwood, and X committed murder to get it . . . well, I think he, or someone working with X, will certainly be back for it."

He reached for her hand. "And you've got to be careful."

When Hank got to the station he found Keisha McAndrews waiting for him. Smiling eagerly, but not saying a word, she followed him into his office. He turned and stared at her.

"You've got something. What?"

She seemed almost unable to begin her story. There was a new folder on his desk and he reached for it.

"We found where she was!" Keisha blurted out.

Hank took his hand from the folder and said, "Tell me about it."

"It *was* the ABC." The Atlantic Beach Club, the popular locals' bar and restaurant next to Easton's Beach. "She came in around 11:30. I talked to the waitress who served her a drink."

"Let me guess. Dewar's on the rocks."

"No twist. It's her. The waitress, Beth Martin is her name, when I showed her the photo, she made the positive ID. Said she was a 'real pretty woman with long reddish brown hair'."

"Was Hackett alone?" Hank asked.

"No. There was a man sitting with her. She described him as being on the thin side with light hair. They were in one of those little booths next to the bar." Hank nodded. He knew the layout. "The man ordered a beer."

"Did you show her Shipley's photograph? Did she recognize him?"

"She stared at it for a while but said she wasn't sure. Wouldn't swear to it. He was the same, but not the same."

"Did she hear him talking? The sound of that voice is pretty unforgettable."

"No. But she swears the woman was Meredith Hackett."

"What time did she leave? Was she alone when she left?"

"That, I'm afraid we don't know. Beth Martin left at 12:30, and she thought they had already left by then. But she didn't notice them leaving. She knew about the murder, Lieutenant. She said she just didn't connect the woman who died with the woman she gave the drink to. I think she was embarrassed."

"How did they pay?"

"They must have paid one of the other servers. Any of the servers would have taken the check to the register. But no one remembers doing it. It's really busy in there on a Friday night."

"And none of the other servers remembers anything about them?" Keisha shook her head. "O.K., we've got a start here. A man. Hackett. A bar next to the beach. She was alive when she left the ABC." He paused. "X."

"Pardon me, Lieutenant? Did you say 'X'?"

"Yeah. And now the description of the man brings us back to Neil Shipley. Why can't he ever leave this case?"

"If it's any help, Beth said they were talking like they were friends or at least on good terms. From what we know of Shipley and Hackett's encounter in The Black Pearl, well that doesn't fit. Plus Shipley claims he was drunk that night. This man wasn't drunk."

"Yeah. But we've got to have Beth Martin take a look at him."

"Do you want me to pick him up?"

Hank thought for a minute, then shook his head. "No, sergeant. I think I'll do that."

Spider Shipley's announcement that he was working for Gen. Patterson had surprised his mother. He had seen the questioning look on Irene's face and ignored it. She had wanted him to get a job, and he had a job.

His mother began her own work day at 8 a.m., and since they shared the same car, Spider was forced to do the same. Getting up early didn't matter. At his court appearance the day before he had been fined $150 for creating a public nuisance, and he was broke. There would be no going out drinking at night until he got paid by the general, and no one said when that was going to be. He couldn't borrow any more money from his mother.

And like in the TV police shows he was fond of watching, he couldn't leave town. Not while he was suspected of murder.

Hank hadn't said it exactly in that way. It was all that gibberish from that lady sergeant about "where were you on the night in question?" It was just like on TV. Only worse. It was happening to him. And all because of that Meredith Hackett. She had to make fun of him. Well, he contented himself with knowing that she got what was coming to her.

Spider surveyed the fence he was supposed to repair. Igor—and Spider wouldn't be able to stop calling Jason Forman that name inside his head—had set him up yesterday afternoon with tools and instructions. The fencing was ripped, and the rocks which formed part of the wall were crumbling. It was a major project, and Spider would take his time about doing it. After all, he was being paid by the hour.

Yesterday Spider had managed to start his task by pulling a section of the fence away from the rocks. Today he was just about ready to begin shifting some of the stones when he spied Will Patterson coming across the lawn.

"Hey, Spider, how's it going?" Will called out.

"Oh, all right. I got to get this old fence out of here. It's hard to do all by myself." He paused, but Will didn't take any hint that he could offer his own pair of arms to help. "It's going to take me a long time," Spider added. "You can see that." May as well lay the groundwork for a long operation and more pay.

"I thought I'd better tip you off," Will said, not even looking at the fence and the rocks. "There's a policeman up at the house looking for you."

"What? Ah, shit. Did my mother see him?"

"I don't think so. He's talking to my father, but I heard him say it's you he came to see."

"Damn," Spider said, stamping his foot on the ground, "your father's gonna be pissed. How did this cop know I was here?"

"I think he went by your house this morning, and one of the neighbors said you and your mother had gone to work together. I guess he asked where you worked maybe."

"I betcha anything my mother told that nosey old bag next door that I was working out here with her. And she must have told Hank."

"Who's Hank?"

"This guy who came, does he have black hair? He's tall, kind of good-looking?" Will nodded twice. "Yeah, that's Hank. He's an old buddy of mine." Spider smiled now as if it was no big deal a cop wanted to see him. "Yeah, Hank Nightingale. He's a lieutenant now in the Newport Police."

"Why's he coming to see you, Spider?"

Spider didn't like the look on Will's face. It suggested that Spider had some contagious disease that Will might catch.

"Oh, some case he's working on. That's all." Spider tried to sound disinterested. "Thinks I can help him. Maybe you read about it in the papers. That woman who was found murdered over the week-end across from the 7-Eleven. Hank's investigating that."

"How can you help him?" Will looked at Hank with fresh interest. "Did you know her?"

"Ah, we was out together," Spider answered with a grin.

"You were?" Will looked doubtful.

"Yeah. You think I wasn't?"

"It's just that the TV said she was an actress from New York. How did you know her? She was just visiting Newport. How did you meet her?"

"We was out that night with Hank and his girlfriend. Having a few drinks together."

"You were?" Will looked truly surprised. He had a weak chin, which sagged, but his mouth was a moving barometer of his thoughts.

"The ice lady I called her. She didn't like that." Spider grinned. "Nah. Not one bit did she like me saying that."

"What do you know," Will said, shaking his head. Spider liked the new look in the general's son's eyes. Spider was sure Will was realizing he had underestimated his new friend's reputation as a ladies' man. "And you were with her on the night of the murder?" Spider nodded. "Wow, you ought to sell your story to the newspapers."

"I could? For money?"

"Sure."

"What do you mean?"

"You know. You were the last person to see her alive, weren't you? Those TV shows would pay a lot for a story like that."

"Well, I don't know," Spider said uneasily. "I wouldn't want to say that I was really the last person to see her alive." He laughed nervously. "Somebody might think I killed her."

"Did you?" Will looked directly at him.

"Nah. You crazy? Why would I kill her?"

"Do you know who did? Is that why the police want to talk to you?"

"Um," Spider hesitated. "I . . . I'm not at liberty to talk about that. Hank and me, like I said, we been friends a long time. I'm just trying to help him out."

"Well," Will said "Here he comes now."

Spider turned and saw Hank striding across the lawn. Shit, Spider thought to himself. This is nothing but bad news.

CHAPTER XII

Gen. Patterson was an intriguing man to Hank, despite his physical immobility and confinement to a wheelchair. The small brown eyes were hard, and the jaw set in an unrelenting lock. Hank thought Charles Patterson would be a tough man if you crossed him. Despite his love of police work, Hank was uncomfortable with military men. The professional soldier was trained to kill, and Hank, as a police officer, could be called upon to take another person's life in the line of duty. While such an occasion had never happened, the detective was prepared if it did. It was killing as the military's job that Hank found at odds with his own sworn obligation to bring killers to justice in the civil world.

Gen. Patterson seemed disinterested in the purpose of Hank's visit. He accepted the policeman's explanation that he needed to question Neil Shipley in connection with a case he was working on. The older man didn't ask any questions, and Hank didn't volunteer any information. The policeman had been impressed that Spider had found a job, and he hoped nothing that happened that afternoon would interfere with that.

The general's intimidating chauffeur had told Hank where Spider was working on the estate. Jason Forman seemed disinclined to leave the general's side, and Hank thanked them both for their time and found his own way outside. He liked the house. Windward was a name which suited it. There was a breathtaking view of the ocean. As he crossed the back lawn, Hank looked out at the sea. Several sails dotted the horizon, and he was jealous of those sailors whose day could be given over to such diverting labors.

He spotted Spider by the broken fencing and observed that there was another man standing beside him.

"Hey, Hank," Spider said nervously when Hank joined the two men by the fence.

"Hello, Spider."

"I'm working out here at Windward. I guess you heard."

"Yeah. I wonder if we might talk." Hank saw the second man exchange a knowing glance with Spider before extending his hand.

"Hi, Hank. Will Patterson. Gen. Patterson is my father." Hank felt his hand being shaken vigorously. "Spider says you're a cop," Will said.

"That's right. Lieutenant Hank Nightingale."

"Is this an official visit?" Will asked.

"You might say that," Hank answered. He turned to Spider. "I need to ask you some questions."

"Sure, Hank," Spider said. "Listen, Will, me and Hank got to talk a bit. How about excusing yourself?"

Hank thought that Will Patterson was irritated with the speedy dismissal, but the general's son only shrugged and ambled off in the direction of the house.

"I'll see you for lunch, Spider," he called. "I guess your mother'll feed you up at the house again today."

"Sure thing," Spider said uneasily. He turned to Hank. "Am I going to be here for lunch?"

"That depends. I've got a witness who needs to take a look at you."

"What do you mean, a witness? To that murder? I told you already, Hank. I ain't done no murder. You're not going to pin that on me."

"Take it easy, Spider. We're nowhere near that place yet. This is just somebody who saw Meredith Hackett later that night. After she left The Black Pearl."

"Don't screw with me, Hank," Spider said plaintively. "We been friends. You got to be my friend still. You know, we're old friends. The old gang and all."

Hank considered his old school buddies. He and Billy Hanigan had been best friends in high school. Everybody called them Butch Cassidy and the Sundance Kid. Another friend had been given the absurd name of Toaster. It was so long ago, another lifetime. Billy worked as a mechanic at one of the gas stations in town. Toaster sold insurance. Hank ran into them and several of the old crowd from time to time, but he was friendly with none of them now.

"Spider, I'm a police officer. I'm investigating a murder case. Whether I like it or not, you were with Meredith Hackett on the night of her murder. Every time I try to eliminate you from this case, I can't."

"But I'm not involved. I swear to you."

"If this witness says she doesn't recognize you, we'll be a lot further to eliminating you from the list of suspects."

"I knew it!" Spider shouted. "I knew it. You do think I did it!" He started to run.

"No," Hank shouted back, grabbing Spider by the arm. The smaller man struggled fiercely to get free, but Hank had the edge in strength, and he held Spider rooted to the spot. "Now don't run, Spider. That'll make it worse."

"What could be worse than being a suspect, like you say I am?"

"Do you remember going to the ABC, the Atlantic Beach Club, last Friday night? After you left me downtown?"

"I'm not saying nothing now. I'm getting me a lawyer. I heard Francie Sikorski's a lawyer now. Remember her, Hank? She had those braces in high school, and everybody called her Weedeater."

"Spider," Hank said firmly.

"Is she a good lawyer, Hank? Being a cop, you ought to know who's a good lawyer."

"I think she does real estate."

"Hell, who's going to help me?"

"Look, you can call a lawyer, but you're not officially a suspect yet. I shouldn't have said that. But, I'm asking you, on your own accord, to come in and have the waitress look at you. If she identifies you, well, then I definitely advise you to get yourself a lawyer."

"It would look that bad, huh, Hank?"

"Yeah, Spider, I'm afraid it would."

Sarah Ryder had made herself uncommonly scarce for the day. She had not been in the house earlier that morning when Hank wanted to talk to her, and all afternoon Caroline monitored the comings and goings of the guests for a sight of Meredith's absent sister.

Molly had finished cleaning the guests' bedrooms by noontime, and Caroline had resisted the strong temptation to enter Sarah's room herself. Caroline knew it was perfectly within her rights as owner of the inn to check on the work done by her staff, but Molly's work was perfect. The only reason to look in Sarah's room was to snoop, and Caroline knew she couldn't do that.

It was after the lunch service was finished and the kitchen was once again quiet, that Caroline had a break in her schedule. She drifted into her office. There was always the business end of running the inn to occupy her spare time. The weather forecast called for rain that evening, a reminder that the estimates for the new roof work ought to be reviewed. The paperwork lay on a corner of the desk, but she didn't pick it up. Instead she reached for the telephone and punched in the number she had for Tom Benton in New York.

"Caroline," Tom said after she said hello. "I'm glad you called."

"You heard about Meredith?"

"I missed the item in the newspaper, but there was a text message from Randi James, telling me. I couldn't believe it."

"Have you talked to the Newport Police? They were going to contact you."

"I had a phone message from them. Just got back into New York today from Richmond. You caught me as I was coming in the door. I've been on the road doing summer stock."

"Did Lt. Nightingale call you?" Caroline asked.

"A sergeant, I think."

"But you haven't spoken to him?"

"No. I kept planning to call back, but you know how it is. We were doing the show and packing to come home." His voice trailed off.

"You should call them, Tom."

"Randi's message said Meredith was strangled. That's incredible. Do they know who did it?"

"No. They are looking for information about Meredith's life in New York. Who is her manager these days?"

"Ethan Samuels. You remember him."

"I don't think so," Caroline answered, as she wrote down the unfamiliar name. "Did you say you've been gone all summer?"

"Practically. I had a good supporting part in *The Lion In Winter*. We took it as far as St. Louis—"

"But I thought you had just seen Meredith before she came up here to Newport," she said, interrupting his travelogue.

"Did she say that?"

"She said she had talked to you, and you told her that I was running an inn up here, and she decided to come to stay because she needed a break from New York. I took it for granted it had been only recently that she learned I was living in Newport."

"Gee, I haven't seen Meredith since early in the summer. We ran into each other at a party. I don't even remember telling her about you and the inn, but I guess I did. You know how it is when you run into another actor. You want to know what everybody's doing, who has a job, who's doing something in TV or they got a commercial. I knew I was going into *Lion*, and that's all I wanted to talk about."

"That's very interesting," Caroline said. Meredith had known that she was living in Newport as far back as June.

"Poor Meredith. Was it some random thing? Robbery, what?"

"The police don't know the motive."

"Why did they call me?"

"To see if you knew anybody who might have wanted to harm her, I think."

"But she was killed in Newport," Tom said. There was bewilderment in his voice.

"Someone might have followed her here. An enemy."

"What kind of enemy? Meredith was an actress."

"That's just the point. Was there something else going on with her besides acting? What do you think, Tom? You knew her."

"That sounds crazy. What do you mean?"

"Did she have a boyfriend?" Caroline asked.

"I honestly don't know. Never saw her with anyone who seemed special. Meredith was dedicated to her career. Selfish about that."

"Did you know she had a sister?"

There was a short silence on the other end of the line. Caroline waited patiently.

"Ye-ah," he said in two syllables. "Her sister. I met her once. She came backstage when Meredith was doing that play at the Irish Rep last year. I didn't talk to her. She didn't hang around."

"Do you remember her name?"

Again the pause before Tom's voice came on again. "Rebecca. Emily, something old-fashioned. No, no, Sarah. I'm pretty sure Sarah sounds right."

"Sarah Ryder," Caroline offered.

"I don't know. Hackett wasn't Meredith's real last name, you know." Caroline didn't know.

The sound of Tom's sigh was audible from the other end of the conversation. Caroline guessed it was not because he wanted to solve the mystery of Meredith Hackett's death. Tom had been gone from his apartment for a couple of months, and he would be looking around while he was talking to her, wishing he could begin to catch things up in his own existence.

"Tom?" Caroline prompted. "The police will want to know all this, if you have information."

"I don't know what Meredith's real name was. Once she joked that it was Hasselgruber or Hickenlouper, or some such name that the press would misspell, she said. That's why she changed it to Hackett."

Tom had little else to tell her, and Caroline let him go. She wasn't giving up that there was a clue back in Meredith's life in New York. Maybe Tom would think of something later on.

"I wish I had the time to go to Manhattan myself," Caroline said as she replaced the phone in its cradle. She was ticking off names in her head, names of theater people who might have some piece of information about Meredith's life or who may have had contact with Sarah Ryder. "We could chat, gossip about the business. They would tell me things, I bet." She could drop in on Meredith's manager. Ben was telephoning for information. Caroline would have a better chance in person. Could she spare a few days to go down to New York to look up some old friends?

One thing was clear in Caroline's mind. Meredith must have had to leave Manhattan suddenly last week. It was too strange that her conversation with Tom Benton about Caroline had been three months ago. Why had she suddenly decided to visit her in Newport?

Caroline racked her brain to remember every detail from the conversations she and Meredith had shared for a clue to the mystery. Caroline was sure no man's name had been mentioned. Not even the suggestion that Meredith was having an affair, let alone with some mysterious and crooked stockbroker. And Tom had shrugged off the suggestion.

Meredith was selfish, he had said. Selfish. What did that mean? Was she also greedy? Was her need for money involved in this riddle? Meredith had never appeared to be well off. She didn't act in films or commercials where the fees were so much higher than those from her stage work.

Sarah had been looking for something at Kenwood. Caroline returned to that. It proved that Meredith must have been carrying information with her which contributed to her murder. Caroline was sure that Meredith had been followed to Newport. An ugly thought came into her mind. Blackmail. Was it possible that Meredith had some incriminating document, which she was intending to use to extort money? Sarah Ryder must have known what her sister was doing. Otherwise Sarah wouldn't have made up that ridiculous story of the mob's being after Meredith. Was Sarah's unwillingness to tell the truth due to her desire to shield her dead sister's reputation? Or was Sarah planning to do a little blackmailing on her own? She might have even been the target of the blackmail herself.

As her head spun with the possibilities, Caroline realized that it was time she began searching Kenwood for the mysterious material herself.

CHAPTER XIII

"Lieutenant?"

Hank looked up from his desk to see Officer Sue Edwards standing in the doorway.

"Yes? What is it?"

"Chief wants to see you, sir." Hank nodded his head and put the folder he had been reading down on his desk. He wondered what the chief wanted. No doubt, a new report on his progress on the Hackett murder.

It had been twenty-four hours since Spider Shipley had been viewed by Beth Martin, the waitress at the ABC.

"No," she had said with some disappointment while she studied Spider's face. "That other guy's hair was longer, I think." Beth shook her head. "His face was different maybe."

The other promising lead, the sister Sarah Ryder, was also going nowhere. Hank had just returned from Kenwood where he had gone to interview her. Sarah had obstinately stuck to the same account she had given Caroline. Meredith had a boyfriend, who was a stockbroker, who did owe money to a drug dealer. Hank couldn't shake the story.

"That's what she told me," Sarah had said mulishly. He did see the resemblance to her sister, the actress, but Sarah had gotten the short end of her sibling's handsome looks and the long end of the sour attitude which Hank had found so unattractive in the living Meredith Hackett.

"Didn't you think the story sounded like something out of fiction?" Hank had asked Sarah Ryder.

"I'm from New York," she had answered tartly. "Maybe you don't have such things up here in Newport, but in the city, cocaine users are a dime a dozen. Everybody owes their supplier."

Hank speculated as to whether Sarah did, also. Perhaps coke or something kin to it entered into the case somewhere. The autopsy had shown no traces of drugs in Meredith's system, however, and the whole thing suggested a convenient fairy tale.

"What about your late night visit to the conservatory? What were you looking for, Ms. Ryder?" he had asked, and that, too, had been explained away.

"I told Mrs. Kent I had lost an earring. You both are too suspicious. Should I have reported it to the police?" Did Sarah Ryder suppose he really was a Rhode Island bumpkin?

As Hank reached the chief's office, the thought of Meredith's sister dismissing him as a hick still rankled.

"Go right in, Lieutenant," Greta Rossler, the chief's secretary said as he already had his hand on the door. Hank smiled obligingly. Greta was in the best tradition of an official gatekeeper.

Inside the office Hank was surprised to see that Chief Williams was not alone. If he was expecting a report on the Hackett case, Hank wondered who this second man was and what connection he might possess to the murder.

"Good, Lt. Nightingale," the chief said as he rose from the chair. Barton Williams was a large man, and he didn't move his bulk unnecessarily. "Come in."

The chief put a comradely arm on his subordinate officer. Hank met the chief's eyes, looking for direction. Who was this visitor? He was formally dressed. Dark brown suit, with a starched white shirt and an olive green tie. Hank had felt his scrutiny as soon as he had entered the room.

"Lt. Nightingale," the chief continued, "this is FBI Agent Broglio."

FBI. Hank nodded to Broglio.

"Ernie Broglio," the dark-suited man said crisply. "I'm from the Providence office." The two men shook hands. "Sit down, Lt. Nightingale."

With a quick glance at his chief, Hank sat down. The chief resumed his place behind the desk, and Broglio walked toward the window. He was a few years Hank's senior, lean and muscular, with a dark receding hairline.

"Newport's a nice town," he observed. "My wife and I come sometimes for a week-end."

Silence met his comment. Finally Agent Broglio turned around.

"Why don't you tell Lt. Nightingale why I'm here, Chief?"

"I'd rather you did," the chief answered. "I'm still digesting the facts myself. You'll have the story clear."

Hank couldn't wait to hear it.

"Name Phoebe Harrington mean anything to you, Lieutenant?" Broglio asked, his jaw tight. He was staring right at Hank now, and he had clearly ceased thinking of week-ends at one of the local B & B's. Hank had the feeling he was expected to know the answer, but he didn't.

But the FBI man from Providence was patient. Hank made himself think. He wondered if Barton Williams had to answer this same question. Phoebe Harrington. Hank repeated the name several times in his head. And then he knew.

"The kidnap case," he said.

"*The* kidnap case," Broglio said. His lips curled over the words.

Hank had long forgotten Phoebe Harrington's name even though for several months her face had dominated the front pages of newspapers and she was usually part of the lead story on the evening news. When would it have been? Fifteen years ago? No, longer.

"It must have been twenty years ago," Hank said, shaking his head at the passage of time in his life.

"1991," Broglio said.

"That was well before I became a policeman."

"Were you in Newport then, Chief?" Broglio asked Barton.

"No, before my time here. Let me see. I would have been in Cincinnati in '91. But I remember the case. Who doesn't? It was a sensational kidnapping."

"You remember who it was that Phoebe and her two pals kidnapped, Lt. Nightingale?" Broglio asked.

"Katherine Patterson was her name, wasn't it? Her father was serving in the first Bush administration."

"It seems that her father lives in Newport now, Lt. Nightingale," the chief said.

Charles Patterson's daughter, Hank said to himself in astonishment. He would never have connected the invalid in the wheelchair with the kidnap victim's father who had appeared standing at his wife's side during the very public ordeal.

"What did Katherine's kidnappers want?" Hank asked. "I've forgotten the details." He tried not to make eye contact with the chief. Barton Williams didn't know that in looking for Spider Shipley Hank had by chance talked to Charles Patterson only the day before.

"Charles Patterson was an assistant secretary in the Energy Department in Washington, D.C.," Broglio said. "He had the responsibility for federal nuclear facilities. There started to be a lot of charges in the press claiming that people living around these facilities had a high incidence of illnesses like cancer and leukemia. There were doctors who said the diseases might be related to those facilities, and that their safety ought to be investigated. Radioactive waste was being dumped in the water. A lot of local activist groups sprung up. Said there were cover-ups that needed to be exposed. They got a lot of media attention."

"There were the usual campus demonstrations in several parts of the country, and the idea spread," the agent continued. "The students wanted action. With a capital A. The media hounded Gen. Patterson."

"Katherine Patterson was a freshman at a small private college in Maine," the chief observed.

"Some leftists up at that college made the connection between her and her father's job," Broglio said.

"So they kidnapped the general's daughter," Barton Williams explained to Hank, taking up the story. "The students thought that would force her father to listen to them. They said they would murder Katherine if he didn't do what they wanted." The chief shook his head sadly. He and his wife had two daughters, one of whom was starting college this month, and he had taken his last year's vacation to make the rounds of the schools which she was interested in attending.

"What were their exact demands?" Hank asked.

"Shut down the nuclear plants," Broglio said. "Stop the supposed contamination of the water. Of course that was all ridiculous. The kidnappers didn't realize there was no way that the general could make that decision on his own."

"No," the chief agreed.

"There were three kidnappers," the FBI agent continued. "At least that's what the FBI thought at the time. Three students. Phoebe Harrington was Katherine Patterson's roommate. And there was a young black kid, Darnell Stewart. Both of them were eighteen. The third member of the gang was twenty-one, an older student who had been the point man on campus for all the demonstrations. His name was Josh Ware. It was always thought that he was the one who planned the enterprise." Broglio paused again and cleared his throat before resuming.

"Phoebe Harrington was the one who got Katherine to come with her to the cottage in New Hampshire where she was held. It was a summer house belonging to Phoebe's great aunt."

Hank was listening attentively, but he was still confused as to why he was being told all of this.

"The Harringtons issued a public plea for their daughter to turn herself in," the chief said. "They promised they would get her the best legal defense money could buy."

"But she ignored them," Broglio said.

Hank remembered seeing footage of Katherine's Patterson's parents on TV. There was a mother then. She had been tearful, begging the kidnappers to release her daughter. Katherine's father had appeared imperturbable by her mother's side, never flinching.

"But I remember that Gen. Patterson refused to listen to the kidnappers' demands," Hank said.

"I've already told you. He couldn't." Broglio scowled.

The saga had kept the nation riveted to the story for months.

"But Katherine was never released," Hank said. Ernie Broglio shook his head. "And it was ultimately believed that she was killed."

Katherine's abductors had threatened her murder if the general didn't follow their orders, but would three college kids have killed because of her father's intransigence? Could Phoebe Harrington have executed her freshman roommate as a political prisoner?

"You know in police work we never assume anything, Lieutenant, but it was the simplest explanation," the agent said. "Katherine Patterson was never seen after she left the campus the night of her kidnapping in October of 1991. The bureau always suspected that one of the students got nervous, did something stupid."

"Were you with the bureau then?" Hank asked.

"I'd just joined, still doing my training. We followed the Patterson case closely."

"I'm sure it was very instructive."

"But you never found a body," the chief said. "Which means Katherine Patterson *could* still be alive somewhere."

"Katherine has never contacted her family," Broglio said. "They have had every reason to think that she is dead. Me? I think she was killed, and her body was buried somewhere in the woods. The cottage was in a remote part of the state. Or maybe the body's at the bottom of a lake up there."

Hank thought of the general sitting stiffly in his wheelchair in that lonely house out on the cliff. What did he believe after all these years? "And what happened to the kidnappers, Agent Broglio?" he asked. "They weren't apprehended at the time, were they?" Even though their pictures were on the front page of every newspaper. "Despite her parents' pleas, Phoebe never turned herself in, did she?"

"The bureau finally got a tip on the cottage location around Christmas. By the time the FBI arrived, everyone was gone. There were plenty of fingerprints in the cottage so we knew who to look for. Josh Ware turned up dead in Chicago a year later. Drug overdose. The FBI managed to trace Stewart to Amsterdam. But he disappeared into the underground over there. Today? Who knows where he is."

"And Phoebe Harrington?" Hank felt the beat of his heart quicken. "Where is she?"

"You've got her, Lt. Nightingale. Her body's right here in your morgue."

CHAPTER XIV

Phoebe Harrington's identity had been confirmed once more through her fingerprints. All of the prints that the Newport Police had taken from Caroline's BMW had been sent to the FBI registry in the hopes that the murderer's identity might be learned from them. Instead the prints had revealed the stunning information that the victim had another name, was another person.

Meredith Hackett's identity was being researched back to 1991. The FBI had already begun the spade work. So far she was known to have been acting in New York City as early as 1997. Prior to that she was non-existent. Six years to account for. Six years when she had been running, hiding, making the transition to another name. Another person. Meredith Hackett, who came to know Caroline Kent as a fellow actor in the New York theater.

The bureau had found no birth certificate for the dead actress. Meredith Hackett had a Social Security number and a membership card in Actors' Equity. FBI agents had already been to her Manhattan apartment where they found two U.S. passports, one in Meredith's name, the other in the name of Mary Morgan.

Hank studied the photograph of Phoebe Harrington which Broglio had handed him. It was a professional studio portrait, probably her high school yearbook photo. The girl in the picture had long red and gold hair. Her large, serious eyes looked at the camera through rimless aviator glasses.

"I've explained to Chief Williams that the FBI won't interfere in your murder investigation," Ernie Broglio told Hank.

"Are you going on the assumption that there is a connection to her death and this old business?" Hank asked, momentarily forgetting that police officers do not assume. His mind was whirling with new possibilities. Caroline had believed that Meredith was followed from New York to Newport. Charles Patterson was in Newport. Had Meredith known that Katherine's father was living in Newport?

"It would be interesting to know if the general had ever met Katherine's roommate," Hank said. Would Charles Patterson have recognized Phoebe if he had seen her as Meredith Hackett twenty years later?

"I don't know that," Broglio answered, "but I think we can find out."

"I'm also curious," Hank asked the agent, "if Katherine's parents were living in Newport at the time of her kidnapping."

"During the time the general was working in the Energy Department, they lived in an apartment in one of the Washington hotels. After the kidnapping period, a friend lent them a place in Maryland where they could be secluded from the press. But Mrs. Patterson's family did once own an estate in Newport, and she came here as a young woman. In 1991, though, there was no connection to the city of Newport that we know of."

"I see," Hank said. "I'd like to go back and read the files on the case. Also see the newspaper clippings, whatever you've got."

"I can tell you that the general didn't stay in his government job after the kidnapping news died down. Who knows?" Broglio shook his head. "He might have been eased out of the administration. The Pattersons left the Washington area, and he and his wife bought the estate in Newport. I believe it's called Windward. Marjorie Patterson died about a year or so after they moved here."

"Katherine had a brother, Will," Hank said.

"Did she, Lieutenant? I'm not sure. I don't think he was part of the events in the kidnapping."

"And Charles Patterson was a former military man," the chief remarked. "What was his record?"

"Oh, good," Ernie said quickly. "He was decorated in Viet Nam. He was severely wounded during an extremely dangerous mission."

Top secret, Hank thought, by the look on your face.

"When he retired from the Army, Charles Patterson went to work for one of the nuclear energy companies. That's how President Bush came to appoint him to the post in the Energy Department."

"What does the FBI want out of this, Agent Broglio?" Hank asked.

"We'd like to close our files on Katherine Patterson's kidnapping."

"Agent Broglio is going out to see Gen. Patterson after he leaves here, Hank."

"My superiors thought that the former assistant secretary was entitled to that courtesy."

"I've asked Agent Broglio if you can go along." Hank knew he couldn't wait any longer to explain how he'd already met the general. The chief frowned as Hank gave a quick account of his visit to Windward to see Spider Shipley in connection with the Hackett case.

"That's how you knew about the brother," Broglio said.

Hank nodded.

"What about Meredith Hackett's murder?" Hank looked back at the agent.

"I thought I made that clear, Lieutenant. That's Newport's case."

"I don't think we can eliminate the possibility that her past life could have something to do with her death."

"That's true enough," Broglio said. "That's why the FBI assigned me to the file. We want to keep up with what you are doing. In case anything does lead back to the kidnapping."

"Like evidence that Katherine was killed in 1991? I don't think Phoebe Harrington can tell you about that."

"No," Ernie Broglio agreed, "but you might turn up someone who's still alive in this case who can. Don't forget Darnell Stewart. As far as we know he is still alive. We'd like to find someone who could tell us a lot more about what happened than the FBI was ever able to uncover."

The idea that Meredith had hidden something at Kenwood before she died continued to preoccupy Caroline's thoughts. Systematically she had gone over the interiors of the rooms in the house which the late actress had seemed to favor, looking for the mysterious object.

Of course, Caroline would have been helped immeasurably if she knew what it was she was looking for. Papers, Sarah had said, but Caroline was determined not to be misled by that hint. Sarah was most definitely a woman capable of telling lies. Caroline believed nothing Meredith's sister had told her. It was only Sarah's actions which were truthful. She had been looking for something in the conservatory. And since she continued to occupy a guest bedroom at Kenwood, Caroline knew that whatever Sarah was looking for, it was clear she had not found it. Otherwise, she would have settled her bill and checked out of the inn.

"Papers," Caroline said to herself as she stood in the doorway of the billiard room that same day. "But it could be something entirely different." She surveyed the room, allowing her eyes to go from left to right, slowly taking in the contents. It was a wonderful old space, the past scene of many late night games between the gentlemen of the house and their guests. Her father-in-law had been a skillful player. His inlaid cues still rested in the circular oak stand, a picturesque reminder of the house's past glories. Now, if the guests at the inn wandered inside, it was only to admire the heavy, ornate table, the smooth ivory billiard balls and the antique counter. Encouraged to play, they would protest. The old mahogany table with its claw feet and richly carved panels was too intimidating to use.

Caroline began the task of looking around the room. Again, the question nagged at her. What was she looking for?

"Anything I don't expect to find," she said, lifting the cues from their holder and peering in. "What doesn't belong?"

She bent over to push her fingers into the deep recesses of the brown velvet cushions of the long upholstered divan. Getting down on her knees, she reached under the furniture, hoping for the feel of some object. Nothing. Lamps, boxes, even the fireplace. Lastly, she turned to the billiard table itself. Would it be worth looking in the pockets where the balls traveled inside the interior? Who on earth could be entrusted to eviscerate the ancient billiard table?

"Caroline, what are you doing?" Louise was standing in the doorway, watching her daughter-in-law trying to push her hand into one of the billiard table's corner pockets.

"Oh, Louise," Caroline answered, withdrawing her hand and rubbing her fingers. "I'm not going mad."

"No, dear, I didn't think you were." Louise came over to the table and looked into the dark hole. "Did you drop something?"

"I'm looking for what Sarah Ryder is trying to find."

"Any luck?"

"No," Caroline said in a disappointed voice. "It would help if I knew *what* I was looking for."

"Yes, I have been trying to think that out myself."

"My turn to ask. Any luck?"

"No, but I can't get over the feeling that it has something to do with money. Maybe jewelry. Sarah did say she lost an earring.

Perhaps that was one of those slips you make when you want to conceal something but say a thing that is almost true."

"It's possible. It can't be anything big. That's for sure. It couldn't be large and still be concealed in our house without our seeing it." Caroline looked around the room.

"A case of hide-in-plain-sight," Louise suggested.

"I was wondering if it is stuffed down in the pockets of the billiard table."

Louise looked at the old table. Her eyebrows narrowed. "We could push something through, I suppose. With a wire contraption. See if it dislodges anything."

"You think it's possible?" Caroline asked, brightening.

"I think it's unlikely," Louise answered. "Perhaps the police ought to be looking, instead of us."

"Hank didn't seem that interested in Sarah's story. I think he believes the whole thing was a fabrication. But I know she's looking for something. That's why she's staying on."

"Cool as a cucumber that one. I asked her at breakfast this morning how she was planning to spend the day, and she told me she was going to The Breakers for the new audio tour she saw advertised. Honestly, Caroline. She must think I've got the brain of a rabbit. I saw her coming out of the garages yesterday afternoon. While I was gardening. She waved to me."

"She has that attitude. I've never met anyone quite like her."

"She's immoral, Caroline."

"Immoral? What do you mean?"

"She doesn't care about right or wrong. She's entirely motivated by her own selfish needs."

"You might mean that she is amoral, Louise."

"Is there a big difference?"

"I don't know. I've never been much for philosophical questions. I've always thought that immoral was more evil, and amoral was, well, just unconcerned about morals."

"I don't like her," Louise said, "whichever word is correct to use."

"Neither do I," Caroline responded. "I wonder if we could get her in some dark room and make her talk."

Louise laughed. "Give her the third degree, you mean?"

"Sarah knows a lot about her sister's activities, and what Meredith was hiding, and I would give anything to get that information out of her. Hank hasn't had any luck."

"I never thought I'd see the suspect who could fight Hank Nightingale to a draw."

"I suppose he has other leads he is following."

"That man Spider."

"I don't know." Caroline hadn't talked to Hank recently, and she was missing the connection to the case and what he was doing.

Louise was squinting into one of the side pockets of the billiard table.

"Drop something, Mrs. Kent?"

Both women turned to see Molly coming into the room. She was wearing her apron and carrying a bucket stocked with cleaning materials.

"No, Molly," Caroline answered on her mother-in-law's behalf. "We were just looking in the table." She started to say for the maid not to be concerned when she had an entirely new idea.

"Molly?"

"Yes, Mrs. Kent."

"You remember when my friend Meredith was staying here, I'm sure. You were working during that week and saw her in the house."

"Oh, yes. So sad that." Molly looked sincerely distressed. "She was so beautiful, and so young. It isn't safe for a woman to be out on the streets alone at night."

"You have to be careful," Caroline said kindly.

"I don't go out at night alone if I can help it."

"I'm sure that's wise," Louise said.

"Molly," Caroline began again. "When Ms. Hackett was still alive, and you saw her here at the inn, where did you see her usually spending her time?"

"Is it important to the murder investigation?" Molly asked. Her grey eyes widened.

"It might be," Louise said. "Did you ever see her in this room, Molly?"

"Oh, no," the maid answered quickly. "I mostly saw her in the plant room."

"The conservatory," Louise said.

"What you call it, Mrs. Kent. She liked to sit in there after breakfast, but of course once the dining room table was cleared, I liked to take the vacuum around the downstairs and do my dusting. Then once the guests come out of their bedrooms again, I can do up there. Change the linen and do the bathrooms."

"Yes, Molly," Caroline said, hoping she successfully concealed the impatience in her voice. She knew the household's routine as well as anyone. "But you did see her in the plant room. Every morning, would you say?"

"Well, I think so. I mean, I must have. Because I did realize how irritated she was to see me coming in. It made me nervous, I can tell you. Although it was only for ten or fifteen minutes. I mean, them plants is dirty anyway, so you can't be so particular about getting all the dust up. I mean, I just swept the floor and ran the dusting cloth over the furniture. Don't do the cushions every day—"

"Molly, back to Ms. Hackett, what did—"

But Molly's narrative was not to be interrupted by Louise.

"—no point. Once a week is fine. But I could see her give me that look when I come in. I knew I was interrupting her writing in that book of hers, but like I said. It was only ten or fifteen minutes I was going to be there. But once she saw me coming, she slammed up that book and after the first day, she would pick herself up off the chair and take herself out of the plant room." Molly was staring at Caroline, now at Louise. The maid looked puzzled.

Caroline looked at her mother-in-law's open-mouthed expression and had the feeling that if there was a mirror in the room, she would have been able to see the same astonished expression on her own face.

Writing in a book.

"Don't know where she went," Molly added while the two other women in the room remained speechless, gaping at each other. "Because after that I like to do the powder room off the front hall. And she was never in there."

Meredith had been writing in a book.

"Molly," Caroline said slowly, at last recovering her voice. "Did you see this book up close?"

"No, Mrs. Kent."

"Think carefully. Did you ever see it in Ms. Hackett's bedroom?"

"Oh, no. Only with her holding on to it like it was the crown jewels."

"What color was it?" Louise asked.

"Green. It was light green with a paper cover. Like one of them school notebooks with the spiral wire."

"How big was it?" Louise held her hands about ten inches apart.

"Smaller than that," Molly answered. She held her own hands about six inches apart.

"Ms. Hackett was writing in this book?" Caroline asked.

"Every time I went in there. Like I said before."

"A diary," Louise said, her eyes bright with excitement.

"Of course," Caroline said. "Meredith kept a diary."

"And that's what her sister is looking for."

CHAPTER XV

Spider Shipley was impatient for the first week of his employment at Windward to end. It was hard getting back to steady work, and being hounded by the police at the same time hadn't helped. Tomorrow was Friday, a good night to go out and get plastered. He hoped he would be paid and would have the cash to get good and drunk.

But it was only Thursday, and he had the afternoon ahead of him, plus all the next day. Spider put down his shovel and surveyed the work he had so far accomplished on the fence. The enclosure looked worse than when he had started to repair it. Everything was in pieces, and he was only digging aimlessly in the earth to give the appearance of being busy. In truth, he hadn't a clue as to how he was going to restore the deterioration in the wall.

Not that anyone seemed to care. The chauffeur Jason, who had gotten Spider started on the job, hadn't been out to see its progress after the first day's work had ended. From time to time, Will Patterson came out to chat with Spider. The general's son appeared to have little to occupy himself, and he frequently sauntered across the lawn to talk to Spider about nothing very important. The weather, baseball, movies Spider had never bothered to see.

Growing up in Newport, Spider had never liked the rich kids he saw around town. They had new cars and expensive clothes. And a certain look that said *don't touch*. And he hadn't. But Will seemed different, friendlier. He didn't dress like he was rich and his old van was in worse shape than Irene's Taurus.

Spider's lunch break had been over an hour ago. He had forgotten to refill his water bottle when he had been in the kitchen to eat the sandwiches his mother had prepared for him. A man couldn't work outdoors at hard labor without water. Wasn't healthy. Walking back up to the house to get some water seemed like a good use of his present time.

Windward still fascinated him. The house had so many interesting parts. Growing up in Newport hadn't given him the opportunity to get inside any of the mansions where people actually lived. None of his friends lived on any of the big estates, and he'd never bothered to take a tour of one of the places open to the public. That was for the tourists.

Spider especially liked Windward's studio. He hadn't been there since that first day he had met Will unloading his van, but he wished Will would invite him up there again. Spider liked the space and still pictured himself one day moving into it. In L.A., people had been impressed when he told them he was from Newport, Rhode Island. Now that he was back home, he thought it was time he lived in a mansion. He had a feeling that Will wouldn't be hanging around much longer. With a little bit of luck, Spider could find himself as live-in help in possession of the studio by Christmas. That was the set-up he wanted.

To kill more time on his water break, Spider took the long way around the house. Passing the open French windows of the general's study, he heard voices. The sounds were clear. Will and his father were arguing.

Slowly Spider crept toward the window, finding a nook behind a tall shrub in which to hide his small body. He could see partially inside the room, which was as dark as he remembered its being on his first meeting with the general. Spider crouched down in the shrubbery. He was curious about the old man, and Spider had no reservations against eavesdropping to satisfy his curiosity. His mother had been no help when he had questioned her about the Pattersons. She felt sorry for the general, but she had little interest in him.

". . . always do this to me." Will's voice. Spider strained to listen. The property was secluded, quiet. With concentration, he got his ear to hear everything that was being said inside the house.

"You do it to yourself," the general replied in a surprisingly strong voice.

"I don't know why you bothered to have children. I guess Mother wanted them."

"A man likes a son."

"But not a daughter."

"You've no right to say that."

"You killed your daughter."

The words shocked Spider, and he strained to see what was the scene inside the room. The general was in his wheelchair, and the slight figure of Will stood in the shadows across from him. Finally the old man spoke in a low, hard voice.

"I did not kill Katherine. Those people did."

"Those people were your instrument." Will's voice was shrill now. "You could have saved her."

There was another silence, and Spider craned his neck to see Will's face.

"You were very young, William," the general said. "You never understood what was at stake."

"My sister's life," Will cried out. Spider still couldn't see his new friend's face clearly, but he didn't need to.

"I had a duty to the government. You can't negotiate with terrorists."

"They weren't terrorists, Father. They were people Katherine knew. If you had only met with them, listened to what they wanted.

Respected what they were doing. No. Instead you held your head up high and pretended to be doing your precious duty—"

"You couldn't respect them. Those people told scare stories. There was nothing to their claims that nuclear plants are dangerous. Exposure to low level radiation is not dangerous. They were fear-mongers. They tried to use Katherine." Now the general's voice was also rising, and Spider saw him pushing his chair toward Will. "You should be angry at *them*."

"I hate you," Will said, backing up from the approaching chair. He had reached the fireplace, and there was no place for him to go. "You killed her," he shouted again.

"No. They will always bear the guilt for what happened. I can't take that away."

"The guilt is yours, Father. No matter what you say now. Mother knew. She knew you killed Katherine."

"The people who kidnapped Katherine are to blame for what happened to her. They had no right—"

"You had no right to play God," Will screamed.

The sound of shouting had summoned Jason Forman, who now rushed into the room. Spider jumped back from the window as he saw Igor run rapidly toward the wheelchair and push it back across the room. While he was being propelled, the man in the chair was still as a statue. He let himself be handled without protesting.

"That's enough, Will," Jason said.

"Leave us alone, Jason," Will answered him.

"No," came the answer. "Your father needs his rest."

"All he does is rest. It's time he faced up to his crimes."

"You're hysterical, Will," the chauffeur said.

"I've never been more calm," the general's son said. "I know the truth." He turned and ran from the room.

Spider eased back from the window and also began running. He wanted to reach the safety of the kitchen before anyone discovered his presence at a family quarrel. As he ran he tried to make sense of what he had just heard.

Who was Katherine? It sounded like she was Will's sister, and she was dead. Will had said his father had murdered her, but that couldn't be right. There was more to this story than Spider understood from this short argument. He wished his mother knew the details, but he was pretty sure she had not bothered to learn them.

If Ernie Broglio had believed that his announcement to the father of Katherine Patterson that one of her kidnappers had been found dead would please him, the FBI agent was in for a big disappointment. The news, delivered in somber tones to the general in his study at Windward, was absorbed with cold silence.

Nightingale was glad to be a bystander while Broglio gave a quick, but efficient account of the purpose of his visit. He watched the general's military bearing unflinching as the news was delivered. Hank could not tell his reaction; Patterson's face was that rigid.

"The bureau sent me over from Providence to tell you personally, Gen. Patterson," Broglio concluded. At this show of respect for his former position in the government, the master of Windward nodded. "Is there anything further you would like to know, sir?" Broglio asked.

"Thank you for coming," the general replied without emotion. "I appreciate the bureau's courtesy. Jason will show you out."

The muscular figure of Jason Forman had been standing vigilant by the general's side.

"Yes, sir," he answered.

"Gen. Patterson, excuse me," Hank said. "I wonder if I could ask you something."

The general turned his head toward Hank, and it was his turn to study the other man's face. "You were here on Tuesday," Charles Patterson said.

"Yes, sir."

"Did you speak to Mr. Shipley?"

"I did."

"And you were satisfied?"

"Yes. Thank you."

"He is still working here. I trust that is all right. He isn't dangerous, is he?"

"No, sir. I needed his statement in connection with an investigation. He was a witness."

"Good." The general began studying the folds of the blanket over his knees.

"General," Hank began. "Had you ever met your daughter's roommate? Phoebe Harrington."

"No," the older man answered. He had not taken his eyes from his legs.

"You didn't visit your daughter at college?"

"I was working in Washington, and I was extremely busy. Katherine was only away at the college for two months before the kidnapping."

"I see."

"My wife drove her up there when the semester began," he added as if he was remembering it for the first time since it happened. The effort seemed to tire him. His shoulders drooped slightly.

"You would have seen the photographs of her in the news at the time, however," Hank pressed gently.

"I'm sure I did, Lieutenant, but I wasn't interested in the news coverage that much." He looked up and straight into Hank's eyes. "We kept everything away from Mrs. Patterson."

"Do you think you could have recognized Phoebe from the photographs?"

"Then or now?" The general's eyes were alert.

"Now," Hank replied.

The general sighed. "I doubt it. It was a long time ago. People's appearances change over the years." He waved at his lifeless legs. "Look at me."

"So you don't think you would recognize Phoebe Harrington today?"

"Young women become older. Their faces age. They dye their hair."

"You're right, sir," Broglio said unnecessarily. Hank frowned at his interruption.

The general had shifted his gaze to the agent, and Broglio was nodding his good-byes. Hank gave in. He would do some homework and come to question the general again, this time without Broglio. But he was curious to know if it was only a guess by the general that Meredith Hackett had changed the original color of her hair.

"He's a cool customer," Broglio said as Forman closed the door behind them. "What do you think?"

Hank was surprised to be asked his opinion by Ernie Broglio.

"It's a type."

"You don't like military men, Lieutenant?"

"Why don't you call me Hank, Ernie?"

"Sure. I can do that, Hank. No problem."

"I don't like the general because he is cold and calculating, Ernie. He didn't move a muscle when you mentioned his daughter's name and the kidnapping. You might have said his neighbor's dog was missing."

"It's their training, the military culture. I wouldn't put too much stock in it."

"No, of course not," Hank said. "But then he didn't seem happy to learn that his old enemy was dead, either."

"I don't follow you."

"Why didn't he show some emotion when you told him that Phoebe Harrington was dead?"

"I said—he's a military man."

"No."

"What then?"

"Maybe he already knew that Phoebe Harrington was dead."

CHAPTER XVI

⸺⸺❈⸺⸺

While Charles Patterson showed no emotion at Ernie Broglio's revelation of Meredith Hackett's real identity, Hank had the satisfaction of being the bearer of a genuine bombshell when he delivered the same news to Caroline a few hours later.

"My God, Hank," she said after he had told her what he knew of the kidnapping and Meredith's role in it. "It is utterly unbelievable."

Caroline had been upstairs when he arrived at Kenwood, and Louise had directed him to go up to the second floor to find her. Caroline had taken him into the sitting room which she and her mother-in-law shared.

Caroline was standing, staring at him incredulously.

"What do you think of it?" he asked.

"I can't think of anything to say," she answered. Her head was reeling, with Meredith's face crowding her mind. She sat down in one of the armchairs.

"Do you remember Katherine Patterson's kidnapping?"

"I was in high school at the time. I don't think I followed the news that closely. I do remember the name, though."

"Whose? Katherine's or Phoebe's?"

"Both, I guess. They were so linked. They were college roommates, weren't they?"

"Yes, but only for a couple of months. They were both first year students."

"And you're sure? There's no chance of error? Meredith is . . . was Phoebe?"

"The FBI has the fingerprint match. There may be the chance of getting a DNA match, but I don't know why they need to. No, Meredith was Phoebe."

Caroline was quiet, still absorbing the shock.

"Did you ever suspect anything was wrong about Meredith?" Hank asked.

"In what way?"

"Look, I know this is a hell of a surprise, but I've got to start somewhere. Meredith Hackett was only using that name since the mid-nineties. Before that, well, we're not sure what she was doing, but if you could think back. Remember things she said that might give us a clue."

"A clue to what?"

"How she got to be an actress for one thing. You said she was good. She must have had training somewhere."

"I don't know." Caroline was genuinely puzzled. "It's all so confusing. But I guess it does explain a lot of things now."

"What things?"

"I know for certain she had at least one film offer that she turned down. At the time it seemed reasonable enough. She said the money wasn't right. And then not doing TV. She always explained that she loved working on the stage, mostly off-Broadway. Said she had time for the other stuff later on, when theater work dried up. At the time I admired her dedication to the craft."

"Instead, the reason was that she didn't want her picture broadcast across the country on the television or her face on a giant movie screen."

"No, of course not. That would have been really risky. She wouldn't do commercials either, and everybody took those in New York to pay the rent."

"Well, she was successful in remaining anonymous."

"But how does this all come into her murder? Does it tell you who murdered her, Hank?"

"No, not at all."

"But that story that Sarah Ryder told us. What about that? Running from the mob and the boyfriend. Was she really talking about something in this old kidnapping business?"

"There's another part to this puzzle, Caroline."

"What is that?"

"Do you know Charles Patterson? He has a big house called Windward out on Ocean Drive."

"No, I don't think so. Who is he? Oh! Patterson. You don't mean that—"

"Yes, I do. Katherine Patterson's father lives in Newport."

"Mr. X!"

"What?"

"We kept saying there was a Mr. X in this case, Hank. It makes perfect sense."

"Charles Patterson is a retired general in the United States Army. He is confined to a wheelchair."

"Is he rich? He could have had her killed."

"I'd say that anything's possible after what I learned today. The case has become much too complicated. Anybody who knew Meredith as Phoebe Harrington has to be considered a suspect now."

"Do you think Meredith knew Katherine's father was here in Newport? I thought she was running away from something or someone in New York."

"When Phoebe knew Katherine, her parents lived in Washington. Her father worked for the federal government then."

"Why did Meredith come to Newport, Hank?"

"To see you?" he suggested.

"Why me?"

"I don't know the answer to that. To tell you something . . . to confide in you. You said she was upset and preoccupied. Would she confide in you?"

"Time heals," Caroline said, her own words to Meredith coming back to her suddenly.

"What?"

"Last week, when we were sitting, talking in the gazebo. I said that to her, Hank. Remember? I told you. And what did she say? That it didn't work that way. She didn't believe it."

"Guilt?"

"Maybe. Good Lord, there's something else. Something I only found out about today. Meredith kept a diary."

"A diary? How do you know?"

"Molly, one of the maids, saw her writing in it. I said to you that Meredith had a book, but we never found it when we looked for it in her room. I thought it was a novel. She told me she was reading a book every night. Not reading. *Writing*."

"Where is the diary now?"

"That's just it. We don't know."

"The diary could answer a lot of these question." Hank shook his head. "You say you never saw this diary?"

"I don't think so. According to Molly it is the size of a small school notebook."

"Well, we'll have to search for it. I'm not sure I can put anybody on it today. Tomorrow's Friday. I'll have to see what I can do. Have you been looking for it?"

"Of course. But I haven't found anything yet."

"And that's what the sister is looking for, I presume."

"I'm sure of it. Oh, Hank, this is fantastic. I'm starting to feel excited. That's awful, isn't it? But I still can't believe that Meredith was part of a kidnapping. She was very young at the time. And it does seem as if Katherine Patterson died because those students botched things up. Meredith must have felt tremendous guilt."

"I didn't think she looked so remorseful the night I met her in The Black Pearl."

"Hank, she was an actress. When she wanted to, she could hide her feelings very well."

"Well," he frowned. "You knew her better than I did."

"That's rather an ironic comment in view of the circumstances, don't you think?"

"People don't change character just because they change their names," Hank said.

"Do you think there are clues to what happened in the kidnapping in her diary?"

"That's information for the FBI. I was hoping it would have a clue to who she was meeting that night after she left The Black Pearl."

"Of course. Her murderer. Her killer would want that diary."

"Assuming he or she knows it exists."

"We've got to find it first, Hank."

"Where is Sarah Ryder? Is she in the house?"

"I'm not sure." Caroline looked at her watch. It was ten past five. "Some of the guests go into the library for a drink at five. We always have it set up for cocktails."

"Then let's go down for cocktails, Mrs. Kent."

"Do you think Sarah Ryder could have . . . I almost can't say it . . . done away with her sister?"

"Anything's possible," Hank said grimly. "Finding out about the kidnapping gives us our first solid motive in the case."

"But her own sister," Caroline began, realizing immediately how much she herself disliked Sarah and how, only earlier, had been saying that the woman was a liar. "A killer?"

"Katherine Patterson was presumed to have been killed by her kidnappers, Caroline. It's very possible that your friend Meredith was a killer."

"You're saying that it runs in the family?"

"I'm saying that a woman is dead. Her body's in the morgue, and I want to find out who killed her. I've got the FBI around my neck and a chief who's on my tail. There's a woman staying here at your inn who would do well to cooperate with my investigation. I'm through playing games with Ms. Sarah Ryder. If indeed, that is her real name."

They found Sarah Ryder sitting on the small veranda outside the library. She had a drink in her hand, and she was staring up at the sky. The sun was on this side of the house, getting ready to sink out of view. Sarah was relaxed, and Caroline studied her silhouette. The resemblance to Meredith—Caroline couldn't get used to thinking of her as Phoebe—was strong in the late afternoon brightness of the sun.

"Ms. Ryder," Hank began, and Sarah started forward in the chair. She turned slowly and looked up at Hank. There was a guarded manner about her.

"I expected you to come in to identify your sister's body. I thought we had agreed that you would do that," Hank said.

"You agreed, Lieutenant. I have no desire to see her body." Sarah looked suddenly grim, and Caroline felt the first feeling of sympathy toward the woman seated in the chair.

"It's a formality that needs to be attended to."

Sarah looked at Caroline. "You knew her."

"I wanted the next of kin."

Sarah remained silent, and Caroline wondered what Hank had planned that would draw her out. Sarah turned back and stared at the horizon.

"I sat out here last night and saw the sun set. It was very beautiful, all orange and dazzling in your eyes." She sipped her drink and looked ahead as if she were still alone. Hank sat down in the chair beside her.

"I didn't come here to watch the sunset, Ms. Ryder. I'm investigating a murder, and it's time you helped me with that." Sarah took another drink from her glass. "Since you don't want to be forthcoming on your own, I'm going to start. We know who your sister is." He waited, and Sarah's lower lip quivered. "Now why don't we talk about that?"

If Caroline expected Sarah to go on the offensive, exactly the opposite happened.

"I always wondered how it would end. I was always fearing there would be a sensational arrest." Sarah bit her lip to stop it from trembling. "Never this way, never the way it did."

"I would appreciate your cooperation," Hank said patiently.

"Phoebe's dead," Sarah said. "You can't hurt her anymore."

"It's not my job, and never was, to hurt your sister. I want to find her killer. To begin I've got to follow the lead of this kidnapping mystery."

"The kidnapping was a terrible mistake," Sarah said, staring with difficulty into the sun's rays. "She was only eighteen, you know."

"Tell me about it, Ms. Ryder."

She sighed heavily and raised the glass to her lips. "I was in college then myself. Boston University. I'm two years older." She faltered, and Caroline slipped into a chair on the other side of Hank.

"Is Sarah Ryder your real name?" he asked.

"Yes. My ex-husband's name was Ryder, and I've never changed it back."

"What do you know about what happened in October of 1991?"

"Phoebe had always been passionate about things. Growing up, she hated to see a dead animal lying in the road. She would get physically sick if its guts were spilled out. I never thought of her as being politically involved. I suppose it was the stories about the people living around those plants who were made sick that got to her. Anyway, all of a sudden, there was my sister's picture on every newspaper and TV news program. I couldn't believe the kidnapping at first. I thought it was some crazy mistake."

"But it wasn't," Caroline said.

"No. And then when they wouldn't release Katherine Patterson, I really got scared. My parents were alive then, and they said publicly that they would support her no matter what she had done. I was sure she would come forward, give herself up. She couldn't know the seriousness of what she was doing. She was practically a child still. It was that Josh Ware character who manipulated her into helping him. I'm sure of that."

"When did you first see her again?" Hank asked.

"What will you do with this information, Lieutenant?"

"I need help in finding your sister's killer. I want to understand the background. What you tell me could help."

"If I tell you what happened, I could be in big trouble."

"How do you mean?" Caroline asked.

Sarah looked at Hank. "You understand, don't you?"

Hank nodded.

"Sarah helped her sister to hide, Caroline, and she could be prosecuted for that."

"But that was years ago," Caroline protested. And Meredith's gone now. What would be the sense in prosecuting now?"

"Meredith was my sister, and I didn't turn my back on her. But I don't want to go to jail for it."

"I'm not taking notes," Hank said. "If the FBI decides to question you, Ms. Ryder, you can answer their questions for the record."

Sarah clasped her drink.

"Well, if you remember, there was a period when the kidnappers stopped giving out those taped messages. Meredith . . . I've had to think of her by that name, call her that. It was important that I never make a slip, for her sake. Anyway, Meredith was the one who recorded them, with Katherine's voice added at the end to show she was with them and alive. Ware mailed them to somebody he knew in Chicago, who re-mailed them to the press in a new envelope so there was a Chicago postmark" Cassettes detailing the demands of the students had been regularly sent to one of the Chicago newspapers at various times during the episode. "Then the police, maybe it was the FBI. I don't know. Anyway, they got some kind of tip that led them to my Great-Aunt Lorraine's cottage in New Hampshire. She didn't use it in the winter, only the summer. It wasn't heated. But, of course, when the authorities broke in, everybody was gone."

"That was around Christmas," Hank said.

"What a horrible holiday that was. No word from Meredith. My parents were frantic. Anyway, I went back to school after the first of the year. Then, in February, I got this letter. Block printing, no return address, telling me to come to one of the public parks in Boston at a certain time. I did, and Meredith was there."

"By herself?" Caroline asked.

"Yeah. She looked awful. She was thin and dirty. She hadn't been eating properly. She wouldn't tell me where she had been. And she was limping. Said she had hurt her ankle, but wouldn't tell me how." Sarah bit her lip. "I wanted to know everything that had happened, but she said the kidnappers had sworn each other to secrecy, and she wouldn't tell me anything. She was wild-eyed and said she had given her promise. She frightened me. I had never seen her like that. I said all right, and then we faced what to do with her."

"Which was?" Hank asked.

Sarah hesitated before continuing, looking at Hank once more for another confirmation that he could be trusted.

"I knew this guy in Boston whose brother used to do work for the IRA in this country. He knew the network of people who helped send the money and all back to Ireland. He arranged for Meredith to go to Ireland."

"I can't believe it," Caroline said.

"It happened quickly," Sarah explained. "The guy had a whole set-up to give her papers and everything." Meredith's sister smiled ruefully. "All it took was money. I sold some family jewelry that I had. Meredith was gone in two weeks. I never told my parents until she was over there, and I knew she was safe. It broke their hearts that they never saw her."

"But you still didn't know what happened in the kidnapping? What happened to Katherine Patterson?" Sarah shook her head "How long was Meredith in Ireland?"

"Four years."

"What did she do?" Caroline asked. "Where did she live?"

"At first, undercover, with somebody's family in a little town outside of Cork. I think everybody was hiding somebody those days in the countryside. Then she gradually blended into the landscape. That's where Meredith took up acting."

"In Ireland?"

"In a little storefront theater in Cork. I think it saved her sanity."

Caroline, who had traveled in Ireland, could picture it all in her own mind. The little whitewashed cottage, the green countryside, the small city look of Cork. And most of all, the small, dark theater. It was probably sandwiched in between two noisy, colorful pubs on one of the narrow side streets. The Irish loved and revered their theater. Meredith Hackett had been lucky to stumble into that territory. She had come away from her exile with nothing less than a solid grounding in the craft of acting.

Hank was quiet. But Caroline knew he wasn't thinking of dark, musty theaters and worn black floorboards. Sarah had finished her drink and was squinting back at the setting sun.

"I understand you're looking for your sister's diary," Hank said. When Sarah didn't answer him, he continued. "Have you ever read it?"

"No," Sarah answered. "I've never even seen it."

"How do you know it exists?"

"Meredith told me she had kept one during the kidnapping. She said she had recently started writing in it again. It wasn't in her apartment in New York. I checked after she died. She had it with her. I'm sure."

"But you haven't found it, Ms. Ryder?" Hank asked.

"I don't have it, Lieutenant. But I think it's mine now. I'm her next of kin, as you have pointed out."

"Katherine Patterson's family would like to know what happened to their daughter," Hank said.

"I can understand that. But how do I know there aren't incriminating entries in that diary that I don't want the FBI to get their hands on?"

"We can't help that now," Hank said. "The diary is evidence. I can't let you destroy it."

"I won't promise not to, if I find it first," Sarah said in a reckless tone. She had resumed the persona she had been when she first arrived at Kenwood.

"Why did your sister decide to come to Newport last week?" Hank asked.

"I didn't even know Meredith was here until I read in the newspaper in New York that she was dead."

CHAPTER XVII

"How about a beer, Spider?" Will asked. He had been standing for the last fifteen minutes watching while Spider packed up his tools and supplies. He had been making a habit of hanging around, watching Spider work. But never offering his help.

"Ah, I don't know, Will. I usually go home with my Ma."

"Come on over to the studio. I've got plenty of beer there," Will said as Spider started walking up the back lawn, carrying his load alone. "I'll buy you one. More than one, even." He grinned, and Spider decided to return the smile. A free beer was a free beer.

As they climbed the steps to the studio, Spider looked around with the eyes of a prospective tenant. Will hadn't done much to the interior since Spider had first seen it on Sunday. The plastic garbage bags still dotted the walls, and boxes remained unpacked. Some clothes were flung over a chair, but the camp bed was made in a neat and orderly fashion.

"Let's have some music," Will suggested. "I've got a real great system. I built it myself. The sound's great. I want you to hear it."

Spider studied the set-up. There was an old turntable and tuners with lots of knobs. Two huge speakers were wired to give the sound from opposite ends of the room.

"Why do you have records? Nobody has them anymore."

"Music sounds best on vinyl records. That's why I had to do this all myself. Everything, including that turntable, is from the 70s. That's when things were made the best, you know."

Spider didn't know. He had a cheap MP3 Player he had bought out in L.A..

"What kind of music do you like? Take a look at the records and pick something while I get us some beer." He gestured to the boxes on the floor that held the brightly colored cardboard sleeves of albums. "I pick them up wherever I travel," he said proudly. "It's a great collection."

While Spider looked through the boxes, Will opened blue plastic tub and withdrew two green bottles of beer. Imported. Spider liked that. He usually bought Budweiser because it was always on sale.

"You got a lot of music here," Spider said as he picked up a Metallica album and began to take the record out of the sleeve. "Do these cost a lot of money?"

"That's one of the best," Will said as he took the album from Spider's hand. "You'll really hear the clearness of the original tracks." Carefully he withdrew the record and placed it gently on the turntable. Spider took a swig of beer. He didn't like Will's grabbing the record from him.

Spider took another long, cool drink. The music had started. The volume was high, but the sound was diffused into the entire room, so it wrapped around them. Spider looked for a place to sit. There was only one chair besides the one covered with clothes, and Spider sat down on it, moving his head and tapping his feet to the beat of the music. Will stretched out on the bed.

"Have any more trouble from that policeman friend of yours, Spider?"

"No, why should I?" Spider asked.

"You're not helping him with that murder case anymore?"

Spider glanced sideways at Will, trying to read the languid look on his new friend's face.

"I already talked to Hank about all I know about that. I never saw her after ten o'clock that night. She was killed around midnight, the TV said." He drank some of his beer. "She wasn't my type anyway."

"Sure you weren't her type?" Will asked with a sarcastic laugh in his voice.

"Nice place you got here," Spider said, looking up at the skylights. The subject of the murder was closed. He didn't even want to think about it now. He hated remembering that night.

"What did you say this room was? Some kind of painter's place?"

"My mother had it set up for her painting. She had the skylights put in so she could have light. Artists need a lot of light." He said the words reverently, and Spider remembered the argument he had overheard between Will and his father. It had been about someone called Katherine who Will said was his sister. But Spider remembered that Will had mentioned his mother, too. But where was the general's wife? Spider knew he shouldn't reveal anything he had listened to, so he played the innocent to satisfy his curiosity.

"Don't your mother use it anymore?"

"No," Will said, frowning to himself. "She can't."

"Oh, is she injured like your father or something?"

"No, Spider, she's dead," Will said.

"Geez, I'm sorry, Will. I didn't know." Had he misunderstood the quarrel? Was the dead Katherine his mother? No, he was sure Will had said she was his sister. Spider tried another tack. "Your father leads kind of a lonely life. I guess he was glad you came back from Montana like you did."

"I thought so. But he doesn't say much these days. You don't know my father very well, Spider. He's been a mean son of a bitch in his life."

"That's 'cause he was a general."

"What do you mean?"

"Soldiers are like that. I had an uncle who was a career guy in the Marines. He was a mean bastard. Used to beat the crap out of my aunt. My mother's sister, you know?" He paused. "Your father didn't beat your ma or anything like that, did he?" For an instant, he'd forgotten about the general's being in a wheelchair, but Will's father hadn't always been a cripple if he had served in the army. The bad shit could have happened when he'd been able to walk.

"No, he would never lay a hand on her. It wasn't that, Spider. My father just likes to have his own way. I think the shrinks would call it emotional abuse."

"Oh," Spider said knowingly, as if he understood perfectly. He didn't, but he listened for more.

"My mother couldn't have a life of her own. He didn't like her painting, and she stopped doing it. The only life that counted in our family was his. His stupid damned career."

"But I don't understand," Spider said, looking around the studio. His eyes rested on the paint-splattered table. "She never did any paintings here after all?"

"Oh, well you don't know, do you? Well," he stammered slightly. "My sister died. And afterwards my mother tried to start painting again. To try to get over things. She set this place up here, away from the main house. Away from my father."

"Your sister, huh? Wow. Geez, I'm certainly sorry to hear that." It seemed to Spider that Will's family had a run of very bad luck when it came to staying alive.

"It happened a long time ago. Before my parents moved to Newport. They were living in Washington, and . . . well, my sister . . . oh, it's a long story, and I hate talking about it."

"Oh, don't then," Spider said, trying to sound sympathetic even though he wanted the details. During their argument, Will had accused his father of murdering this Katherine. "Your Mom dead and your sister, too. You had it real hard." He finished his beer and noticed that Will's bottle was empty, also. "Let me get you another beer, Will." Maybe alcohol would keep loosening his tongue.

Will, still silent, gave up his empty, and Spider went to the tub. There were about a dozen bottles on ice, and he took out two and opened them.

"I'm sorry about your old man," he said. "But mine was no saint either. Ran off when I was twelve, and my Mom only heard from him when he had a lawyer send her some divorce papers. She's had it tough, my Mom. Works real hard. Well, you know that. You see what she does around your house."

"I try to stay out of the house. In fact, I'm thinking about leaving here altogether."

"You are? Going back out west again?"

"I guess so. I got some friends out there. Maybe Colorado this time. I might just pack up the van again this week-end and head out sometime next week." He looked around the room and smiled. "I didn't exactly unpack, did I?"

"No," Spider agreed.

They sat in silence for several minutes. Will was drinking his beer, staring in the direction of the old painter's easel.

"She was nice, your Mom?" Spider asked.

"The best. My father was away a lot in the Army. I guess that was the good part. My sister was a lot older than me, and my Mom spent a lot of time with me when I was little."

"Not like your Dad, huh?" Spider laughed. He could imagine the hard ass general and the artsy fartsy mother. He had no doubt which one he would have preferred to hang out with.

"I told you, Spider," Will said angrily. "My father is a real son of a bitch."

"Like I said, mine—"

"But did he ignore you your whole life? Send you away to school to get rid of you?"

"Me? I went to school right here in Newport. Rogers High. But I know a lot of rich kids get sent away to school."

"It wasn't because we were rich," Will said. The beer bottle was empty and he tossed it on the floor. "My father sent me away after my mother died. He didn't want me around anymore."

"Yeah, well maybe you were lucky," Spider said.

"Luck?" Will turned on him, his eyes hard. "You think I had any luck in my life?"

No, Spider thought, not the way you see things. You're probably thinking to yourself that your father should have been the one member of the Patterson family who ought to be dead. Not your mother, and not your sister. No, that was real bad luck for you, Will Patterson. And you know what? I, Spider Shipley, am sure as hell sorry for you.

The Metallica album was finished, and Will got up to change it.

"Let's have another beer, Will."

"Sure. I'll put something else on. What do you want to hear?"

"You got any Ozzy Osbourne in that box?"

On Friday afternoon Caroline found her mother-in-law planting the last of the chrysanthemums around the entrance to the gazebo. The flowers made for a cheery burst of color which was visible to Caroline as she came down the back pathway from the kitchen.

"Hello, Louise," she called as she approached the back of the figure bent over, gently tapping dirt around the thick clumps of mums. A bag of mulch lay unopened in the nearby wheelbarrow. "I've brought you some iced tea."

Louise turned and looked up from her task. There was a large smear of dirt on her cheek where her gloved hand had undoubtedly brushed against it.

"Thank you, dear," she said, rising to her feet with some difficulty, which Caroline pretended not to notice. Louise took the glass of liquid and drank several large swallows. "Oh," she said with a loud sigh. "I needed that." She pointed to the crescent of flowers on either side of the open doorway. "What do you think?"

"They look lovely," Caroline said. "You can see the colors all the way from the house. Have you finally finished getting them all in the ground?"

"Yes. I've got to put the mulch around them, but George is coming tomorrow, and I'm tempted to let him do it. It's cool today, and I feel a bit achy from the bending already."

"Why not?" Caroline responded. "You've done a lot this week. Come on, let's sit in the gazebo. We can both do with a break."

Louise followed Caroline into the summerhouse, and they took seats on two of the old wicker chairs. Caroline saw that Louise had selected one of the long chaises in order to put her feet up. They sat in silence for a few minutes, content to be listening to the sounds made by the ocean waves lapping at the rocks below the cliffs just beyond the gazebo.

"How many guests are in for dinner tonight, Caroline?"

Her mother-in-law's question focused her back to the present, and Caroline answered in a voice that sounded lifeless to her own ears. "Only two. Everyone else has made plans to eat at one of the restaurants downtown. I honestly wish there were none."

"Well, it shouldn't be too difficult to get them fed. I'm sure Mattie's cooking for an army, dear. Why don't you ask Hank to join us for our dinner afterwards? I'm sure he could use a home-cooked meal after this long week of work."

"That's a very kind suggestion," Caroline said, her spirits rising. "I was thinking earlier that it would be nice to go out with him for the evening, but it was last Friday that I did that . . ." Her voice trailed off.

"I know. So have Hank come here. You two can have our sitting room tonight. I'll take one of Mattie's bubble baths and go right to bed," she added, with a twinkle in her eye.

"I do love you," Caroline said. She sniffed in the tear she felt materializing in her right eye. "It's nice that you understand about Hank and me, Louise."

"Please." Louise held up her hand. "You don't have to say anything about that."

Caroline nodded, listening to the rhythmic sound made by the ocean. If Louise didn't want to talk, Caroline would accept that.

"Actually I just got a text from Hank on the telephone," Caroline said. "He's coming out tomorrow to search the house for Meredith's diary."

Caroline had told Louise about Meredith's true identity as soon as she had learned of it from Hank, and her mother-in-law had not seemed especially surprised at the news. Instead Louise had taken the information as confirmation of her belief that something had been terribly wrong about the actress from the beginning of her stay.

"She was always acting while she was here with us," Louise had said with unconcealed satisfaction last night. "I used to wonder who she really was. Of course I never suspected she was a criminal, and on the run all those years. But it does add up, you know, Caroline. If she hadn't gotten that acting training in Ireland, I wonder if she could have pulled off such a deception for so long."

Caroline had agreed with Louise, and had been thinking of the fact all day long.

Where was Meredith's diary? Caroline wished she could find it and read it. Did it detail the years in Ireland? What was Phoebe thinking as she lived in exile? Had she ever expected to come home? What was the turning point when she thought it was safe to return to the United States?

Caroline listened to the swelling waves and remembered last Friday when she and Meredith had sat in this same room together. Her old friend had said Caroline had been strong to go on after her husband died. Phoebe had gone on . . . as Meredith. That had taken strength. But, Meredith had looked tired that afternoon. Was she running out of the strength which had sustained her since she had turned up in Boston, dirty and shabby, to ask her sister for help?

"I knew Marjorie Patterson, you know," Louise said. "I'd almost forgotten, but I thought of her last night, just as I was falling asleep."

"Did you know her well?" Caroline asked, her interest turning from Phoebe to Katherine's mother.

"No, not well. I never saw her after she and her husband moved to Newport. I was living with Reed in New York by then, before you were married. And, of course, she died shortly after they came here. Cancer. So sad. I knew her when Frederick and I first were married and spent our summers up here. Her parents had a large house right on Bellevue Avenue. It's been turned into condominiums now."

"What was she like?"

"Quiet. Shy. She was artistic. Her parents had sent her to school in Italy to study painting. They encouraged her, but I don't think she ever exhibited. She might have had talent, but I don't really know."

"When did she marry?"

"I'm not sure. Let me think."

"An artist and a general," Caroline said thoughtfully. "That doesn't sound like a good combination."

"Of course it wasn't," Louise said. "But now that I think back, I believe they met not long after Marjorie returned from Italy. Charles had been to West Point. He was real Army. And I suppose he was handsome in a rugged way."

"And you met him, also?"

"When they were engaged, at parties." Caroline tried to picture two people she had never seen in the flesh. "We still came up here for the summers then," Louise added. "It would have been in the sixties."

"Before he went to Viet Nam. Hank said that Gen. Patterson was there during the war."

"I expect he would have been, dear. West Point graduates were certain to want to be posted there."

"Why?"

"Charles Patterson was ambitious. They didn't make you a general if you sat behind a desk in Washington during wartime."

"I see," Caroline said. "Did Marjorie devote herself to his career?" Louise nodded. "And I'll bet she didn't have much time for her painting."

"I don't think so. And, of course, she had the children to look after." She paused before continuing. "Like everyone else I was horrified by the kidnapping. I remember Phoebe Harrington's picture being in all the papers. But, I would never have matched it to the face of that woman who was staying here last week."

"Why was Meredith killed, Louise?" Caroline asked suddenly. She saw Meredith alive on the stage, that magnificent profile and rich voice. Caroline couldn't think of her as a criminal on the run. "Was she killed because of the kidnapping?"

"I should say it's impossible for us to know, my dear. What does Hank think?"

"He has theories, but he has no real evidence yet. Do you think Gen. Patterson is involved? Could he have wanted revenge so badly?"

Louise shook her head slowly from side to side. "Is there ever really vengeance for the death of a child?" she asked quietly.

CHAPTER XVIII

"So the FBI is in on our case," Ben said. "We're big time now."

"They want us to develop information on what happened to Katherine Patterson," Hank said. The team was assembled back in his office so Hank could explain this new twist in the case.

"And they get the credit?" Keisha asked. She exchanged a glance with Ben.

"I don't care," Hank said. "I want a killer."

"Katherine Patterson," Ben said. "Well, I never. That was a sensational case." Ben was in his late forties, and would have been on the force in Newport at the time it happened.

"You followed it?" Hank asked.

"Sure. It was big news in the papers all over New England."

"It was big news everywhere," Hank said.

"Those were the days when people still used the word hippies to describe anyone who was counter-culture. Those students were heroes to some."

"Because they kidnapped an innocent young woman?" Keisha asked in disgust. "Whose heroes were they?"

"The movement's," Ben answered. "You're too young to understand."

"I don't remember the case at all," Keisha said. "I was ten years old."

"Bush's policies weren't that popular in this part of the country," Ben explained. "A lot of people agreed with the kidnappers that those nuclear plants were dangerous. But then, when the students wouldn't release Katherine, people turned against them."

"And now one of the kidnappers is our murder victim," Keisha said in amazement.

"The Patterson kidnapping makes us change our thinking," Ben said.

"What do you mean?" Hank asked.

"There's got to be a connection between it and to this murder. Something goes back to 1991 here. Josh Ware is dead, right?" Hank nodded. "But this other guy, Darnell Stewart. Nobody knows where he is."

Hank looked at Keisha for agreement. "I still lean to the angle that Meredith met someone here in Newport, and something went wrong."

"Well," Hank said wearily. "Let's take what we know about that first."

"Neil Shipley," Ben said. "Do you want to start with him?" Hank nodded and studied the paper clips he kept on his desk. They were in an old metal ash tray, and the layer of dust at the bottom was beginning to form small, fluffy balls. While Ben read from his pad, Hank dumped out the clips onto a sheet of paper and shook the dust balls into his waste basket. Keisha watched in fascination.

"We know the cab took him home at two in the morning," Ben said, trying not to notice the lieutenant's preoccupation with the paper clips. "And we know he was put in that cab by somebody in front of O'Brien's on Thames Street. Not especially close to where we found Mrs. Kent's car with the body."

"We haven't found anybody who drank with him that night?" Hank asked, shaking his ash tray to settle the clips in a neat arrangement.

"No," Keisha said, reluctantly taking her attention away from the ash tray, "but I think people are afraid to come forward and get involved with the police. The bartender at O'Brien's doesn't remember him coming in. A bartender at Busker's who knows him says he saw him in the bar probably around eleven. But he remembers him leaving, and it was before midnight."

"There is one thing that connects him to the crime," Hank said.

"The clothing he was wearing that night was found to have a hair, which has been identified as belonging to Meredith Hackett," Keisha said. Hank had seen Spider fall against Meredith in The Black Pearl when his feet had gotten tangled in her bar stool's legs.

"But," Hank said, "I'm a witness to an incident earlier in the evening which could explain that."

"Yes, sir," Keisha said.

"There's nothing in that BMW to connect him to the crime," Ben said, as if he was reading Hank's mind. "I'm beginning to think he's out of it, Lieutenant."

"What about the report on the fibers and hairs found in the BMW?" Hank asked.

"They identified Meredith Hackett, you, Mrs. Kent and her mother-in-law. But there are some samples with no match."

"Not Shipley?" Hank asked.

"No, nothing matches him."

"And the waitress at the ABC told me that he's not the man who was with Hackett on Friday night."

Hank continued to ask about the routine work to which both Keisha and Ben had been assigned.

There was nothing new to report from the house-to-house questioning which had been done in the areas around the 7-Eleven and First Beach. A check on the residents' names in the area around the beach had not turned up anyone suspicious with a record of violence. Another check with the authorities in California had revealed no police record for Spider Shipley.

"Let's go to Meredith's life next," Hank said with a nod to Ben. "What have you turned up out of New York?"

"I talked to her manager and got lots of fine comments about what a good actress she was, disciplined, professional, never fired from a show. Everybody liked working with her. Of course I talked to him before we knew Meredith was Phoebe. I think he might have said something different if he knew that."

"No old rivalries?" Hank asked with a smile.

"Not according to Ethan Samuels," Ben said. "By him, she was a jewel. But don't forget he gets 15% of her earnings."

"What about fellow actors?"

"Nothing there. Shock at her death mostly. I talked to that fellow named Tom Benton who gave me the names to check with. Benton knows Mrs. Kent, and I guess she had called him. He knew all about Hackett's coming up here to stay at Kenwood Court. He asked me if there was going to be a memorial service. How the hell would I know?"

"What about her cell phone?" Hank asked, turning to Keisha.

"It's not turned up yet, but we got the records. The only calls she got while she was here were from this guy Samuels. I checked with him and he said everything was about her next play. Apparently she was due back in Manhattan the beginning of next week to begin rehearsals. He had no reason to believe she wasn't planning to return to New York City."

"New York sounds like a dead end," Hank said. "Let's get back to Newport. We need to concentrate on the missing time that evening. Between about 10:15 when she left Mrs. Kent, Shipley and me at The Black Pearl and then was seen at the ABC around 11:30. Where did she go? And more importantly, who did she see? No one saw her come back to the Inn at Kenwood Court."

"She could have been walking the beach," Keisha said. "Then walked over to the ABC for a drink, even something to eat."

"Is that when the killer first saw her?" Hank ran his fingers pensively through the ash tray of paper clips. "Let's remind the papers that we're still asking anyone who may have seen her that night to come forward."

Keisha said she would take care of it.

"Can we talk about how the kidnapping changes the case, Lieutenant?" Ben asked.

"It gives us ideas about a motive, Sgt. Davies," Hank answered. "That much I know."

"And who has the motive?" Ben asked.

"Anyone connected with the kidnapping who is still alive. You mentioned the Stewart kid, but you'd have to say Gen. Patterson has a pretty strong motive."

"The guy in the wheelchair?" This skeptical remark came from Keisha.

"He has that chauffeur," Ben explained to her. "The lieutenant said he appears devoted to his master." He turned to Hank. "Could he be the guy at the ABC?"

"No way. Jason Forman, the man in question, is over six feet tall, very muscular and very bald. Also his coloring is dark."

"The man at the ABC could be a red herring, just somebody who asked to buy her a drink. That happens," Ben said, leaning forward. "A lot of single people go in there. If she was alone for a while on the beach, she may have wanted company when she got to the bar. There was nothing in the statement from the waitress that the two of them were arguing or anything like that. They were sitting quietly and talking."

"We've got to find that man," Hank said. "Why don't these people come forward?"

"Let's get back to the general," Ben continued. "Say the general was following Meredith that night in his car. He and his chauffeur could have been waiting for her as she left the ABC. Grabbed her as she was getting into the car she was driving, which we think was parked at the beach lot because of the sand we found inside Mrs. Kent's BMW."

"Gen. Patterson was just driving around that night," Hank said. "And he just happened to see the woman who kidnapped his daughter twenty years ago."

"He must have known she was in Newport, Lieutenant. Maybe he saw her earlier in the week and had the chauffeur follow her. Gen. Patterson, since he is an invalid, doesn't go out much, and the chauffeur has a lot of free time on his hands. He's been following her a while."

Hank's mind was beginning to spin. Charles Patterson had said that Meredith Hackett would look different after twenty years, even mentioning changing the color of her hair, but he couldn't see yet how the general and Meredith could have found each other by chance. That would have been a coincidence of major proportions.

"The general served in Viet Nam," Ben was saying. "Didn't those soldiers do a lot of guerilla fighting where you would sneak up behind someone with a rope or wire and strangle them?"

"We're still talking about a guy in a wheelchair," Keisha repeated. "Sneaking up behind someone?"

"Suppose Hackett was in the passenger seat," Ben continued, ignoring Keisha. "She got in the general's car because she recognized Katherine's father." Keisha frowned, but Ben persevered. "The chauffeur's driving, and the general was in the back seat. Right? Patterson reaches over and puts the wire around her neck." Ben pantomimed the killing motion.

"O.K.," Hank said. "Let's do that check on Forman."

In his mind Hank saw the neck of Meredith Hackett bruised and discolored with the deep marks of the strangling. He remembered

Charles Patterson's powerful hands lying limp on top of the green blanket covering his legs in the wheelchair.

"I want to talk to him again. That's for sure. And this time, without Broglio around to interrupt, maybe I can find something out."

"Where's Broglio now?" Ben asked.

"Back in Providence. I said I'd keep him updated. He can easily come back if something develops. By the way, the bureau is releasing the story of Meredith's identity. They're holding a press conference at 2 p.m. today to make the announcement. The chief is going to be there."

"That should get some coverage," Ben said. "Matthews will have a circus on his hands tomorrow." Sgt. Everett Matthews was the department's public information officer. Hank knew he had spent the morning being briefed by Chief Williams on how to handle the press when the story was made public by the FBI.

"The chief is going to assign an officer to be out at Windward. He's expecting the press to stake out the house."

"Smart thinking," Ben said.

"I don't suppose either of you have thought of this one," Keisha said. She had been quiet for the last several minutes.

"What?"

"Somebody else involved in the kidnapping has a motive for killing Meredith Hackett."

"Who do you mean?" Ben asked. "Darnell Stewart? The FBI lost him in Amsterdam. He could be back in the states. But why would he want Phoebe Harrington dead after all these years?"

Keisha shook her head. "Katherine Patterson."

"But she's dead," Ben said.

"You're only assuming that, Sergeant," Hank pointed out. "Her body was never found."

"You mean she's alive? You think she killed Meredith Hackett?"

"I think she could have killed Phoebe Harrington," Keisha said with satisfaction. "Think about it. Phoebe aged and changed her appearance and her name. Katherine could have, also."

Hank saw that Ben was looking at Keisha with admiration. "By God, you've hit on something. Katherine Patterson had to have the strongest motive of all to want revenge on Meredith Hackett," the sergeant said.

Hank closed his eyes again, and this time Meredith's dead body did not appear in his mind. Instead he saw two young women, both eighteen years old, who started college as roommates. Phoebe's young face was clear. He had seen her photograph. Katherine's features were not. He would have to get the files on the kidnapping and study her face.

Was she alive? Had Katherine Patterson been in Newport on last Friday evening when her old roommate Phoebe Harrington had met her brutal death?

CHAPTER XIX

Caroline's telephoned invitation to come out to Kenwood to have a quiet dinner was a welcome summons, and Hank was on the verge of accepting it, when Keisha burst into his office. He looked up in annoyance, his hand over the instrument's mouthpiece.

"Lieutenant," Keisha said breathlessly. "All hell's broken out at Windward, sir."

Hank held up his hand to interrupt her report and spoke quickly into the phone.

"Listen, I'll call you back when I have a chance, but it sounds like I'm going to have to pass on this evening."

The other end of the line was quiet after he finished. There was more Hank wanted to say, but there wasn't time for it now. "I'm sorry," he added. "I'll call you as soon as I can."

Caroline finally answered that she understood, and he said good-by. He heard the disappointment in her voice. It mirrored his own feelings, but he was all officialdom as he switched his attention to Sgt. McAndrews.

"O.K.," he said.

"The media is out there in full force," she began. "The chief just got a call from the owner."

"Gen. Patterson?" Keisha nodded. "I thought we sent an officer out there earlier today."

"Officer Edwards is out there, but it's more than she can handle. I just talked to her over the radio. There are camera crews all over the road. She said it's a mob scene. We'll need more than one officer to keep order. Right now the road's blocked to thru traffic on the Drive."

"And Patterson called the chief?"

"Yes, sir. No one in the house wants to speak with the press. Chief Williams wants us to get out there to provide Edwards with some reinforcements. And he's setting up another detail for the night shift."

The FBI's Washington news conference had been held at 2 p.m. It had been carried live on the cable news channels as a breaking story. Hank looked at his watch. It was a few minutes before six. Quick work if there were TV news people already in place, covering the story on the Newport end.

"Has anybody been monitoring the TV news to see how the story's been carried so far?" Hank had closeted himself in his office for the last two hours, going over every scrap of information he had on the kidnapping case, preparing for his interview with Gen. Patterson.

"Sgt. Mathews has, sir. He's been getting calls all afternoon. I don't think anybody realized the size of the coverage the story's getting."

"We should have," Hank said ruefully.

They had failed to consider the impact that the Newport angle, with its photogenic mansions and scenery, would have on the story. The news of the murdered Meredith Hackett's true identity as a wanted federal criminal had been treated as sensational stuff, almost lurid. The Newport locale and shots of Windward, combined with the 1991 kidnapping footage from the archives, would keep any and all news channels going for days.

He let out a long, loud sigh and rose from his desk.

"We're in for a long siege, you know. It might feel exciting now," he said, acknowledging Keisha's heightened energy level, "but we're going to get tired of it pretty quickly."

"Yes, sir," was Keisha's chastised reply.

"It gives us all the more incentive to catch our killer and put these news people back in the FBI's bailiwick."

They made their trip out to Ocean Drive rapidly despite the Friday night rush hour. Hank let Keisha put on the siren, so that they navigated the usually slow-moving Bellevue Avenue traffic in record time. They had barely made the right turn past Belcourt Castle when they spied the first of the news vans parked on the highway. A crowd of people were milling about on the stretch of land below the imposing front columns of Crossways, the Stuyvesant Fish house. Keisha blew the horn as she maneuvered the highly visible black and white police car towards the entrance to Windward. The usual deference to their official vehicle was definitely lacking in the manners of the crowd of news crews and the curious onlookers who were their camp followers.

"Look, sir," Keisha said. "There's the Sundance Kid."

"What?" Hank's annoyance at the scene was compounded by his bewilderment over the sergeant's remark. "What are you talking about?"

"Over there," she answered as she parked the police car on the shoulder behind Edwards' black and white. "See the TV lights and the Fox camera over there. The Kid's giving an interview to one of the reporters."

Hank's eyes went to the lights and saw the familiar figure of Spider basking in the haze of the TV lights. "He's not the Sundance Kid," he said irritably.

"I thought he was the Kid and you were Butch Cassidy," Keisha said.

"Billy Hanigan was the Sundance Kid, Sergeant." The absurdity of making the correction combined with the scene of Spider's being interviewed by Fox News made him laugh out loud.

"But you *were* Butch," Keisha said, deciding that she was allowed to enjoy the joke with him.

"Yes, I was," he said with mock gravity. "But it was a high school nickname, and I don't use it anymore. As far as that instant celebrity over there, the one being interviewed for national TV, his nickname is Spider, and I believe he still likes to use it."

"Noted, sir," Keisha said as Officer Sue Edwards joined them.

Hank listened as Edwards explained conditions. Gen. Patterson's request was that the reporters were to be kept off the private property. He would not meet with them. As would be expected, the reporters had no intention of leaving and were busy filming segments which reported this fact to their viewers.

"What about that situation?" Hank gestured to where Spider was being interviewed.

"He came up the driveway a little while ago. Naturally the news people rushed him, and he agreed to speak to them. I don't know who he is."

"He works for the family," Hank said. "I'll go over there. You and Sgt. McAndrews see what you can do to get these people off the road and see that any of the TV vehicles that have to stay are parked out of the right of way. I want this road cleared, and you can call for back-up to take anybody who won't comply down to the station."

Hank made his way slowly through the crowd toward where the interview was being filmed. Without his uniform, the curious crowd impeded his way. A young man of about twenty-five was holding a microphone as Spider spoke into it. His face was flushed and animated. He looked like he had been drinking, and Hank scowled. Spider's drinking had already figured too much in this case.

"—didn't know her all that well, no," Spider was saying. "You could have knocked me over with a feather when I heard she was wanted by the FBI."

"You didn't know the woman calling herself Meredith Hackett was an escaped fugitive?"

"You crazy?" Spider asked with real alarm. "I never go to the post office. How would I know that?"

Hank stood in front of interviewer and interviewee, coughing to get Spider's attention. The reporter frowned at the sound, but Spider shot a momentary look of panic in Hank's direction. Hank smiled back, and the reporter asked another question.

"Would you say you were the last person to see Phoebe Harrington alive that night, Mr. Shipley?"

Spider shot Hank another cautious glance and swallowed hard.

"Hey, now that would be the killer, don't you know? Wait up. I'm just saying her and me, we had some drinks together that night. We was just getting to know each other. Like I said."

"Where did you leave her that night? What can you tell us of those final moments of her life?"

Hank and millions of TV viewers waited for the answer.

"Mr. Shipley?" the Fox reporter prodded.

"Yeah, yeah. I'm getting to that part." Spider was thinking, the wheels turning visibly in his head. "We were downtown. Now that was a way away from where"—he paused dramatically—"the body was found." From the corner of his left eye, Spider glanced at Hank.

"But you weren't there?"

"Shit, no," Spider said excitedly. Hank saw the look of exasperation on the reporter's face. They'd have to bleep the expletive.

"Where were you?" the reporter asked. He didn't look happy now, and he stared at Spider as if he were a hostile witness in court. "At the time of the murder."

"I was drinking with my buddies. Downtown. That's my story all along," he added. It was an unnecessary addition, and called for the immediate ending of the interview. Whatever first-hand information that the reporter had gotten Spider to pass on at the beginning of the interview, his remarks now were becoming muddled. The reporter impatiently signaled the camera operator to stop filming. Without further comment the TV crew moved off, and Spider was left standing bewildered in the sudden darkness left by the removal of the bright lights. Hank approached him.

"Hey there, Hank," Spider said in an overly friendly tone. "Thought you'd want to be here for this. Did you see me getting interviewed? It's gonna be on TV later tonight."

Up close, Hank smelled the beer on Spider's breath.

"You got a car with you?" Hank asked.

"Nah, my mother went on home, and I stayed to have a beer or two with Will. Might see someone I know, though. Pretty good crowd, huh?"

"I see you haven't had any memories come back to you as to where you were that night after you left The Black Pearl?"

"Huh? Oh, no, not at all. Sorry. But I know I'm innocent, and you can't prove I did it, Hank. You told me that already."

"I hope you're not planning to leave town. We might have some more questions."

"Nah. Matter of fact, I'm hoping to stay on here with the general. Nice job I got out here, and I'm thinking I'll keep it. Might even be moving in soon." Hank raised his eyebrows. "Yeah, his son Will's gonna move out of that studio, and I might get in there so I can be on call, like. You know. If they need me at the house to take care of anything." Spider smiled. He was starting to look a little unsteady on his feet. "I'm hungry," he said suddenly as if he had just thought of it. "Think I'll see if I can catch a ride back to town."

He tottered off, and Hank watched the wobbly movements of his walk. It reminded him of the night at The Black Pearl. Murderers usually knew their victims. But which victim did this killer know? Meredith Hackett or Phoebe Harrington?

Caroline wasn't sure which bothered her more: that Hank could not join her for dinner or that he had to go rushing off on his case and she was not included in the chase.

It was late, almost midnight. The house had settled into an easy, dark quiet. Caroline had been glad that the people for whom Kenwood was an appealing accommodation never kept late hours. She liked the chance to wander around the rooms in the silent hush when no one was about. Standing in the mansion's grand hall, it pleased her to imagine being among the voices of the past. Sometimes she thought of Reed's grandparents who had lived here before Louise and Frederick. Other times, Caroline reached even further back to the Gilded Age and tried to picture the Kents' spectacular nineteenth century parties with their fashionable guests and opulent settings. Tonight, in her peevish mood, it suited her brain to envy an era where women were pampered and had little responsibility. That their role during that period was chiefly one of ornamentation she carefully ignored.

Leaving the grand hall, Caroline started up the main staircase to the lonely prospect of bed and a book. Halfway up the treads she remembered that she had finished the novel she had been reading, and if she planned to settle herself to sleep with a book, another one was going to be required. Reluctantly she retraced her steps downward and went into the library.

The shelves of the room held well over two thousand books. At one time a great effort had been made to shelve them in an orderly system. No doubt some former member of the Kent family with unlimited time and an intellectual bent had devised a catalog. The interests and hobbies of several Kents were obvious. Someone had been an amateur naturalist, another a student of Frederick the Great. A third had been interested in the Chautauqua Movement.

The novels were clustered in one corner of the room, and Caroline went in their direction. Louise's late mother-in-law had been a fan of mystery writing, and there were at least a hundred or more of these cloth-bound volumes of thrillers written in the nineteen twenties and thirties. While Caroline had an interest in real life mystery, she had read few of these. Tonight she decided she was in a mood for Henry James, and her eyes scanned the shelves for the collection of nineteenth century fiction.

Caroline found Edith Wharton and Mark Twain, but no James. She moved further along the shelves, looking to find James in British fiction, but found herself instead among books on the American Presidency. Several volumes on Lincoln, an entire shelf devoted to Theodore Roosevelt. Someone had most certainly admired TR.

The quirk on the bottom shelf almost escaped her eyes. The book was the last one on the shelf, slid in next to a copy of John Gunther's *Eisenhower,* the title proclaimed in big bold capital letters. The cover of the neighboring book which caught Caroline's eye was royal blue. It had no dust jacket but she easily recognized the volume because she owned a copy of this same book. But Caroline knew that hers was in the boxes in the third floor attics that she had moved to Newport from Manhattan. Whose copy of *Profiles In Courage* was this? Caroline was sure that no blue blood Republican member of the Kent family had ever shelved a book written by a Democratic President next to accounts of the life and times of Dwight D. Eisenhower.

Confused, Caroline withdrew the familiar copy of John F. Kennedy's book which had been written in 1955. But the object in her hands felt unfamiliar and bulky, as if it had gotten wet and dried unevenly. Caroline frowned as she opened the cover.

The pages of the book had been cut out in a huge, neat rectangle. Nestled tightly in the space left by their removal was a thick green spiral notebook. There was no writing on the faded paper cover, and the corners of the book showed the wear and tear of years of handling. Caroline had no need to open the cover of this book to know what she was holding in her hands.

Her killer did not have Meredith's diary, nor did her sister. Caroline had beaten them all to the prize.

CHAPTER XX

―――∞∞∞―――

"I've got to get this somewhere safe," Caroline murmured to herself.

From the instant she realized what she had found, Caroline had been fighting the panic that Sarah Ryder might instantly materialize in the room and seize the book from her. Upstairs. Caroline needed to go quickly up to her own quarters.

The house was unaware of her anxious movements as she ran through the grand hall and took the back stairs which led up to the hallway outside Louise's bedroom. The next doorway led into their shared sitting room, and she locked the door behind her. It was a useless gesture unless she bolted both her own and Louise's bedroom, as doors from each joined the parlor room, but it made her feel momentarily safe.

Caroline stood, taking several deep breaths to calm her racing heart. She put the copy of *Profiles In Courage* on a table, opened it again and gently lifted the diary from its cradle. Too late she worried about fingerprints. But she couldn't stop now. Her fingers eagerly grasped the edge of the cover of the worn notebook.

I can't believe we actually did it.

The diary's first entry was scrawled in a large, loopy handwriting on its first yellowed page. There was no date above it. Further down, in the middle of the page, was a second entry. This one held a date: October 24, 1991.

The notebook had been innocently purchased for her freshman classes, Caroline guessed. The lines on the pages were narrowly spaced, and Meredith's handwriting often took up two lines.

Phoebe. This is Phoebe Harrington who is writing, Caroline reminded herself. But it was hard not to think of her as the Meredith she had met in the theater.

"October 24, 1991. The waiting is so intense. Josh says we must be patient. The pigs will make us sweat. Katherine and I are trying to be cool about things, but Darnell is nervous. He knows he will lose his scholarship."

At the bottom of the page, another entry began.

"October 27. We're finally on TV today. I guess Katherine's parents waited before they called the police. She said her father would be like that."

"October 28. Katherine is angry with her father. He doesn't seem to be doing what we want to get her back."

"October 29. Darnell wants to leave, but Josh got angry and told him he would kill him if he tried. I don't think he means it. Darnell said he would stay until the week-end."

"October 31. Nothing today or yesterday."

"November 2. Darnell is still here."

"November 5. We made another tape. Josh made me say we would kill Katherine. It was hard to do, but he said we had to think of all the people who are dying because of the nuclear plants. Katherine knows I had to say it."

Caroline wondered what the scene inside the New Hampshire cottage was like. What did they do all day to keep busy? Where did they get their food? She remembered Sarah's saying that the house had no heat. Perhaps the two men chopped wood. Did Meredith have to do the cooking? Caroline tried to picture her as Phoebe, as she would have been at eighteen.

Suddenly the authenticity of Katherine's abduction became awful and real. Caroline tried hard to appreciate Meredith's youthful frame of mind. Self-righteous, she had thought only good would come from their actions. Jeopardizing a life was a price that someone had to pay. A political kidnapping was a just cause if the people living near the nuclear plants would be helped by it.

The pages of the diary were well-handled. How many times had Meredith re-read her record of the past? Had she always carried this book with her or had it been hidden and taken out for her fatal trip to Newport?

"November 7. There has been no answer from Katherine's parents to our tape. I don't understand. They must want her to be released. All Gen. Patterson has to do is stop the pollution caused by those plants. Doesn't he realize how important that is? Why is he ignoring us? NUCLEAR WASTE IS A TICKING BOMB!!!"

The last sentence was printed in large, bold capital letters.

The next several entries into mid November revealed no progress in the kidnapping.

Then: "November 13. Katherine is upset. She thinks her parents don't want her back. I can't believe that!"

And there were disputes among the fugitives.

"November 14. Darnell talked to Josh again last night about leaving. I want to leave, too, but Josh keeps telling us we are like the Viet Cong in the jungle of Viet Nam."

"November 15. The waiting is awful. Katherine's father refuses to speak to the press now. Josh is furious. We watched the news tonight. They said that Gen. Patterson will never negotiate with us because he thinks we are like those terrorists who hijack airplanes. That's not who we are. I wish he would meet with us. Katherine could make him understand why we had to do this."

"November 20. I told Josh I wanted to give up. It's almost a month now. Things didn't work out."

"November 21. I'm afraid of Josh." There was something begun, then crossed out. Caroline held the page close to her eyes and made out what looked like "He" and then something in lower case. Perhaps a *b* or an *h*. "I only know I want to leave. But I can't say anything. I can't let them know."

"November 25. Josh sent me in to town today for supplies. I wanted Darnell to go with me, but Josh said people would notice us because he is black. I thought about calling my parents, but I was afraid of what Josh would do to me again."

The entries stopped for November, and the next one was on December 9.

"December 9. I feel so bad inside. I think there is something wrong with me. I've started throwing up my food. It's so cold at night."

"December 10. I want to go home. I want to see my family. I don't know how Josh and Katherine can stay so calm."

"December 14. Josh left us here to go into town, and I think there was some trouble. I hope this means we can leave. He must have gotten into an argument with someone. He thinks we've been spotted. We all took a pledge of secrecy if we get caught."

"December 15. We all realize nothing will be done. Katherine's father is not going to do what we want him to do. This has all been for nothing. We're going to break our camp here. Josh is very angry. He wants to move to another hideout, but we don't know where. He says he has a friend in Chicago who would take us in. I'm not going. Darnell and I won't go. We talked about it last night after Josh and Katherine went to sleep."

"December 16. On our way to Chicago today. Darnell and I have a plan. I pray it works."

"December 17. We are free. Darnell and I went to the bathrooms at the rest stop and told a trucker that we had been part of a cult and we wanted to get away. We look pretty awful, so it was believable. Josh saw us running to the truck with the driver when we came out and started screaming after us. It made the trucker believe us. He had a gun in the cab and pulled it on Josh. I never saw him scared before, but he was of the gun. I sprained my ankle running for the cab and jumping up. He took us to Pennsylvania. We drove all night. I wish Katherine could have left with us. I hope Josh takes care of her. I'm sorry, but we had to go without her."

Darnell, as it turned out, was from Philadelphia, and the two runaways found refuge with an uncle who was a small time drug dealer. He seemed to live in a never land of junkies, petty criminals and homeless vagrants whom the police never quite discovered. Caroline sensed that Phoebe must have had something close to a breakdown. She wrote of sleeping on rags in vacant houses. Her stomach upsets continued. Darnell stayed with her, and Caroline suspected they had become lovers. Caroline's heart ached for Phoebe. She was lost and abandoned like the houses where she and Darnell hid from the world. Caroline stopped reading and focused on the Meredith she had known in New York City. She couldn't recognize her in the pages of the notebook.

The diary was kept faithfully, if sporadically. There were often gaps, as Phoebe shut out the world to crawl in her hole and lick her wounds. Eventually Darnell was ready to move on. The manhunt for them had turned up too many dead ends. They were off the front pages. The FBI was keeping up the chase, but the trail had gotten cold.

There was only one more mention of Katherine, and Caroline read it over several times.

"January 10, 1992. A new year. It feels like the old one. I keep wondering how Katherine is. Is she still with Josh? The police haven't found them."

In February, as Sarah had told Hank, Phoebe went to Boston to find her sister. Darnell had left Philadelphia, and the uncle had given them both money to travel. Caroline sensed that while Phoebe was strong enough to be on her own, it was just barely.

Her passage to Ireland was arranged, and Phoebe wrote dispassionately of it. Sarah's story of the Irish connection secreting her sister out of the country had seemed exciting to Caroline. Meredith's diary, however, recounted it as if it were no more than one of the trips to the grocery store in New Hampshire. She appeared indifferent to the risk being taken on her behalf. Sarah Ryder's role in her sister's escape was barely acknowledged, and no other names were mentioned. Caroline doubted that the FBI could use the diary in a case against Sarah.

Ireland welcomed Phoebe. She was an exile from home, accepted as another political prisoner. The tone of the diary entries improved and Phoebe was soon describing her life in glowing and happy terms. The previous scraps of anxious notations became long and vivid descriptions of the tranquil green countryside and her new friends among the Irish people.

"April 12. Noreen is wonderful. She fusses over me as if I were one of her children. I drink lots of strong tea and eat lots of sweet cakes and biscuits. I am gaining weight, but I needed to. She found me some clothes which fit me that Brian's mother had worn. They are all pastels, colors I would never wear at home. I feel like another person when I put them on."

The spring stretched into the summer and then the fall.

Phoebe ate and slept and exercised, all under the watchful eyes of the couple whose last name was carefully left unmentioned. Caroline wondered if Brian and Noreen were even their true first names. There was no hint, either, of where in Ireland Phoebe was staying.

The theater in Cork, although the city itself was not identified, entered Phoebe's life the following spring when Rose, a friend of her hosts who was working on one of the plays, invited Phoebe to come to the theater with her one afternoon to paint scenery. With strength, Phoebe had become restless in her banishment. "I shall go mad without work," she had dramatically declared in a diary entry for May 2, 1993. Brian had not thought the outing a good idea, but his wife supported it, and Brian angrily relented.

The members of the drama group offered an easy comradeship to anyone willing to lend a hand to their labors of love, and Meredith made several trips to the theater before her work on the show was completed. No one questioned who she was or why this young American had time on her hands, and Meredith decided to risk attending opening night. And when her second Irish summer began, she wrote that she was preparing for a small part in the group's next production. That Brian was fearful was obvious.

"July 28. I wish Brian would understand how I feel about this play. I have to have something to focus on, or I will be sad again, and I can't be that sad ever again. Noreen understands, as a woman would. I might stay in town with Rose, but Brian says that would be unfair to involve her as she has no idea who I am."

Phoebe did move in with Rose, whose husband James was the director of the play. Brian continued to be angry, but dismissed his concerns. He and Noreen had served their purpose, and Phoebe was moving on. She explained her presence in Ireland to her new hosts as a student who had dropped out of school and was traveling. That Americans were free to follow such whims apparently was reasonable, and there was no further question of who Phoebe was or why she had surfaced in Cork.

James, the director, recognized Phoebe's raw acting talent and began his mission to develop it. For the next year and a half Phoebe appeared in a half dozen of his plays, taking on larger roles and drawing closer to his person. The diary was now a collection of jottings on rehearsals and passionate praise for the mysterious James. What Rose thought of all this was never mentioned. It was only in one of the last entries made in Ireland that Caroline learned that Phoebe had been calling herself Mary Morgan.

"May 10, 1996. Mary Morgan is going home. I want to try it. I can act now, and I want to go back home and reclaim my life. I think I can do it."

Back in New York, if indeed that was her initial destination, Phoebe stopped keeping the diary. The years when she was making her name in the theater as Meredith Hackett were not described. Instead the entry which followed the last one made in Ireland in 1996 was dated August 22 of the current year.

"My dreams are terrorizing me. They've suddenly taken over my whole being. I can't work. I'm afraid to go to sleep. I see Katherine's face when I close my eyes. Where is she? Why is she haunting me? Is she dead? Did Josh do something to her?"

"August 28. I don't know why Katherine is doing this to me? Can she be dead? It is the only explanation. I must know whether she is dead or alive. I can't think of anything else in my life right now."

"September 3. Katherine was in my dreams again last night. I felt myself touching her, hugging her. She is smiling. Does that mean she is dead and at peace? Or is she somewhere alive? What does she want from me?"

"September 7. Katherine visits me now in my dreams almost every night. She is trying to tell me something."

"September 11. I have found out that Katherine's father is still alive and must see him to find out if she is dead or alive."

"September 13. I was thinking today how much was changed by the plans we made in 1991. My parents died without seeing me again. Katherine's mother died. We hurt our parents so much. I must see Katherine's father before he dies and explain things."

And then Meredith had learned where the general lived, and she arrived on Caroline's doorstep at Kenwood.

"September 20. Newport is wonderful. Caroline is so kind. I remember again what it means to have friends who care for you. I came yesterday and it seems that we have so much catching up to do. I would like to tell her why I have come, but she seems so happy to see me that I want her to think it was just because I missed her."

Caroline winced and wondered if, to Meredith, she had appeared so in need of a friend of her own. The time spent with her old colleague had been pleasant, but what unhappy impression had she given? She read on.

"Caroline's still sad over Reed. I can see the sadness in her eyes when she talks about him. Why did that terrible accident have to happen? Unlike me, Reed and Caroline never hurt anyone in this life. I wish there was some way I could help her get over his death. Perhaps she needs to come back to New York and the theater. She is such a wonderful actress and is wasting her talents. I don't think this is the right place for her. She is so lonely. The work is hard, and I don't see what she is getting out of it. Perhaps when this is over we can do a play together like the old days."

"September 21. I'm going to see Katherine's father tomorrow night. He doesn't know my new name, and I'm sure he wouldn't see me if I told him who I was. I called him from the phone in the conservatory today and said Katherine and I had been at school together and I wanted to pay my respects to him. That didn't sound right, but he didn't seem to care. I'm afraid of seeing him, but I must do it for Katherine. I will have to think of a way to explain to Caroline why I am going out alone tomorrow night."

"Last night I had a dream about Katherine again, and this time she didn't hug me or smile. I can't get over that she might be dead. I never felt right about letting her go with Josh to Chicago that day, but he was so mean and Darnell and I had to get away and were only thinking of ourselves. How much we thought about ourselves then. We didn't know what we were getting into. Nobody ever considered that the FBI would be after us. Isn't that stupid? I have almost forgotten how we talked every night at school about the plan and how Josh made us believe it would work. I do know we were right to want to help those people who were being hurt because the government didn't care. I hope Gen. Patterson understands that now."

Several paragraphs followed describing the general's job in the government and how the kidnappers had convinced themselves that they could get to him through his daughter. Meredith was trying to justify their actions once more to herself. Was she rehearsing what she would say to Charles Patterson when she met him the following night?

September 22 had been the day Meredith died. The day's entry, probably written that morning in the conservatory, continued with her thoughts on the role she had played in the kidnapping and what she hoped would be the outcome of her planned visit to Katherine's father that night.

The dreams would stop when Phoebe Harrington, now Meredith Hackett, confessed her part in the kidnapping and asked for Gen. Patterson's forgiveness.

"I will tell him who I am," she wrote with a strong hand. "It is the cleansing I need to move on with my life. I will stand in front of him and ask his forgiveness for the pain and sorrow we caused him. Her father must forgive us. Otherwise I don't think I can go on like this any longer."

The last pages of the notebook were blank. The diary ended here. What had happened on the last night of Meredith's life when she finally met Katherine's father? Meredith had yearned for forgiveness, but instead met death. Had Gen. Patterson truly found it possible to forgive Phoebe Harrington for the massive pain she must have caused him?

Meredith had been alive when she left Windward. She was seen later at the Atlantic Beach Club. And her dead body was found in a street nearby. Still Caroline couldn't shake the feeling that Meredith's death was somehow connected to her visit to the general's house. Hadn't Hank believed that the last entry in the diary would tell them who killed Meredith?

The reference to her appointment with Charles Patterson was the last entry in the notebook.

CHAPTER XXI

———⊶⊷———

"There's something strange about this diary," Caroline said to Hank. "I hardly slept all last night, thinking about it."

Hank was reading the last entries in Meredith Hackett's diary in Caroline's office at Kenwood the next morning. While Hank sat, Caroline paced the room nervously.

To save time he'd asked her to summarize the journal's long first part, the section kept by Phoebe Harrington at the time of the kidnapping. But his curiosity was too strong, and before Caroline had finished her account, he'd already flipped to the back pages and begun reading the entries Meredith had written this year, hoping it held the clues he needed to solve her murder.

"What's so strange to me is what the beginning says about Katherine," he could hear Caroline saying. "I read it all over again first thing this morning. It doesn't seem to me that she is right."

"Hmmn," Hank said, only half-listening. Meredith's handwriting was difficult to decipher. He re-read Meredith's sudden and urgent determination to see Gen. Patterson at all costs.

The last entry was staring up at him in the big, arched words on the page he held in his hand. "I will tell him who I am."

"Meredith went to see Charles Patterson," Hank said, closing the diary. "On the night she was killed. That's the missing hour and a half.

She went out to Windward to tell him that she was sorry that she helped to kidnap his daughter."

"I know. That's the reason she came to Newport." Caroline's eyes searched his. "She called him from the extension in the conservatory. She didn't use her own phone."

"Yes," he said grimly. "Meredith made an appointment to see him on Friday night. Late, I'm sure, because Patterson likes to sleep late into the day. He's awake in the evening hours. So she looked at her watch in The Black Pearl right in front of us and said 'Good night, Hank, Caroline and Spider, you bore me, I'm leaving.' And she took your car and went out to the house on Ocean Drive."

"That confused me when I first read it, but it shows that she must have been alive when she left him," Caroline said, "because she was seen afterwards at the Atlantic Beach Club."

"Yeah, her death was shortly after. But the connection to the general is there." He frowned.

"I know, Hank. It feels like it ought to be part of this."

"After she told Charles Patterson what she had come to tell him, something happened. I've met the general. He wouldn't be one to say thanks for stopping by."

Ben had his scenario where the chauffeur had followed Meredith, and he—or possibly the general - had murdered her in their car. Could Hank get a search warrant to look at the car? He'd have to go to the chief.

"Hank, will you listen to me about something?"

"What about?"

"It's about the first part of the diary, the part you haven't read yet. I don't know exactly how to say this, but I'm getting this feeling that the kidnapping wasn't exactly what everybody thought it was."

"What are you talking about?"

"It's because I can't get a picture of Katherine. She's not clear, not in the way I had understood her. Suppose I were playing her on the stage? That's what I ask myself."

"Meredith was writing about herself," Hank pointed out. "Not Katherine."

"Yes, but she mentions Katherine a lot. But all the diary entries don't call her a political prisoner, or use any rhetoric that makes it seem like she was the victim." Caroline took the notebook from his hands. "Here, let me show you this entry at the beginning of 1992."

She found the passage and read it aloud. "'A new year. It feels like the old one. I wonder how Katherine is. Is she still with Josh? Does she still believe he was right?'" Hank didn't see what she was getting at. "The character of Katherine," Caroline said. "What do I learn from the text? In her diary, Phoebe asks, 'Is she still with Josh?' What does that sound like? To me, I read that Katherine agreed with Josh from the beginning. Katherine participated in her own kidnapping."

Caroline paused, giving Hank time while her idea sunk in. "The kidnapping would force her father to do what they wanted. What they *all* wanted."

"You think the kidnapping was a fake? That she wasn't held against her will?"

Hank recalled the back files he had earlier been reading relating to the Patterson kidnapping. The old newspaper photographs of Katherine, furnished by her family and friends to the press in 1991, had not especially interested him. With her light hair and pale skin, Katherine had appeared to resemble her brother Will. Not a beautiful or even pretty face. Hank remembered one of the file photographs in particular now. The general's daughter had been with several other students, and she had been caught staring insolently at the camera. There was a distinct look of impudence in Katherine's grey eyes. Did that expression reveal more of her true personality?

"I think it's all there, throughout the diary entries," Caroline said." There's another part that says how Phoebe and Darnell were afraid, but Josh and Katherine weren't. Now why wouldn't Katherine be afraid if she were the one who was being kidnapped? The tape Phoebe made said they would kill her if the pollution didn't stop. The whole thing was a ticking bomb, they said. So tell me. Why wasn't Katherine frightened if a bomb was about to go off?"

Hank found Keisha and Ben enjoying a huge breakfast in the kitchen.

"Can I get you something, Lt. Nightingale?" Mattie asked. Hank knew the cook was an adversary of Caroline, but to him Mattie Logan was always sweetness itself.

"No, thanks," he said with some reluctance. The aroma of sausages and fresh coffee pervaded the room, and the smell was intoxicating. He saw there were blueberry muffins in a basket, the steam still rising above them. "We've got work to do," he said to the two sergeants busy with their knives and forks.

While they cleaned the last of the food from their plates, Hank told them about the diary and its contents. He had spent the last half an hour reading it in Caroline's office.

"I knew it," Keisha said. "Katherine Patterson is still alive."

"She might be," Hank conceded. "At least she was alive and on her way to Chicago when Phoebe Harrington last saw her. If the diary's genuine, of course."

"You think it might be a fake, Lieutenant?" Ben asked.

"No," he sighed, "not really. It strikes me as being authentic."

"And Meredith Hackett was going out to see Gen. Patterson the night she was killed?" There was no mistaking the look of satisfaction on Ben's face. Both he and Keisha were each thinking of their pet theories in the case. For Keisha, that Katherine hadn't been killed by her so-called kidnappers, was alive, and had stalked Meredith. For Ben, that Charles Patterson had somehow engineered the death. Which did Hank believe? Right now he wasn't sure.

"Yes. Now we have to see what happened when she got there. I'm going out to Windward. Sgt. McAndrews, you come with me," Hank looked at his watch. It was only 9:30 in the morning. "We're going to talk to everyone at the house If the general's not up yet, we'll start with that chauffeur, who never seems to leave his side."

"The one who beat his girlfriend in Atlantic City a few years ago?" Ben said with scorn in his voice.

They had run a records check on Forman and found that he had been involved in a domestic violence incident four years ago. The woman had refused to testify against him, and there was no conviction.

"Who else is in the house?" Keisha asked.

"The son is living there now, Katherine's brother. We'll talk to him, also. We need to find out what he might know about Meredith Hackett's paying a visit to his father on the Friday night of her death."

"Gen. Patterson is still in bed," Jason Forman told Hank when he and Keisha arrived at Windward about twenty minutes later. The information was given in an impersonal tone, and the chauffeur cum whatever-else-he-was stood waiting in the doorway for Hank's response.

The two Newport police officers had driven up the driveway, past the flanks of news people waiting for anything to happen, no matter how trivial, to relieve the boredom of their watch. Hank had driven his own unmarked car to the estate, and their arrival was greeted with only mild curiosity.

"I have important information to share with Gen. Patterson," Hank explained to Forman. "And also some important questions to ask him." Hank pointedly checked the time on his watch. Just past ten o'clock. "What time does he usually wake up, Mr. Forman?"

"Generally, not before noon," the chauffeur said. Hank's tone had been polite, and Forman added, "The pain in his legs always seems at its worst during the night. By the time the painkillers kick in, it's morning. There's no reason why the general needs to adhere to any schedule, so we let him make his own."

Hank wondered who *we* was. The detective was also curious about the nature of the general's leg injuries. He debated whether to ask Forman, but decided the general ought to have the first chance to answer that question.

"Is Gen. Patterson's son around now? Will, I believe is his name." Hank looked around the dark foyer where they were standing. Forman hadn't invited them further into the house.

"He's staying in the studio, not the main house." The tone had become superior. "Will doesn't come on this side often. You'll have to call for him at his own door." The general's driver made a move as if to show the police officers back outside, but Hank stood rigidly, ignoring the hint to leave.

"Fine, we can see him after we talk to you, Mr. Forman."

"Me?" The surprise was genuine. The huge chest muscles became taut, and the face which had looked so confident now lost some of its composure.

"Is there somewhere we can talk?" Hank asked.

Without answering, Forman led them through a door off the foyer into a small anteroom. It was simply furnished in blue with a soft look to it. There was a writing table, some occasional chairs, and a walnut credenza.

Without being asked, Hank sat down on one of the chairs. It was uncomfortable. Keisha took out her notebook and sat across from him.

"I have some questions," Hank began.

"About what?" Forman asked, not bothering to hide his irritation. "What's this all about? Has it got anything to do with the FBI? That agent who was here last week?"

"No, not really," Hank answered, his demeanor outwardly cordial. "Do you mind sitting down?" He indicated another of the fragile looking chairs. It was as if Hank were the host, and Jason Forman the caller.

Slowly Forman stretched his large body onto the chair's small, striped silk seat.

"Good, now I'll explain why I'm here, Mr. Forman. I'm investigating the murder of a young woman in Newport. It happened a week ago, last Friday. It was all in the news, so I'm sure you know about it. Her body was found in town. She was strangled." He paused. Forman, his brow furrowed, was being attentive. "The victim's name was Meredith Hackett. Recognize that name?"

Forman hesitated.

"I said her name was Hackett. Have you ever met her?"

"The newspaper said she was visiting here," the general's driver said carefully. "She was from New York, right?"

Hank reached into his pocket and took out the studio portrait of Meredith.

"Here, take a look at her." Forman's hands remained fixed on his knees.

"Why do you think I know her? I never go to New York."

"According to information that's been developed in the case, Ms. Hackett planned to visit Gen. Patterson. That's the reason she came to Newport." Hank paused for a several seconds, then said evenly, "Do you answer the telephone in the house?"

"Usually," the chauffeur responded. It was hard to miss the caution in his voice.

"Ms. Hackett would have telephoned beforehand, most likely that Thursday, the twenty-first." Hank paused again, watching Forman consider his answer. "I'm pretty sure it would have been sometime on Thursday."

"I can't remember."

"Try to remember."

"Mrs. Shipley was here those days. If I'm busy with the general, she picks up the calls."

"We can check with her," Hank said. He looked around the room. It was cold, impersonal. Unused. "I don't expect you get many visitors out here. Ms. Hackett would have arrived around 10:30 in the evening on Friday. Ring a bell? That's late for a caller. I don't think Mrs. Shipley stays that late. You would have had to answer the door yourself, I think."

There was a long silence while the chauffeur looked to be weighing his options.

"Do you want to wake the general now, Mr. Forman? An hour before my victim met her death, she came to this house. Her business was with Gen. Patterson, not you. I'm going to need his statement and yours, whether it's done here or down at the police station. I'll ask you again. Did you see this woman?" Hank offered the picture, but Forman was meticulously rubbing his palms together. "Was she in this house on the night of Friday, September 22? It's a simple question."

"You'd better ask Gen. Patterson," Forman said without looking up. "Give me a some time to go upstairs and tell him you're here."

"All right," Hank said. Keisha stood up to go along with the general's chauffeur.

"Is she coming with me?"

"She doesn't have to," Hank said. He nodded to Keisha and she sat down. "You can tell Gen. Patterson about the questions I've asked you."

Forman, relieved, started for the door.

"And you can tell him one other thing." Forman hesitated in the doorway. Slowly, and warily, he turned back to Hank. "You can tell him that I have another reason for wanting to speak to him. It concerns information that's also come my way in this case. New information about the kidnapping of his daughter. I think he'll be interested to hear what I know."

CHAPTER XXII

The laptop's screen was glowing as Caroline checked her email. The inn's web site had been a useful investment, and almost daily she answered requests for information about Kenwood's facilities. Today she also had a few personal items in her mailbox, and she gave herself the luxury of time to correspond with a couple of friends around the country.

Caroline felt good, energized despite the hours of sleep she had missed. She couldn't stop thinking of the idea that Katherine Patterson had participated in her own kidnapping. In 1991, the country had been shocked by the crime and had immediately given their support to the young woman whom they believed was being held against her will. The threats to murder her if her father failed to respond to the demands of a band of radical college students had been believed by the public.

Caroline's fingers moved over the keyboard as she went into the web site of *The New York Times* to look for information on the kidnapping. The files before 1996 were not readily available, however, and she tried *The Washington Post* news site. Searching back to 1991 was a laborious process of going into the archives, and several attempts to find what she wanted failed. Finally she typed in Katherine's name in her search engine and first came up with the Wikipedia entry. Reading it didn't tell her much she didn't know, and she knew relying on the information posted could be questionable.

Another link took her to an article written for a Massachusetts weekly in 2006 on the fifteenth anniversary of the kidnapping. She started reading it with high hopes but soon realized it was more of a comparison to present day pressure tactics by a frustrated environmental activist. The writer did point out that Katherine Patterson, alive or dead, had never been found. But the writer found this fact less interesting when compared to the present day problems of worsening pollution in Boston harbor. A look at a *Time* magazine story on the top 25 crimes of the 20th century, published five years ago, showed the kidnapping didn't merit a mention on the list.

She was about to give up when another approach suggested itself.

She Googled *nuclear waste*. Immediately she got a screen full of possibilities. Entries from the government as well as groups working against nuclear power, lists of research articles and notices of upcoming conferences. Caroline clicked on one of the headings and read about attempts by native Americans to keep nuclear waste off their reservations. *Nuclear Power and Waste* was another heading in hypertext, and she clicked on that.

This brought up an even longer listing of items, which included stories from several newspapers around the country about related news in their local areas. Caroline scanned them, unsure which would give useful information. She wondered if Phoebe's campus friends had been part of a national group with a name or an acronym. Would there be remnants of the organization still active? It seemed like looking for a needle in a haystack.

"Excuse me, Mrs. Kent," Karen said, tapping on the door frame. "Do you have a minute? I need you."

"Come in, Karen," Caroline said, turning from the computer. "What is it?"

"There's something wrong with the drain in one of the guest rooms. I can't get the water to go down in the tub."

"Damn," Caroline muttered under her breath. She hated plumbing problems because the guests hated malfunctioning plumbing. Nothing made hotel accommodations less inviting than a backed-up drain. "I'll get the plunger," Caroline said reluctantly. Unclogging drains was one of the first skills she had learned as an innkeeper, and she had a variety of tools to aid her. "Let me get out of this screen."

"It's up in the Newcombes' room. I think they've gone out for the day."

"Yes, they're renting a boat to go sailing. Something I wouldn't mind doing today."

Karen followed Caroline up the back stairs, and they crossed the second floor gallery to the west wing.

"The plunger is in the big linen closet. Let's get this over with."

Jason Forman had left the two Newport police officers alone in the small anteroom for almost half an hour. Hank was getting impatient, his mind imagining several possibilities, none of them good ones. Would Charles Patterson refuse to see them? Was he calling his attorney? Hank shifted uncomfortably in the chair. When at last Forman returned, the chauffeur announced that he was instructed to take the visitors to his master's bedroom.

The general was sitting in his wheelchair when Hank and Keisha were shown into the room, which was located in a distant wing on the first floor. Charles Patterson was dressed and groomed, his face clean-shaven, the smell of some aftershave lingering in the air. Hank was surprised at the care the military man had taken with his appearance. It reminded him of the spit and polish of the parade ground.

The room was furnished with heavy, old mahogany pieces. The draperies and the bedspread were pattered in colors predominated by purple and navy blue. Like the room Hank had just left, this one looked indifferent and cold. He glanced around, looking for pictures or mementos of the past, but there was nothing. Hank had yet to see any family photographs at Windward. A lone book, its title turned away, was placed on the general's bedside table next to an old fashioned wind-up clock.

"Bring another chair, Jason," the general commanded. There was only one in the room, placed in a corner, and the servant quickly returned with another. Hank moved both chairs near to the general's wheelchair, and he and Keisha sat down. Forman stepped back from them, becoming almost invisible in a dark corner away from the window.

"Thank you for seeing me, Gen. Patterson," Hank began. "I'm sorry if I woke you, but my business is important."

"I sleep very poorly, Lt. Nightingale. No apology is needed." Patterson said the words slowly, and Hank caught a note of caution in the older man's voice.

"I'll get down to my business, if you don't mind, sir." The general nodded. "Although I suspect your man has already told you why I'm here." Hank paused, waiting for Patterson to give an answer. When none came quickly, Hank took a gamble. "Yes, I'm sure he has." The general nodded slightly, and Hank smiled back "Good, we won't waste time then. I need the details of the visit to this house of Ms. Meredith Hackett on the night of Friday, September 22."

"It was a private matter between us." No hesitations. The answer was ready on his lips.

"Between you and Ms. Hackett, you mean?"

"Yes." The general said the word sharply, his dark brown eyes leveled directly at Hank. There was a challenge in them "I'm afraid I have to ask you what that private matter was, General."

"Why?" Again, the sharp staccato.

"I expect you follow the news, and you know that Meredith Hackett was murdered on the night of September 22."

"I have no information for the police about that."

"You may have been the last person to see her alive that evening."

"I'm sure that I wasn't."

"How do you know?"

"The newspapers keep asking for the man to come forward who was seen in the bar with her later that night."

"You're right," Hank said. "So I think you have nothing to fear from describing what you know about her activities prior to that time. She came here to Windward, spent some time here, and I want to know the details. When did she arrive?" Hank gestured to Keisha and she steadied her notebook on her lap and held her pen over the page.

"We had an appointment for 10:30 p.m.," Patterson answered. "She was prompt."

"Good," Hank said. "Now when did she leave you that evening?" He peered over at Forman to let him know his presence had not been forgotten.

"I would say that she was here about fifteen minutes. No more. It was not a long conversation, Lieutenant."

"I wish you would tell me the purpose of her visit, Gen. Patterson . . . although I think I can guess it." He paused while the other man looked curiously back at him. "Meredith Hackett came here to ask about your daughter, Katherine. Whether you have been in touch with her since the fall of 1991. Am I right?"

"She didn't deserve to say her name!" The words were spit out angrily.

"She wanted to know if Katherine is alive, didn't she, Gen. Patterson?"

There was no response, and Hank leaned forward in his chair.

"When she called to make her appointment with you, Ms. Hackett gave you the new name she was using, said she was an old friend of Katherine. After she arrived, did Meredith tell you her true identity, that she was Phoebe Harrington?"

"I should have called the police that night."

"Why didn't you? Phoebe Harrington would probably still be alive if you had."

"Do you think I care if she's alive or dead?"

"I'm sure I can understand your feeling that way, Gen. Patterson, but the fact remains that someone did kill that young woman. Meredith, Phoebe, however we name her. I want to know if anyone in this house took a part in her murder."

"That's an absurd suggestion. Only Jason and I are here, and he never leaves my side, especially at night."

Forman nodded his agreement to this statement, and Hank sighed.

"I'm going to ask again about the details of the conversation you had with the dead woman, General. Mr. Forman, were you a witness to that encounter? Will you tell me what was said?" Jason looked at his master for direction. "I'd hate to have to ask you both to come down to the station. I suggested earlier that an interview here ought to be preferable to that, but the other can be arranged just as easily. There is such a thing as obstruction of justice, you know."

"I don't want trouble," Forman said unexpectedly.

"All right, Jason," the general said. "Don't become upset. I'll tell the lieutenant about it. But I want your word, Lieutenant, that you will treat this confidentially. I do not want to read about this matter in the newspapers."

"It's not my job to give out information on my interviews to the press."

"Phoebe Harrington came here to get information, as you said you already knew. I told her I had no information about Katherine."

"What happened next?"

"I told her to leave. You can imagine that I was furious that she had come to my house, stood in my home, after all that they did to my daughter."

"The general's right," Jason said. "He told me to show her out right after he knew who she was. I said we should call the police, the FBI, turn her in. She was a wanted criminal."

"But you didn't?" Hank asked Charles Patterson. "I'm curious. Why?"

"She got hysterical," the general said coldly. His dark eyes were two nuggets of hardened indifference. "She threw herself onto the floor in front of my feet." Patterson looked at his lifeless legs, supported by the chair's foot rests. "She was begging me to forgive her. Forgive her! They killed my daughter."

"But the police should have been notified, General. It was your duty to see that she was brought to justice."

"My daughter is dead. I deserve closure."

Closure. Hank repeated the word to himself. Did Katherine's father think refusing to deal with the past gave closure?

Aloud he said, "Gen. Patterson, I need to ask you another personal question."

Katherine's father's face stiffened, the line of his closed lips became thin and straight.

"What kind of personal question?"

"Your legs, sir. Are they completely useless? Can you walk at all? I'm sure I can get a court order for your medical records, but I'd appreciate your telling me yourself."

"My legs are weak as a result of a serious wound I received in Viet Nam. Over the years they have continued to deteriorate, and I can't rely on them anymore. I've become a prisoner in this wheelchair."

"I see," Hank said. The answer was not definitive, but he wouldn't press further. "How did you end it with Phoebe Harrington? How did you finally get her to leave that night?"

The general didn't answer, instead he shifted his eyes toward the window and kneaded the fingers of his right hand. Hank looked at Forman.

"Mr. Forman? Did you show her out?"

"That woman was screaming, like the general said. Yelling that she needed his forgiveness. I told her she had to leave. She was upsetting him, and she had no right to do that. I had to pick her up from the floor. It was like she was in a trance or something."

"Do you know what time this was?" Keisha asked. It was the first thing she had said since they had entered the room.

"I have no idea. Like the general said, she was supposed to come at 10:30. It had to be before eleven o'clock."

"So you put her out," Hank said.

"I picked her up, like I said, and carried her to the front door. She was kicking me to put her down, but I got her there and tossed her out." This could be the explanation of the bruises which the autopsy found on Meredith Hackett's body.

"And closed the door?" Keisha asked.

"Yeah," Forman said defiantly. "I threw her ass outa here."

"Jason," the general said, turning back from the window. "I don't approve of that language in the house."

"Sorry, sir." The voice was penitent. "But I knew she upset you, and the doctor said your heart can't have that."

Hank sighed. Where was the truth? The two men living at Windward would have the same story, and nothing would break it. Their statement that Meredith had asked the general to forgive her actions in the kidnapping was born out by the diary entry. But would the general have been merely content to have her leave his home? Or would he have exacted some punishment of his own design? There was one other possible witness at Windward to interview.

"Where is your son Will, Gen. Patterson? Is he at home?"

"William?" the general asked. He frowned. "What do you want with William?"

"I'll have to ask him if he was home that night. If he heard or saw anything pertinent to my investigation."

"He stays in the studio. The entrance is around the back side of the house. William wouldn't hear or see anything that was going on inside the house."

"Your son may have seen Ms. Hackett's car. He may have heard her leaving if she was screaming as loud as Mr. Forman says she was. To complete my report, I must speak with him."

"As you wish," the general said. "You obviously have your job to do."

"That's right, Gen. Patterson. I have my assignment from my superiors. I have no wish to harass you or inconvenience you in any way. I'm sorry to bring up the matter of your daughter. I see it upsets you." Charles Patterson closed his eyes. "I do have one other piece of information which I can share with you."

"I don't care to continue to discuss that woman any further."

"Not about Phoebe Harrington, but about some notes she left behind." The general's eyes opened, and Hank thought he saw curiosity flickering. But the interest was being well controlled. "They refer to your daughter."

"My daughter . . . what about Katherine?"

"Phoebe Harrington kept a diary during the time of the kidnapping." Charles Patterson swallowed hard. "I won't prolong this, General. There's nothing in the diary which definitely states that your daughter was killed by her kidnappers. According to the diary, Phoebe and Darnell Stewart escaped from the gang while Katherine was still alive. Do you understand what I'm saying? The last time Phoebe saw Katherine, she was with Josh Ware and she was still alive. Did Phoebe tell you that?"

"Katherine was killed after that. You said Phoebe left the gang, but Josh Ware killed her. That's what the FBI always thought, that he was capable of murder."

"The FBI could be wrong. They've never found a body," Hank said. The words came out more harshly than he had intended.

"My daughter is dead, I tell you. It's what I've known all these years."

"It's what you've *believed* all these years, Gen. Patterson. That diary is not evidence of her death."

The man in the wheelchair trembled as if a cold wind had blown across his chest. But the bedroom was warm, and there was no window open to have let in the draft of fresh air. For the first time, Hank smelled the odor of the sick room.

"The FBI will want to follow up with this new information," he said. "It may be found to be the truth. Your daughter Katherine may be alive." Charles Patterson remained silent and still, and Hank rose slowly from his chair.

Why was Charles Patterson so sure that Katherine was dead? Was it because he had never heard a word from her after she was kidnapped?

Or was it because he was haunted by the memory of his unbending intransigence to meeting her kidnappers' demands?

CHAPTER XXIII

"This is an awesome house," Keisha said as she and Hank made their way to the studio. The day was chilly, windswept, and the imposing house looked indestructibly splendid.

"It's a very strong looking house," Hank said. "And it could be a warm family home."

"But it's not, is it?"

Hank shook his head. "No, I think the general is an unhappy man. Tormented, you might say."

"He was so strange when you told him his daughter could be alive. Almost as if he didn't want her to be."

"And why do you think that is, Sergeant?"

"Well . . ." She paused thoughtfully. "I guess if she's alive and she has never contacted him . . . well, that's got to hurt."

"It's still your theory that Katherine Patterson isn't dead?"

"I haven't disregarded that at all," Keisha said. "But if she hasn't been in touch with her father, how would we begin to look for her? We don't know what she might look like after all this time. And the feds never found her, with all their resources."

"That's true. However, if Katherine did kill Meredith Hackett on September 22, my guess is that she is far away from Newport now."

They had reached the courtyard at the back of the house. The battered black van was parked in front of the studio, and the side door was pulled open. A large cardboard box was on the ground next to it.

"Will the FBI try again to find Katherine now?" Keisha asked. "If the diary tells them she could be alive, won't they want to track her down?"

"I sure would think so," Hank said. Caroline had her ideas about Katherine's part in the kidnapping, and Hank thought they had merit. Would the Bureau come to the same conclusion? The diary's evidence might make Katherine into a fugitive herself for participating in the scheme to blackmail her father.

"Hi, Hank." Will Patterson stuck his head out of the van. His face held a friendly grin as he climbed out of the vehicle. Hank saw it had Montana license plates. Will looked inquiringly at Keisha, appraising her uniform.

"We've come to ask you some questions, Mr. Patterson. This is Sgt. McAndrews."

"Questions?" The smile faded. "Is something wrong? Spider's not in trouble again, is he?"

"No," Hank said. "Why would you assume that?"

"Oh, he's told me a few things about his life. I thought maybe he got in another fight and was in jail. Maybe he needs bail or something? I know he'd think I would help him out."

"No," Hank said again.

"Oh." Will looked down at the box and after some hesitation, he lifted it and slid it into the van. For a few seconds he disappeared. The scraping sound of the box being pushed along the floor could be heard. Hank glared, and Keisha moved toward the open door.

"Mr. Patterson," she called. "The lieutenant wants to speak with you. Would you please come out?"

Will reappeared, the smile back on his face. Hank wondered if the general's son were high. He appeared inattentive and unfocused.

"Sorry," Will said. "I'm packing up, and I wanted to get that in the van." He looked up at the grey sky. "It looks like rain."

"Are you moving out?" Hank asked.

"Planning to."

"When?"

"Probably the first of the week."

"Newport doesn't suit you?"

"Not really."

"You headed back to Montana?"

"I'm not sure," Will said. He was studying the van's worn front tires.

"Looks like your tires ought to be replaced if you're going to go very far," Hank said. In his opinion, the reliability of the entire vehicle was suspect.

Will shrugged. "Before, you said you had some questions for me?"

"Yeah, do you want to talk here or go inside?" Hank gestured toward the studio.

"It's kind of a mess up there. Here's fine."

Hank looked up at the sky and saw that rain was imminent. Well, they could stand here until they got wet.

"I've just had a talk with your father and Mr. Forman."

"Jolly," Will interrupted.

"I want to know if you were home, here at Windward, on the night of Friday, September 22."

"Friday? Friday of last week?" Hank nodded. "I'd have to think." There was silence while he thought. "Probably."

"Could you be more specific, Mr. Patterson?"

"What time on Friday?"

"Approximately 10:30 in the evening."

"Yeah, I think so. I just got here on Thursday, and I didn't know anybody in Newport, so I was hanging around here." Will began to close the van's door, but the mechanism wasn't cooperating, and he had to turn full away from Hank to force it shut.

"You didn't go into town to check out the bars?"

"I did the first night I was here, but I wasn't that crazy about the scene."

"On the twenty-second, did you go over to the main house?" Hank wasn't happy not to be able to see the other man's face. "To see your father?"

"I had dinner with him. I came back here afterwards."

"What time was that?"

"He dines at eight." Will said the words in a singsong mocking tone, but Hank pretended not to notice. The door had finally latched, and Will turned slowly around as he spoke.

"So you think you were back here by 10:30?" Hank pointed to the studio's door. Will nodded.

"At dinner, did your father say he was expecting a visitor that evening?"

"Not a word. But he's not much for conversation with me."

"I see," Hank said. "Did you hear anything unusual later that night? I imagine it's pretty quiet here after dark."

"Oh, yeah," Will said. "One of the reasons I'm getting out of here. I might head up to Boston. I got some friends from prep school up there. I could stay with them for a while."

"Did you hear the sound of a car?" Hank asked, getting back to the reason for his visit. "Someone approaching the house?"

Will frowned, and Hank thought he had finally got the young man's attention.

"You heard a car that night?"

"I'm not sure. Like you said. It's quiet here. I might have. Why?"

"Your father had a visitor that night."

"Is that what he told you?" When Hank nodded, Will looked relieved. "Yeah," he shrugged. "I think I heard a car."

"What about the sound of a woman screaming?"

Will frowned again and studied Hank's face very closely. "What did my father say about that?" he asked.

"He says his visitor was screaming when she left."

"Maybe I heard that, too."

"Did you think to investigate the screams?"

"That's what Igor's for."

"Who?"

"Jason. My father's bodyguard."

"You didn't come out of the studio at all later that night? Around 10:30, or after that?"

"You know, I might have been playing some music loud. These old walls are thick. I'm not sure I could hear much else over the sound of that."

"Have you heard from your sister Katherine lately, Mr. Patterson?"

"That's a very bad joke, Hank. My sister's dead."

"How do you know?"

"Everybody knows. It was a big kidnapping case. It was in all the papers."

"You were young at the time. How old?"

"Ten," Will said tersely.

"Does your father ever talk about the case?"

"To me?" Will looked surprised. "No. Why should he? Why are you asking me all this?"

"You ought to be able to put two and two together, Mr. Patterson."

"Yeah? And what is four?"

"The press is camped at the top of this driveway. The woman who was murdered in Newport on September 22 was the same woman who helped to kidnap your sister. A woman visited your father on Friday, September 22, and she was screaming as she left."

"Oh, my God!" Will exclaimed. His pale face blazed red. "He killed her, didn't he?"

"Who do you mean?" Keisha asked. She had been keeping notes of the conversation.

"My father had Jason Forman kill her, didn't he?"

"I haven't suggested—"

"Of course, he would. That's exactly how he would get even for what she did, Lt. Nightingale."

"Ms. Hackett was alive when she left Windward," Keisha said. "She was seen at a bar in Middletown later that night."

"Oh, so that means my father couldn't have had her followed when she left here? He's up half the night. He would have gone in the car with Jason. Directed the operation."

"Do you really believe Jason Forman would have killed a woman on your father's orders?"

"My father's a general, for Chrisakes. He gave orders in Nam all the time for gooks to be killed. He used to brag about it."

"But Forman isn't in your father's army unit."

"My father pays him well," Will hissed.

"All this is conjecture, Mr. Patterson. It would help if you actually saw anything, were a witness and could offer evidence. Did you see any cars, either Ms. Hackett's BMW or your father's, leave Windward that night?"

Will was silent. Thinking. Weighing.

"No," he said at last. "I don't think I'm a witness to anything."

Louise Kent balanced the big tray of glasses against her left forearm and cleared a spot for it on one of the tables in the front foyer. She had been attempting to carry the glasses into the library to replenish the supply in the drinks' cabinet, but had been surprised to find the door to the room unaccountably closed. Now she left her burden on the nearest hall table and went back to open the library door.

As soon as the door opened, Louise saw the reason for its being closed. Sarah Ryder was standing on a chair at the far end of the room. She was pulling books off the top shelf of one of the bookcases. Beside the chair there were books in a jumbled heap. Looking around, Louise saw similar piles on the floor in front of the fireplace and the windows.

"What on earth are you doing?" The sound of the door's opening had not disturbed Sarah, but Louise's exclamation had. Meredith's sister turned on the chair and almost missed her footing. She grabbed for the side of the bookcase and caught herself ungracefully.

"You startled me," Sarah said accusingly to Louise.

"I should hope I did," Louise answered, marching across the room. She stared hard at Sarah's feet, both in their shoes, resting on top of the leather seat of the armchair. Generations of servants had carefully lubricated and preserved its crinkled red hide for over a hundred years. "I'm going to suggest to my daughter-in-law that we begin taking damage deposits from the guests." Sarah looked down virtuously at her antagonist. "Would you please step down from that chair, Ms. Ryder?"

Sarah looked down at the floor.

"Carefully," Louise commanded as her guest jumped off the chair, just missing the pile of books. "What may I ask are you doing?"

"I was looking through your books. Ms. Kent says the guests can do that. It's in your brochure."

"And does it say in the literature that you can stand on the furniture with your shoes on?" Louise was incensed, unable to minimize her anger. "You're looking for your sister's diary."

"It's mine now," Sarah said. She was looking around the room to determine where next to begin her ransacking.

Louise felt some relief from her displeasure as she considered that Caroline had found what Sarah presumed was hers, and that Hank had already taken the diary safely away from Kenwood. Although the detective had not judged it important to tell Meredith's sister of the diary's discovery, Louise thought it ought to be soon if the house was to be spared further maltreatment. She glanced at the shelf where she knew Caroline had found the notebook. It was an area yet untouched by Sarah's probing hands.

"Why do you think the diary's here?" Louise asked.

"It's a book, isn't it? Hide in plain sight. I thought of it this morning. It's an old trick."

"Yes, I see," Louise said, "but there are a lot of books to examine."

"And I suppose you are going to stop me," Sarah said peevishly.

"To save our furniture, yes, I think I should." The older woman brushed off the chair's seat and made an exaggerated examination of the antique leather. "This chair is over a hundred years old. You should respect old things, young lady."

Sarah started to rebut Louise's words, no doubt thinking of some rejoinder that worked *old lady* into the comeback. But that would have been a folly, and instead she began shaking her head. Her face assumed a bitter pallor of sadness. Louise realized that Meredith had not been the only actress in the Harrington family. "I want what's left of my sister's life," Sarah said slowly.

"The police have it," Louise declared. She hadn't meant to give the information away, but the other woman's overdone manner re-irked her.

"How . . . what . . ." Sarah babbled. "Where?"

"Here," Louise said, the note of triumph strong in her voice. "You are a day late, my dear."

"Damn it," Sarah said in an angry voice. "Where is it? Oh, you said the police took it. That Lt. Nightingale, I guess. Well, I'll have to see him about this. I could have been told, don't you think?" She ignored Louise's raised eyebrows and continued muttering, "Damn, damn." Sarah Ryder tapped her foot on the carpet, her fingers clicking as she moved them nervously in front of her. "I have to have that diary." She looked at Louise. "Did you find it?" Louise shook her head. "Ms. Kent then? One of the servants?" Louise remained silent. "Oh, what does it matter who."

"Why do you want to read it so badly?" Louise asked.

"She's my sister, remember?"

"It's possible that your sister may have entered the name of the person she was meeting the night of her death into that diary."

Sarah jerked her head around. "How do you know that?"

"One of the maids saw Meredith writing in the book while she was staying here, in the days before her death."

"Have you read it, Mrs. Kent?"

"No." Caroline had told her the gist of what the diary contained, including the last entry, but Louise could be truthful in saying she hadn't seen the entries herself. "But I'm sure the police have by now."

"Do you know whose name is in that last entry?"

Louise had no intention of answering the question. She examined the other woman's face. The sharp features looked pinched, and the hazel eyes had narrowed. Sarah had told Hank that she was concerned about incriminating facts being in the early diary entries. Did she also fear there could there be even more damaging information in the later passages? Where had she been on the night her sister was killed? Presumably in New York City, but had Hank checked to confirm that? Did Sarah Ryder have an alibi for the night of Meredith Hackett's murder?

Outside in the hallway, Louise stood thinking about the information in Meredith's diary. Hank still hoped a clue to her murderer might be found on its pages, and the FBI wanted to learn new details of Katherine Patterson's kidnapping and Phoebe Harrington's flight to Ireland.

But Louise was beginning to realize that the contents of the diary had another significant value. Book publishers and the news media would pay generously for the right to publish Phoebe's diary of the kidnapping. Sarah, as Meredith's closest relative, was no doubt correct in assuming she was now the diary's rightful owner. Louise knew that Meredith, as a lawbreaker, could not have published a book and reaped its profits. But was there anything to stop Sarah from making money from the diary? She could even write her own book based on the journal, augmenting the story with the sensational tale of how her sister had been spirited out of the country to Ireland. Only Sarah knew the details of that.

Was the sum high enough to make murdering the diary's original author worthwhile? Somehow, Louise couldn't shake the feeling that the woman she had come to know as Sarah Ryder was not incapable of such grisly tactics.

CHAPTER XXIV

Hank shouldn't have been surprised to find Ernie Broglio waiting for him. The FBI agent must have broken every speed limit to travel from Providence to Newport in the time it had taken Hank to interview the three residents of Windward. The intense, muscular figure of the federal investigator was pacing the squad room when Hank and Keisha returned to the police station. Hank motioned Broglio to follow him into his small office.

"Where is it?" The FBI agent's question came without a prefacing hello or a good afternoon. Hank took off his jacket and hug it on the coat tree.

"Want some coffee?" he asked.

"No. I want to see the diary. Nobody here would give me the time of day about it. I've been waiting almost half an hour. You call me and tell me you have it, then you take off."

"It's down in the evidence room. We're getting ready to send it to the lab on Monday to establish that the book is genuine. Age. Her handwriting. Prints. You know the drill on that."

"But you do think it's genuine?" Both Broglio's face and voice gave away his excitement over the find.

"You mean, do I *assume* it's genuine, Ernie?"

209

Ernie Broglio looked startled, then managed a tight laugh. "You got me, Hank. Now, we're even. O.K.?"

Hank smiled. He wasn't trying to make a real enemy of the FBI agent. He didn't make stupid moves like that.

"You know it's evidence in the FBI's case as well, Hank."

"My chief would fight you on its release." Broglio frowned, and Hank said, "But I'm sure you can see it. Let me call him. Do you mind if I do it in private?"

The agent looked surprised, but he left without further conversation.

Hank needed to get rid of Broglio. The entire time the detective had been driving back to the station with Keisha, he had the sensation that he was closing in on the solution to his case. He had been looking for connections. There were people to connect, and there were places where they were joined. Somewhere between Windward and the beach lay the thread. He was determined to pick it up.

Hank closed the door and called Barton Williams at home. The chief seldom came in on the week-ends unless there was an emergency. TV cameras outside an estate in Newport did not constitute such an emergency.

Before Hank told him of the arrival of the FBI agent, he took the opportunity of filling Williams in on today's interviews.

"I'm making progress, sir," the detective said cautiously into the mouthpiece and made his pitch to be able to examine Gen. Patterson's car.

Barton Williams had no problem with the search warrant or making it clear to Ernie Broglio that while he could examine Phoebe Harrington's diary, the notebook couldn't be released to him while Meredith Hackett's murder remained an open investigation.

"Thanks, Chief. I hope you don't mind my putting him on the line."

Broglio left the squad room as soon as he had finished speaking with the chief. The federal agent seemed content for the present, although this was not going to be the last the department heard from the FBI in the matter of the diary. Hank returned to his office and shut the door again. He wanted to think.

Leaning back in his chair, he put his feet up on his desk. He closed his eyes and made a cradle with his clasped hands for the back of his neck. About twenty minutes passed before he finally broke his concentration, and emerged from his meditation.

First what he knew. Meredith coming on Tuesday to stay with Caroline.

On Thursday Meredith telephones Katherine Patterson's father to make the appointment for the following evening.

Friday—Meredith goes to The Black Pearl with Hank and Caroline, adding in the unexpected presence of Spider Shipley, where she leaves just after ten o'clock. Meredith goes out to Windward where Charles Patterson and Jason Forman come into the picture, and she tells Gen. Patterson that she is Phoebe, his daughter's kidnapper. They argue and Meredith departs fifteen minutes after her 10:30 appointment. She is next noticed at the Atlantic Beach Club bar around 11:30.

Now he came to the unknowns.

Meredith leaves Windward. The sand in the car suggests she drove to the beach. It made no sense to him that the ABC was her original destination. But the beach did. He could see her walking on Easton's Beach to calm down and clear her head. Once there she would have seen the lights from the nearby ABC. Then at 11:30 she is seen in their bar. By midnight she is gone.

Did she meet somebody on the beach? Was it the same man in the bar? Or did she meet someone from New York or her past who had been following her? Hank couldn't rule out the presence of two people, the man in the bar *and* the person on the beach who could be man or woman.

He was sure that one of them had murdered Meredith and drove her body in Caroline's car to Freebody Street. Which one was the killer?

Hank took two photographs from the file and placed them side by side on his desk. First he looked at Meredith Hackett's professional portrait. The air-brushed, made-up face with its eyebrows perfectly plucked and red lips artificially full. Beside it the fresh face of the high school girl, Phoebe Harrington, her mouth smaller, almost crooked. Only the eyes truly matched, the two pairs of inquisitive, keen hazel eyes which had stared straight into both cameras' lenses. One woman with two identities.

The detective thought over the scene on Friday night between 10:30 and 10:45, as the general had described it. Both Patterson and Forman acknowledged Meredith's screaming.

Had Meredith played a scene for them in the same theatrical way she had with Spider when she wanted an excuse for an exit? Or was she truly back in the personality of the young college student begging the general for the absolution that would stop her nightmares?

After unblocking the drain in the Newcombes' room, Caroline had gone to her bedroom. She had managed to splash water all over her trousers and was in the act of cleaning herself up and changing out of her clothes when Hank banged on her door. Thinking it was Karen again, with more bad news, she had opened the door a crack.

"Good," Hank had said, not noticing that she was standing half-undressed behind the shelter of the bedroom door. "I need to talk to you." He pushed the door forward, and she jumped back, afraid one of the guests might catch sight of her in her panties. Hank strode into the room. "You've got to answer some questions I have. You're the only one—" He turned, puzzled as to why she was still crouching behind the open door.

"Shut the door," she commanded, and he did.

He was appraising her bare legs as he began to ask about the diary's text, about what she had said told him about how studying it let an actor get into the characters in the play.

Despite the fact that Hank had seen more of her body unclothed than just her legs and feet, Caroline felt herself blushing under his stare.

"I was fixing the plumbing," she explained.

"You should do that more often," he said, contentedly staring. "Next time, though, call me before you start. I could help you with your uniform." He found himself forgetting all about the information he had declared he wanted.

"I had pants on," she said. "They got wet."

"I see."

She went to the closet to take out a clean pair of pants. "My shoes got wet, too," she added.

"I'll help you put those on." He gestured toward the clothing. "Although I don't mind talking to you in your present state of undress." He made a move toward her, and Caroline felt herself getting warm. She dropped the pants on a chair, and they embraced. Softly at first, then with more intensity.

"Is the door locked?" he asked.

"No, should it be?"

"Yes."

Without thinking of anything other than Hank and the moment, Caroline locked the door to the hall and then the door which led to the sitting room.

"Where is Louise?" Hank asked.

"She's out." Louise had gone out to run some errands, and Caroline hurriedly calculated how long it would take her mother-in-law to complete her chores. She looked at Hank. She wanted him.

"I think we've got about an hour and a half."

*   *   *

"Hank, do you think I'm happy?"

"You're asking me that? After we just—"

"I don't mean now," Caroline interrupted.

"Now's a pretty good time to be thinking about happy. What are you trying to do to my male ego?"

They were lying back against the pillows in Caroline's bed. It was the first time Hank Nightingale had ever found himself here. The soft, warm feel of the bed was steeped in the perfumed scent of the woman who slept there. Until a few seconds ago, he had felt relaxed and happy. Now he turned to see Caroline's down-turned mouth and the emerald eyes which looked solemn and without their usual shine.

"Hey," he said, grabbing her and pulling her down under his embrace. "You're not going sad on me, are you? What's wrong? You were delirious a few minutes ago. You didn't fake anything." He gave her a long kiss, and was pleased to feel her give in under the pressure of his lips.

"You read Meredith's diary," she said when their mouths parted. "You know what she said about me."

"Meredith didn't know about me. She didn't know I love you." And as he said the words he suddenly realized how much he did love her.

She took in her breath and studied his face. He saw the green irises in her eyes coming back to their usual depth and intensity.

"I love you, too," she said, touching his cheek with a soft, gliding motion of her fingertips.

Suddenly Hank thought of Reed Kent, and a surprising feeling of panic began to engulf him. He shivered.

"You're cold," she said, pulling up the big over-sized down comforter to his chin. She looked pleased now to be tending to him, and he knew there couldn't be the same thought in her mind. He tightened his chest muscles and managed a smile.

"I'm fine now," he said.

They remained quietly in each other's arms for several warm, tranquil minutes before Caroline said that Louise ought to be returning soon and they should be getting dressed.

When Caroline came out of the bathroom, Hank was standing, looking out of the window. The view from the second floor across the lawns was soothing. He could see the blue sliver of the ocean in a corner of the horizon to the south.

"Did you ever think Phoebe was here?" he asked.

"Phoebe? How do you mean?"

"Did Meredith ever seem different than you remembered her?" He turned around. "That maybe she was behaving like Phoebe? Talking like Phoebe."

"I see what you mean." She was thinking it over, and he waited.

"Once she said I was lucky to be living here. Now that I've read the diary, I know Meredith didn't believe that I was over Reed's death, so I guess that must have been Phoebe talking. Meredith was very reflective that last afternoon. She even called the house a temple. I wonder if Kenwood didn't remind her of the safe harbor she found in Ireland when she was Phoebe."

"I want to know how often she switched back and forth between Phoebe and Meredith. I feel that's important." He told Caroline everything which Charles Patterson had said transpired between him and his daughter's kidnapper on the evening of her death. "Who left the general's house the night she was killed? Was that woman Meredith or Phoebe?"

Caroline looked uncertain.

"I want to understand her mind set after Katherine's father rebuffed her request for forgiveness," he continued. "You know what Meredith wrote in her diary about the nightmares. I need to know how

Meredith would have reacted to the general's rejection of her pleas to forgive her."

"I think she would have been amazed that the general wouldn't forgive her. She was used to having her own way."

"Meredith would have been shocked?"

"Well, yes. That's what I would imagine to have happened that night. But Phoebe, too. I think she would have been shocked as well."

"Why?"

"In her diary . . . remember how Phoebe wrote that the college students had been convinced that they would succeed in shutting down the nuclear plants if they kidnapped Katherine. They didn't believe for a moment they would fail. Oh, I know Phoebe went through that bad time in Philadelphia, but when she got to Ireland, she healed, didn't she? When she became an actress there . . . well, Meredith was able to go on the stage because deep down she had that built-in confidence. Sarah's got it, too, don't you think? It must run in the family."

"So Meredith wasn't used to not getting her own way," he mused, mostly to himself. He was reminded of her relationship with James, the Irish director. "You don't think she would have gotten plain angry?"

"I think she fully expected to meet Gen. Patterson, explain herself and be forgiven. Meredith must have been genuinely surprised when the scene didn't go her way, the way she had rehearsed it. She didn't seem at all nervous in The Black Pearl. She acted herself right into that confrontation with Spider and then did her big exit scene."

"Could she have become vulnerable?"

"In what way, Hank?"

"Afterwards, when she met the man in the bar—damn, I wish we could find him—Meredith had another Scotch with him after the drink she had with us. Were her defenses down? Would she have told him all of her troubles?" He reminded her of how the general's servant had literally thrown Meredith out of the house after she had made her confession. "Her pride, as well as her body, must have hurt like hell."

"I'm not sure she would have trusted a stranger in a bar, but the Scotch could have affected her judgment. I never knew her to drink much. She always said that alcohol didn't mix with keeping your looks."

"If she was intoxicated, did she let down her guard and make our unknown man think he could take advantage of her? Is that what led to her murder? She resisted him, and he killed her. That's always been one of the possible solutions to this case."

"Then her death had nothing to do with her visit to Windward or the kidnapping?"

He frowned. He couldn't let go of the connection to her past as Phoebe Harrington.

"Spider Shipley is definitely eliminated?" Caroline asked.

"There's no evidence to connect to him. We've still got some hairs we took from your BMW which haven't been identified."

"Have you taken any hair samples from Sarah Ryder?" Hank shook his head, and Caroline told Hank about Sarah's continued searching for the diary and Louise's opinion as to what Meredith's sister would do with her discovery.

"A book deal? That's one I didn't think of. Those kinds of books can be big money-makers."

"It's pretty awful to think of someone killing their own sister. Do you think she could have hired X to kill Meredith? I remember her face when you asked her to identify Meredith's body, and I was watching her when she told us about helping her sister when she came to Boston all dirty and everything. I thought that her feelings for Meredith were genuine."

"Not acting?"

"I don't think Sarah's much of an actress."

"You would know, I guess." He was still interested in the character of the woman who went to the ABC. "I wish I could be sure that Meredith was acting that night at Windward."

"I will say," Caroline said thoughtfully, "that it was Meredith who was with us in The Black Pearl earlier that night. If she occasionally said things that were suggestive of the youthful Phoebe while she was here at the inn, well . . . that was when she was relaxed. She wasn't relaxed that night."

"Then you think she was the actress when she began screaming when the general told her to leave Windward?"

"Yes, the more I think on it, she very well could have been giving a performance."

CHAPTER XXV

Monday morning began with Caroline's spirits high. As she wakened to start the early, daily routine at Kenwood, she was aware of an intensified energy in her body. She was in love. The feeling had existed inside her for some time, but it was Hank's declaration to her which allowed the emotion to bloom freely. It was crazy, she thought, as she virtually skipped down the back stairs to the kitchen. Before she faced Mattie, she would have to get some control over her excitement. Caroline felt like a school girl, and the old cook would be quick to notice the change in her young mistress's disposition.

Standing outside the kitchen door, Caroline allowed herself one more smile to herself, her precious secret bursting to get out. Gamely she bit her lip and cleared her throat before entering the room. Mattie was at the stove, her back to the door.

"Good morning, Mattie," Caroline said. "Something smells good. Cinnamon rolls, I think."

Without turning, Mattie grunted. "Some likes 'em," she said. "Missus never did, but I thought I ought to put them out. Them new English guests might like to taste some American sweet goods. We'll see. And I suppose they'll want their tea for breakfast, not coffee." She made another grunting sound. "I won't put them rolls on the tray for Missus. I've got her muffins ready to go in the oven next."

"Perfect," Caroline said.

The arrival of two British couples for a week's stay had provided a welcome diversion from the usual routine at Kenwood. The four well-to-do, middle-aged travelers were extremely interested in the history of both the estate and the Kent family, as well as Newport society in general. In turn the Montgomerys and the Russells were eager to converse with their hosts about nobility and country houses in their own native land. On the previous evening, Caroline and Louise had chatted with their new guests over drinks in the library.

Caroline thoroughly enjoyed their company, thinking as she greeted them again at breakfast, that the Brits were going to be especially interesting guests. After the meal service, satisfied that the household routine was proceeding, Caroline retired to her office to tackle some paperwork.

Unfortunately the inn's web site mail box was empty of requests. It sometimes happened, but Caroline experienced a dim feeling of letdown nonetheless. She stood up to stretch her muscles and went to the window, looking out at the grey sky. There was the chance of rain again.

"I need a vacation." She had said the words, which were only her thoughts, aloud. "I'm tired of working seven days a week."

Needing a distraction, she opened her laptop and went back to her search on the Patterson kidnapping, typing in *nuclear power* and *waste* again as keywords. She quickly found her place back in the headings she had seen on Saturday. This time there was no Karen to arrive with a summons to unplug the drain, so Caroline began scrolling down the listings, skimming words and phrases. There were so many choices—action groups, announcements and information, news sites. Caroline marveled that so many people could be working with such dedication to this one cause. She had a feeling that they didn't take week-ends off. Or complain about it, either.

Caroline was moving the arrow down the text more quickly now, unsure what to click on. Her eye saw the heading only as it began to disappear at the top of the screen. She blinked, not sure what she had actually seen. Quickly she hit the arrow to bring back the screen with the words she thought she had seen.

Ticking Bomb Speech

Caroline's hand trembled as she carefully clicked twice on the blue hypertext of the heading. It seemed the proverbial eternity before the news site she wanted came on in front of her. Caroline read the words on the screen so quickly that she had to go back to the beginning to read them a second time to be sure she understood the meaning of what she had found.

"Oh my God," she said, this time in a loud voice which filled the room. "I can't believe it."

Caroline sat still, her entire body immobilized. Inside her mind, ideas flashed, and her stomach tingled. She thought she might lose her breakfast.

"Katherine," she murmured. There was a bottle of water on her desk, and she drank from it to calm her surging insides. Once again she stared at the screen and her eyes picked out the links to other web sites. There was more. There was much more. But before she went to other links, she would print out a copy of what she had discovered.

The stream of paper came quickly out of the laser printer. Caroline held the sheets in her hand, and the ordinary, neat black words looked up at her. She wanted to read everything again, but she didn't have time. She needed to go to the other links and get as much information as she could. Suddenly time seemed important, and she felt she must hurry.

"Where is he, Sgt. Davies?"

"He's giving a deposition this morning, Mrs. Kent, on an accident case."

"Is he going out to Windward afterwards by any chance?"

"He didn't mention it," Ben answered.

"All right. Thanks. Would you tell him I called, Sergeant? I do need to speak to him. He can reach me on my cell phone. I'm going out to Windward myself."

"Of course, Mrs. Kent. No problem. I'll see that he gets your message."

Caroline hung up. She had purposefully neglected to add that she wanted to talk to the lieutenant about something official. Ben might have asked to have the information given to him over the telephone, and she didn't want to do that. She wasn't sure how she would have put into words what she had just uncovered.

Anyway, she thought, this information deserves to be shared with Katherine Patterson's father. Charles Patterson had a right to know the truth before Ben Davies. Caroline had wanted Hank to know, but things weren't going to happen in that order. She would leave for Windward at once. The inn was quiet, the daily pattern continuing uneventfully. She could slip away for an hour or so. Quickly she sent Hank a text to meet her at Windward as soon as the deposition was over.

Caroline drove Louise's car, her own still sitting in the garage where it had been parked since the police investigators had returned it that morning. Eventually she would begin driving the BMW, but for the present, the idea of sitting in the space where Meredith's dead body had been found unnerved her.

The phalanx of waiting reporters peered into the car as she turned into the long driveway off Ocean Drive. On her way down Bellevue Avenue, Caroline had wondered how she would know which entrance off the Drive led to Windward, but the news presence saved her the trouble of resorting to guesswork.

"Caroline Kent," she identified herself to the young police officer who motioned her to stop at the head of the driveway. She patted the large, thick envelope on the passenger seat. "I've got a packet for Gen. Patterson."

"All right," the officer said. "You can go on."

Caroline smiled and moved on, stopping again when she reached the front door of the imposing house. Gingerly she gathered up the envelope and stepped from the car.

"Hey, Caroline, what are you doing here?"

She knew the sound of Spider Shipley's voice at once.

"Hello, Spider," she said. "I'd almost forgotten that Hank told me you're working out here. I've come to see Gen. Patterson."

"You know him?" Spider asked incredulously. "No kidding." He stroked the top of his meager blond hair.

"Well, I don't exactly know him." Caroline fingered the envelope she held tightly in her left hand. She had been about to choose between using Windward's doorbell or banging the large lion's head doorknocker to rouse the household. "But I do need to see him urgently." She didn't know why she felt compelled to share this last bit of information with Spider. Nerves, no doubt. She had been rehearsing what she would say to the general, and she still hadn't worked out her opening. Quickly she pushed the doorbell's button.

"He won't see you this early," Spider said sagaciously. "He don't see no one 'til he gets out of bed. And that's later this afternoon."

If she had wondered how Spider knew so much about the general's habits, she soon had to accept the authenticity of his remarks. The general, as Spider had said, wasn't seeing anyone this morning. That Caroline had protested she had important information for the owner of the house was summarily dismissed by the tall, muscular man who answered his door. If she desired, she was told that she could leave her envelope and he would see that it was given to Gen. Patterson when he awoke. Pleading was no help, and Caroline felt anger at the man's self-assured manner. His employer ought to be allowed to hear what she had to say. What could be more important?

"All right," she said, not bothering to hide her annoyance. "If I can't see him in person, I can't give you this." She took out one of her business cards from her shoulder bag. "Here," she said, handing it to the man in the doorway. "This is who I am. I live here in Newport. Please tell him to call me. Tell him . . ." She hesitated. "Tell him it's urgent."

The statement was accepted without comment, and the door closed. Caroline found herself standing on the drive, Spider staring curiously across the gravel at her. While she had been talking to the man from the house, she noticed that Spider had made himself very inconspicuous behind some shrubbery. Now he approached her.

"You could talk to Will, you know," Spider said.

"Will?"

"He's the general's son." Katherine's brother.

"Perhaps I could." She stared back at the door.

"Oh, no, don't worry about Igor coming back. Will lives around the other side of the house. Come on, I'll take you to see Will. Me and him's friends."

CHAPTER XXVI

Spider wished that Will Patterson might have shown a little more enthusiasm at their arrival than the chilly greeting he offered. Will was packing up his precious stereo equipment when Spider and Caroline found him inside the almost barren studio which had once belonged to his mother.

"Looks like you're about ready to go," Spider said, making an effort at friendliness. He had introduced Caroline to him, and Will had acknowledged her presence with a slight nod of his head. His attention was totally absorbed in wrapping his speakers with thick sheets of plastic bubble wrap. Methodically he attached strips of heavy clear tape to hold the packaging in place. Spider tapped his foot impatiently, but Caroline seemed content to watch Will at his work. When he had finally wrapped the speakers to his satisfaction, adding in several more strips of tape to corners which seemed well-protected enough already, Will turned to them with a cool inquiring look.

"What can I do for you, Spider?"

"It's Caroline here what needs to talk to you."

"Oh?" Will's eyebrows rose.

Yeah, Spider thought, what do you think I brought her here for? To get some of your tips on gift wrapping. Suddenly the care which Will was taking over the stereo irritated him, and Spider kicked at the long length of disconnected speaker wire which was left on the floor where the speakers once sat.

"Coil that up for me, would you, Spider? There's a spool of it over there on the table, and you can wind that loose piece around on top of it."

"Yeah. Whatever," Spider muttered. Caroline was standing, staring. She looked strange, holding on to that big envelope, and he thought she must be thinking the same thing he was. Will Patterson was a rude son of a bitch.

"When you leaving, Will?" Spider asked. May as well get some good news out of this.

"Tomorrow morning. I was going to come down to say good-by. How's the fence coming along?"

Will knew damn well that the fence wasn't coming along at all. Spider had left that project for the time being, and had been doing some clean-up work on the grounds. No one at Windward particularly monitored what he was doing so he had decided on his own to switch his duties.

"It's O.K . . ." He had wrapped the wire around the spool. "Where you want this?"

"Just sit it back on the table." Will seemed to see Caroline for the first time. "Would you care to sit down? I'm sorry I can't offer you anything, but as you can see I'm packing up to move out."

"That's all right, Mr. Patterson," Caroline answered.

Mister Patterson. Spider laughed.

"Caroline come to see your father, Will, but he's asleep. I told her so, but then Igor come out and told her again."

"You came to see my father?" He was regarding Caroline curiously with his careful grey eyes. At last they came to rest on the envelope she was holding. "Is that for him?"

"I wanted to show him this information. I took it off the Internet this morning." Spider thought Caroline looked really nervous.

"Caroline's a friend . . . was a friend, I mean . . . of that woman who was murdered," Spider offered.

"You don't say?" Will's pale eyes were alert now. "What was her name? Spider knew her, too. Did you know that?" He was studying Caroline with renewed interest.

"Meredith," Caroline said softly. "I knew her as Meredith Hackett. She was staying at my house. My inn, I should say. I'm the proprietor of the Inn at Kenwood Court, here in Newport."

Will shrugged. "I don't know it. I haven't been in Newport long."

"We were all out that night together. Me and Hank and Caroline and that Meredith."

"The plot thickens," Will said. Spider thought his tone was obnoxious given that Caroline had just been introduced as the ice lady's friend, and now she was dead.

"Didn't you hear me, Will? These ladies were friends."

"I'm sorry," Will said. "But I read about the case in the newspapers, and well, you know how these things are. You begin to think you knew the victim yourself, you learn so much about her life. And she was an old friend of yours?" Caroline nodded. "And did you know where she was going that night?"

"You mean after we were out together?" Spider said. He turned to Caroline, his eyes wide.

"No," Caroline said. "She didn't tell me."

"That's odd," Will said. "Because it turns out, you see, that she came here."

"Don't shit me," Spider said. "Are you shittin' me, Will?"

"Matter of fact I'm not," Will said. "Your friend Hank told me. Apparently the big story is that this Meredith came to see my father the night she was killed."

"The truth, Will?" Spider asked. "Don't shit me."

"Oh, yes, it's the truth, Spider. And you know what I realize now? My father was the one who killed her."

"Holy shit." Spider couldn't believe his ears. He looked at Caroline, who was staring incredulously at Will. "Don't you think, Caroline, that we'd better tell Hank about this? Real quick." The sound of her cell phone ringing disrupted Caroline's concentration. She had been standing next to the old paint-splattered table, looking from Spider to Will, unable to trust fully what her brain was in the process of suggesting. For several seconds she did not recognize that the phone, inside her handbag, was what was making the noise. She fumbled with the zipper on the bag and retrieved the instrument.

"Hello," she said cautiously.

"Caroline, it's me." Hank's voice at the other end of the connection seemed very loud.

"Louise, hello," she said as she turned from the two men in the studio and took a few steps toward a corner of the room.

"Louise?" the puzzled voice on the other end asked. "This is Hank. Caroline, is everything all right?"

Of course not, she wanted to say into the mouthpiece. What kind of detective are you? But instead she responded in an easy conversational voice. "I'll be home soon. I just had to run an errand."

"Are you at Windward?" Hank asked anxiously.

"Yes, that's right. I've picked up the dry cleaning, and I'll be on my way home shortly. Is there anything else you need done in town?" She couldn't think what to say. How could she signal Hank? Think, girl, think.

"What's going on out there? Why all this subterfuge? Who are you with? Why can't you talk?"

"You'll never guess who I ran into at the cleaners," she said brightly, composing herself. Will and Spider had stopped their conversation. Her heart was pounding, and she was glad she had her back to the faces of the people who had to be listening to her exchange with Hank.

"The cleaners? Does that mean something, Caroline?"

"My ex," she continued in a cheery voice. Too cheerily she thought. She ought to have delivered that line with less emphasis on delight, more on surprise.

"Your ex?" The tone of Hank's response was certainly surprised. "Your ex what?"

"Yes," she said, "what a coincidence. Well, I'll tell you all about it when I see you. Soon, I hope."

"I'm on my way out there now," Hank said rapidly. "I've just left the lawyer's office downtown." She heard him putting on the siren.

"Good. I'll wait for you if you're going out—"

"Yes, yes. But damn it, be careful. Whatever you're up to out there. Get in your car. Lock the door."

"Yes, I did take your car, Louise. Sorry I left you to handle things by yourself . . . at the inn."

She ended the conversation and grasped the phone tightly in her hand. Hank was coming. He would be here in five minutes or less. What should she do in the meantime? What could she do? She turned back to face Spider and Will.

"Where's Will?" she demanded of Spider, who was standing all alone by the camp bed. "Where did he go, Spider?"

"Oh, he just carried something out to the van." Spider sat on the bed and jumped twice on the thin mattress. "Not bad," he pronounced.

"Is he coming back?"

"Sure. Why not?" Spider looked around the studio, wondering how long it would be before he could suggest he should move in. "He's got more of this stuff to take downstairs."

Caroline reached down for the place on the table where she had put the packet for Gen. Patterson when she'd needed both her hands to open her purse and take out the cell phone. Her heart sank when she saw the flap on the brown envelope lying open, the metal fastener unclasped. She knew what had happened to its contents even before she felt its empty weight in her hand.

Her ex. Hank turned the phrase over and over in his mind as he sped up Coggeshall Avenue. Rain was beginning to fall, and he turned on his windshield wipers, the smooth black diagonals of the rubber blades moving back and forth rhythmically in front of his eyes. What did she mean? Ex what? Usually you referred to an ex-spouse as your ex, but Caroline wouldn't talk about Reed like that. Besides, how could she have met her husband anywhere in Newport? It was a distinct impossibility. No, not that ex. And then he knew. Not ex . . . X . . . *the killer.* Oh, God, he thought. Caroline thinks she's found the murderer. Is with the murderer out at Windward. Rapidly he went over in his mind all the people who could be expected to be found at the Patterson estate . . . the general, the chauffeur, the general's son . . . and of course Spider. Spider worked at Windward, would be there on a Monday morning for sure. Could he have been wrong all along?

He pressed his foot hard on the accelerator as he made the turn onto Ocean Drive. The small band of startled news reporters rushed toward his car as he neared the driveway. He turned off the siren and blew his horn as he continued on, warning everyone out of his way. John Pelella, the uniformed officer on duty, recognized him at once and signaled everyone back off the drive to let him pass.

* * *

"Spider," Caroline said, looking around the studio. "We've got to find Will."

"He's coming back up here. Just wait a minute."

"No. I don't think he is." She held up the empty envelope. "He's taken something from me, and I have to get it back from him. Will you help me?"

"Yeah, sure, Caroline. But what'd he take? You had something important in that envelope there for his father?"

"Yes. Very important. Come on."

She led the way down the steps, back to the courtyard. Spider looked inside the van, but it was empty. Caroline felt raindrops on her face.

"Where do you think he's gone?" Spider asked.

"I think he's taken those papers to his father."

"Isn't that what you wanted?"

"Not quite this way."

She started around the house, back to the front door, with Spider close behind. When they got to the door, she banged loudly with the knocker. After a few seconds, when no one came to the door in answer to her summons, she began ringing the doorbell. Still there was no answer, and she turned to Spider in frustration.

"I've got to see the general and explain things."

"Before Will does?"

"Yes. But he may be doing it right now." She looked around. "Is here another way into the house? What about the kitchen wing?"

"Yeah, yeah," Spider answered. "My ma's probably back in the kitchen. That door's usually unlocked during the day anyways. Follow me."

Caroline followed Spider toward the side of the house where they stepped onto the lawn. The general's home was large, and the path didn't trace the line of the house. Rain was making the grass slippery, and she almost lost her footing. Spider took her by the arm.

"Here, Caroline. Hold on to me." She didn't want to, but she took his hand, and they continued to make their way around to the back of the mansion.

Irene Shipley was in the midst of making an apple pie, and she looked up from her work in surprise as they entered the kitchen.

"Hi, Ma. Ain't got time to talk now. You seen Will in the last couple minutes?"

"Will? No." She looked curiously at Caroline.

"This is Caroline, Ma. Friend of mine. We're looking for Will."

"Have you finished—"

The remainder of Spider's mother's question was unheard as Caroline found her arm being pulled in the direction of the doorway. Spider paused in the hallway, then started left.

"I think we ought to go this way. The other way's the library, and it's too early for the general to be sitting out there yet. I think this way's his bedroom."

In a few seconds they heard the sound of loud voices, and Caroline guessed they were headed in the right direction. They followed the sounds until they came to a long shadowy corridor.

Hank stopped the car in front of the main entrance to Windward. He checked Louise's car, parked in the circle in front of the house, but Caroline was nowhere in sight. He scanned the grounds. There was no sign of life. Damn, he said to himself. He should have asked Officer Pelella if he had seen anything unusual, perhaps Caroline leaving the estate on foot. But he didn't want to waste time to go back or try to reach him on the radio. Instead Hank went to the front door of the house.

When no one came to Windward's front door in response to his knocking, Hank tried the knob. It was locked. He wasn't surprised, but it would have helped if he could have gained a quick entry into the house. He was suddenly convinced that Caroline was inside. Collecting his thoughts, he returned to his car and radioed for back-up. Then he made his way around the side of the house, looking for another entrance. The kitchen door was unlocked, and he knocked and entered the house. Irene Shipley was absorbed in rolling out crusts for a pie. He cleared his throat, and she looked up.

"It's you," she said. Her round black eyes were staring at him with some fear. "You come for Spider?"

"I'm looking for a young woman, Mrs. Shipley. Slender. Long brown hair, light brown—"

"What for?"

"She asked me to come here for her. Have you seen her?"

"What's going on around here? Like the Easter parade today. Never seen so much commotion in my kitchen—"

"You've seen her," he said with some relief. "Where is she?"

"She and Neil come through here just a few minutes ago. Looking for the general's son. Will's his name. They went out that way." She gestured toward the door.

"Do you know where they went? Oh, never mind." He hurried through the door and down a hallway. He saw the room he recognized from his first visit and went in. But the library was empty. He returned to the hallway. "Which way?" He retraced his steps and started down another passageway.

CHAPTER XXVII

The voices stopped as Caroline and Spider were moving along the dark hallway. She had been confused by the lay-out of Windward's interior, but Spider seemed to know his way around very well.

"Which room they in?" Spider asked in a whisper. "I don't hear anything any more."

"I think it's the room at the end," she answered in a low voice, pointing to a door at the back of the passageway. She slowed her pace and stepped softly forward. Spider hung back.

"I ain't going in there if that Igor's there. He's a mean son of a bitch, Caroline. We better be careful. We should have called Hank like I said. I don't like what's going on around here. You heard what Will said. His father's a murderer."

Caroline stopped and bent low to Spider's ear. "I was just talking to Hank. He's on his way." Spider looked in a quandary, but she ignored his perplexed frown. "Trust me, Spider."

"Then let's wait for him." His eyes were pleading with her.

"I don't know what to do," she said. "I feel as though I should talk to Gen. Patterson." Spider looked alarmed now. "If I could just see what's going on in that bedroom."

"No." Spider shook his head vehemently. "If Hank's coming, he'd want you to wait for him. Besides, he'd have my head if I let you go in there and something happened to you."

"I appreciate your protection, Spider, but we can't just stand out here waiting for someone to discover us. Quiet," she commanded as he began to protest again. "I'm going to see if I can look inside that room." Spider tried to lock onto her arm, but she shook him off.

The door was directly in front of her, open about six inches. As she crept closer, she could hear the sound of her own breathing. It seemed like the claps of thunder in the quiet space. Looking through the crack she saw a man lying in the bed, his head supported by several pillows. His face looked pale, almost ghostly. Charles Patterson wasn't moving, and she strained to see if his eyes were open or closed. With a slight twist of her head, she could see Will standing on the other side of the bed.

The papers he had taken from the envelope were clasped in Will's hand like a weapon, and she had no trouble seeing the hate covering his face. Where was the man who had come to the door, the strange Igor whom Spider feared so much?

She stared at the bed again and the man who remained limp against the pillows. How much had Will told him?

Caroline knew that she had come too late to explain things to the general in the way she had wanted. What would Gen. Patterson do when he learned the entire truth about everything that had happened since 1991? What, if any, of his actions would he now regret?

"Can I help you, miss?" Startled by the deep voice, Caroline raised her head and looked straight into Jason Forman's large, questioning eyes.

"I'm not sure," she answered quietly. "I wanted to help, but now I'm not so sure that I can."

*   *   *

By the time Hank found his way through the gloomy maze of Windward's hallways to Charles Patterson's bedroom, his mind had taunted him with every deadly scenario of Caroline's fate in the dark, sinister old house.

Why had she come out to the estate in the first place? If Caroline had figured something out about the case, she should have told him. But of course she had telephoned the station, and of course he himself had involved her in the investigation by continuing to discuss his theories with her and asking her help to analyze the diary. Damn it all. But Caroline should have had sense enough to wait for him to return her call, not to go rushing off to the den of the killer . . . whoever that might be.

Had she no sense of the danger she was in?

"My sister's not dead," a man's voice shouted from somewhere close by. "They didn't kill her."

A door was open at the end of the hallway, the shaft of light visible, and Hank hurried toward it.

While Caroline waited for Hank to find them in Charles Patterson's bedroom, she continued to ache inside, helpless while lives were unraveling before her. She had tried to explain her presence in the house when the man Spider called Igor had grabbed her outside in the hallway a few minutes earlier. Caroline had urged Spider to run, to intercept Hank when he arrived, but unaccountably the little man remained steadfastly by her side, grabbing on to her hand as she was being pushed into the bedroom by the chauffeur.

When Caroline attempted to speak to the general, she was shouted down by Will.

"Leave us alone," he screamed at her.

"Will," she began, but he cut her off in a voice that was now calm.

"She asked me for forgiveness for taking my sister away from me," Will said to his father. Caroline knew that Will was talking about

Meredith. "She told me you said you couldn't forgive her. So she asked me to."

The general made no movement in response to his son's words.

"My sister's not dead," Will shouted loudly to no one in particular. "They didn't kill her." He pushed the papers at his father's face. "This is what you did. You made it so she would never come back. Even to me."

Then the door to the room opened, and at last Hank stood in the doorway.

Hank's eyes went around the room, first to Caroline who stared anxiously at the man in the bed, then to Spider beside her, holding tight to her hand. It was a confusing scene. The general looked drugged as Will Patterson stood over him, waving some papers in the air. Jason Forman was sheltered by the shadows in a far corner of the room. Hank looked to him for some sign of what was going on. Jason nodded to his employer as if to say, this is how he wants it, I don't interfere.

Hank wished he understood what was happening. He had heard Will shout that his sister was alive, but that declaration hadn't surprised Hank. He'd listened to Caroline and Keisha speculate on the very same possibility. The identity of X is what Hank wanted to know. Was there something in the papers Will held so tightly in his hands which answered that question?

Hank looked once more at Will. His thin body was quaking with anger.

"Did you guess she was still alive, Father?"

When there was no response from his father, Will threw the papers on the bed. "Here," he cried. "This is what you caused. This is what you did."

"Mr. Patterson," Hank began, looking at Will. But the general opened his eyes, and the entire room watched as the father focused his dark eyes up at his son.

"I didn't know," Charles Patterson said slowly. "I didn't know."

"Katherine stayed away because of you," Will hissed. "You made her hate you."

The general's eyes closed.

"You drove us all away. Mother to her death." He pointed to the strewn papers on the bed. "Katherine. I went away, but like a fool I came back. As if it mattered to you if you ever saw me again."

"Katherine," Will cried out piteously. "I could have come to you, if only you'd told me where . . ."

Hank had seen enough. He stepped forward and took Will by his narrow shoulders.

"Easy, Will." Will turned to him. "May I see those papers?"

"I'm glad you're here, Hank," Will said, his voice now cold and heavy. "You're just in time to make your arrest. Here's your murderer." He pointed to his father. "He killed my sister's kidnapper. He killed Phoebe Harrington. I can tell you all about what happened that night."

Hank looked over at Jason Forman. "Is that true, Mr. Forman? I think you would know."

All eyes were on Jason Forman.

"I asked is that true, Mr. Forman?" Hank stepped closer to where the chauffeur stood. "What do you have to tell us about the murder of Phoebe Harrington, also known as Meredith Hackett?"

"Don't I have the right to remain silent?" the chauffeur asked in a low voice.

Hank stared at him. Did Forman kill Meredith under the general's orders after all? Was he confessing? "Do you want to make a statement, Mr. Forman?" Hank asked. "I can take you to the station."

"No!" he heard Caroline shout. "No, Hank. Not him."

"Who?" Hank moved toward the general lying prostrate in the bed, his eyes still closed. One man or the other had to be an accessory. Hank took a deep breath and began picking up the papers from the bed. "Is the answer here?"

"No, no," Caroline repeated.

"It's him," Will shouted. "Arrest him, Hank. Arrest my father."

"No, no," Caroline said again, and Hank was beginning to be irritated by the tone of her voice. He turned to face her.

"Stop saying 'no' and tell me. Who is X?"

"Holy shit."

The high-pitched sound of Spider's voice was unexpected, and Hank turned crossly toward him. Was no one going to let him hear the answer? And then he saw. He didn't need to be told the answer anymore.

The drawer to the general's bedside table was open, and the .45 was in Will's right hand. He was holding it surprisingly steady. Hank's fists opened, and the crumpled balls of paper dropped to the floor.

"Will," he said evenly. "Put the gun down."

"I don't think I will, Hank." Will's voice was calm now.

"You won't solve anything with that gun, Will."

"You're not going to arrest him. He's going to get away with everything."

"No, Will, you're wrong. He's been paying the price all these years for what he did."

"He's got to pay the final price for what he did, Hank. Just like I had to make Phoebe Harrington pay. They both took my sister away from me. They both have to pay for that."

Hank thought of many things in that interminable instant. The back-up that was on its way. His own revolver in its shoulder holster. The civilians in the room. Caroline. Department regulations. The last time he had fired his gun on duty.

"Give me the gun, Will," Hank said. "We can talk about all this down—"

The shot was loud, and its mark was cleanly made. The hole in Charles Patterson's forehead opened almost immediately after the sound of firing was heard. Caroline screamed, and Hank willed himself not to rush to her but to keep his head on his job.

The gun remained in Will Patterson's hand. He was staring down at his father, his eyes riveted on the path of the blood as it traveled down the general's cheek and began to seep into the pillowcase.

Hank reached inside his jacket. As the gun came out of its holster, he started to give the order for Will to drop his own weapon. But before he could speak, Spider sprang forward and jumped on Will's back. Will turned, falling, but the gun was still firmly in his hand.

"Get away, Spider," Hank commanded, his gun trained on the scuffling pair. "Get up. I've got him covered. Caroline! Forman! Get back."

He couldn't see Caroline, couldn't take his eyes from Will for even an instant to make sure that she was safely away from the line of fire. Suddenly the room felt claustrophobic. He was aware that Forman had gone to the bed to attend to the general, and that three uniformed officers had entered the room.

And then he heard the bang as the gun in Will's hand went off again.

CHAPTER XXVIII

The blood had soaked through Spider's blue jeans in a wide swath across his left thigh. Somehow he had managed to stay on top of Will, and Caroline, her heart pounding, stared as Hank rushed toward the figures grappling on the floor and kicked the gun out of Will's hand. One of the Newport police officers hurried to Spider's side as Hank grabbed Will.

Quickly the young man was handcuffed. Hank read him his rights and turned him over to Keisha McAndrews who had arrived with the two other officers just as the gun had gone off for the second time. Caroline watched as Will was led out of the room. He seemed unnaturally composed and peaceful.

Charles Patterson's body lay on the bed. Hank was on the telephone, summoning the people and the equipment that would be needed now.

Caroline went to sit on the floor next to Spider, and she held his hand while the uniformed officer administered first aid. Spider was sitting up, looking astonished at the sight of his own blood.

He winced in pain as his pants were cut back to expose his injury. Caroline touched his forehead gently and was rewarded with a smile. She had purposely sat on the floor with her back to the bed to block what was going on behind her. "You know, Caroline, my ma always told me, 'Wear clean underwear in case you got to go to the hospital'."

"We won't look," the young officer said, his voice light and reassuring. The name on his identification badge was Pelella. Caroline recognized him as the officer who had been stationed at the driveway earlier that morning. Only about a hundred hours ago, she thought ruefully.

"Ouch," Spider said. She looked down at the bloody leg and turned away from that sight, too.

"You O.K.?" She felt Hank's hand on her shoulder.

"Sure," she said carelessly. "Don't worry about me."

He got down on his knees.

"How's that?" he asked, pointing to Spider's bony pink leg.

"He's going to be all right," Officer Pelella said. "The ambulance will be here any minute, and they'll fix him up good as new at Newport Hospital."

"Yeah, Spider," Hank said. "You'll be jogging down Bellevue Avenue by Halloween."

"I don't do no running, Hank. You know that. Just want to be able to walk to the bars."

"As soon as you're able, Caroline and I will take you out for dinner and a night on the town," Hank said.

"Sure," Caroline said, hiding her surprise at the suggestion's coming from Hank. "You get your leg better, and we'll all do that."

"Come on," Hank said, taking Caroline by the arm. "I need to talk to you."

She followed him out into the corridor, and they went into a nearby room. Hank shut the door, and she put her arms around him, resting her head against his chest.

"Are you really all right?" he asked.

"Yes," she said in a tired voice. "But I'm glad it's over. I mean, I'm sorry Gen. Patterson is dead, and I hope Spider's all right, but . . . oh, I don't know what I'm saying." She hugged him hard. "I thought you'd never come."

"How did you know?" he asked. She felt him kiss her hair.

"It just came to me when I saw them together."

"Who?"

"Will and Spider."

"Start from the beginning."

She loosened her grip on him.

"I found out something fantastic this morning. I had been doing research on the Internet about the nuclear waste issue and looking for more information about Katherine Patterson and the kidnapping. You were in that deposition so I couldn't tell you what I turned up. I thought Gen. Patterson deserved to know what it was." She shook her head. "I should have waited for you, I know that now."

Before he could ask the question she saw forming on his lips, she told him about her anger at being turned away from the door by Jason Forman, then Spider's taking her up to the studio to meet Will.

"The two of them together, Hank. They look so much alike." He frowned. "Oh, their two personalities are very different, and Spider is a little older than Will. I know you'd never mistake one for the other if you knew them both. But their builds are the same. Short and thin, with the same narrow shoulders. And their coloring. Light-colored eyes. They've each got blond hair."

He shook his head. "What are you getting at?"

"The waitress."

"The waitress at the ABC!" Now his face wore an embarrassed look of understanding. "It was *Will Patterson* Beth Martin saw having a drink with Meredith the night she was killed."

As soon as the ambulance had taken Spider and Irene Shipley away, Hank put his arm gently around Caroline again. "We ought to get your full statement. Now's as good a time as any. I can't do any more here. Do you think you can drive?"

"Please," she said. "I told you I'm fine."

So she drove to the police station, parked her car and went up to Hank's office where she found him studying the computer print-outs he had taken from Gen. Patterson's bedroom.

"You make a great detective," he said in greeting.

"Thank you." Hank moved around the desk and patted her into a chair. "Want some coffee?" She shook her head. "You probably could use a drink."

"Later," she said, with a smile. "I've got to get back to work. I've left Louise with everything at the inn. I thought I'd be gone for about an hour this morning."

"Let's talk about how you worked everything out. I continue to be impressed."

"So you won't be calling me Miss Marple again?"

"But I think I should definitely do that."

Caroline smiled and then her face grew serious.

"The waitress at the ABC told you that she thought Spider's photograph looked like the man who was with Meredith that night. But when she saw him in person, Spider wasn't at all like the man she had actually seen."

"No, he wouldn't be mistaken for Will."

"Will was home the night of the murder, Hank. He heard the commotion when Meredith was leaving, screaming and gone to see what was going on. He must have been very curious to know who Meredith was, why his father had Jason throw her out. Maybe he said why not go for a drink in town and talk about all this." Caroline paused and bit her lip to push thoughts of Meredith dead out of her mind.

"Will would seem so friendly to Meredith after the way his father had treated her, and she would be eager to talk to him. To be forgiven by somebody in that family. When they got to the ABC I bet she told Katherine's brother the same thing she had told Gen. Patterson. Remember Beth Martin said they were talking in a friendly manner."

"And I suppose that Will suggested that he drive his own vehicle so she didn't have to bring him back to Windward."

"Oh, I'm pretty sure he had his van, Hank. That's where he had the spool of speaker wire."

"Speaker wire?"

"Will had brought a big stereo system with him when he moved into the studio the day before. When I was up there with Spider he was taking it apart, to move out. He asked Spider to wind up the speaker wire for him. There was a big length of it lying on the floor."

"You're saying it's the murder weapon?"

"It fits, doesn't it?" He nodded. "When I saw Will and Spider together, and then looked at that wire running across the floor, suddenly I felt I knew what had happened to Meredith. And who did it." Her eyes started to burn with tears, and she swallowed hard to recover her composure.

"The whole scene does fit," she continued. "Meredith asked Will for forgiveness, and he gave it to her. She believed him. They walked on the beach, and she was feeling at peace."

"But Will blamed Meredith for his separation from his sister?"

"He blames his father and Meredith." She shook her head. "Maybe even Katherine for not telling her family what happened to her." She gestured toward the rumpled stack of papers on Hank's desk.

Hank shook his head. "What a story. Somebody ought to write a book."

*   *   *

The FBI had no trouble locating the woman whose disappearance had once been the subject of a frustrating and fruitless nationwide manhunt. This time around, all the federal agents had to do was look up Katherine Patterson's name in the Oak Ridge, Tennessee telephone book.

"Can you believe it?" Ernie Broglio told Hank when they met the following week for lunch in Providence. "It was right there in the bleeping telephone book! K. Patterson, her address and phone number. Practically with a map to her apartment. I still can't get over it. I mean, your girlfriend really deserves the credit. I guess it's sure true. Everything's available online if you know where to look for it."

"Patterson is a common enough name," Hank said evenly, trying hard to ignore Broglio's designation of Caroline as the *girlfriend*. "And Katherine isn't an unusual first name either. Probably a thousand women in the U.S. with the same name."

"But, I mean, her kidnapping was over a protest about nuclear plants, and there she was living right on top the most famous one of all. Where they practically made the original atomic bomb. I'd hate to be the Tennessee bureau guy in Knoxville now. Bet he's going to have to answer for a few things." He laughed wickedly and popped a French fry into his open mouth.

"Probably wasn't the same guy who was there in '91, Ernie."

"Well, he'll still have to give an accounting of himself. I mean, Kate Patterson did get local press and all with that nuclear safety pressure group of hers. They had a file this thick—" He held up his greasy thumb and forefinger in a space three inches apart. "—from the federal Department of Energy. Correspondence signed by her with all her demands that they stop contaminating the environment around Oak Ridge because they said that it caused these health problems and all. There's information circulating that she actually went to see one of the

Tennessee Senators a few years ago to harangue him about it." He smiled again and licked his fingers. "Politicians are such dupes."

Broglio was right about one thing. The information which Caroline had found on the Internet about the activities of Kate Patterson, now the executive director of OREAL, the Oak Ridge Environmental Action League, definitely had resulted in her capture by federal authorities. Kate Patterson had been, according to local newspaper stories and press releases on the organization's own website, a familiar figure in the activities of the citizens' coalition demanding the shutdown of the Oak Ridge nuclear reservation.

The story of the discovery of her present whereabouts had been devoured by the national media. For three days afterwards, the news of her capture and the charge that her kidnapping had been a hoax dominated the news.

Hank had watched the film on TV as the pale, slender figure of the general's daughter had been brought to a Tennessee courtroom to be arraigned. The conspiracy charges had seemed vague to him. After twenty years, Hank doubted that Katherine Patterson would suffer any penalties for her actions. No one had been physically harmed in the kidnapping hoax, and the time which the government had spent on trying to track her down seemed insignificant with passing time. No, Hank thought, all this will do is give her a platform in which to evangelize for the cause which clearly still engulfed her life. While the rest of the kidnappers, Phoebe, Josh and Darnell, had gone their separate ways and met their separate fates, Katherine had remained true to the convictions which had once bound them all together.

The FBI believed that Katherine had arrived in the South at some point in the early 1990s. Documents had been found which conclusively placed a woman called Kate Patterson in the area of the nuclear facility at Oak Ridge in 1995. At that time, the name was mentioned in news articles as one of several committee members of a group demonstrating for a government investigation of nuclear spills and the dumping of radioactive waste into the Clinch River. Once the symbol of the new atomic age during World War II, the Oak Ridge nuclear reservation continued to be embroiled in clashes which pitted a band of determined residents against the muscle of the nuclear industry and the authority of her father's old employer.

Hank had read Caroline's copy of Kate Patterson's 2008 OREAL convention speech entitled *The Ticking Bomb*, which had called on the government to stop the construction of the nuclear waste site at Yucca Mountain, Nevada. The speech continued to be reprinted in its entirety on several web sites maintained by activist groups.

"She's hired Stone Sumner to represent her. Did you know that?" Ernie asked as he pushed his empty plate away from his place. "That'll be a circus, all right."

Stone Sumner, based in San Francisco, had made a long career of representing Black Panthers and other anti-establishment targets of the government's wrath. Hank felt sure that Katherine would gain her acquittal, not to mention unlimited publicity for nuclear safety.

"There's no physical evidence against Katherine Patterson, Ernie. Phoebe Harrington's diary doesn't prove the kidnapping was a hoax. And Phoebe's dead now so she can't testify about what really happened."

"Yeah. Josh Ware is dead, too, and we still don't know what happened to the other one, the one who disappeared in Europe. Too bad."

"You know, I'd kind of like to meet her."

"Who? Katherine Patterson?" Hank nodded. "You might get your wish. Sumner's petitioned the court to have her be allowed to come to Newport to attend the memorial service for her father."

"You're kidding. I didn't know there was going to be one."

"Well, that's what I hear."

"What about her brother? I don't suppose you know if she has any interest in his case. Will Patterson hasn't got a classy lawyer like Sumner. Right now a public defender is handling his defense."

"It doesn't sound so bad. I see they sent him right in for psychiatric evaluation. Sounds like an insanity plea. He'll do his time in the mental ward." He shook his head. "Well, it's your case. Not mine. But, it was good work, Hank. We both did well off this one." He reached for the check.

"This one's on the FBI."

EPILOGUE

"You said you knew my mother, Mrs. Kent."

"Yes, but it was a long time ago. You remind me of her, Katherine."

Caroline studied the soft face of the woman who was sitting next to Louise on the settee, calmly drinking tea in the conservatory at Kenwood. It was a cozy little gathering, and Caroline had been quiet so far, unsure of what she ought to contribute to the conversation. Katherine Patterson wore no make-up and was dressed casually in the manner of one who cares little about her appearance. Like Will, she did not resemble her father. His sister's long, straight hair was the same light yellow color as her brother's, and her eyes had a familiar washed-out paleness. But the facial expression worn by this woman was in spirited contrast to Will's wary look of caution. Caroline had the feeling that this member of the Patterson family would feed a stray kitten and give money to a street person. Was it her old friend Marjorie's personality that Louise was seeing in her daughter? Had Katherine inherited her compassionate nature from her mother?

"Was it before she married my father?"

"Yes," Louise answered. "I'm afraid I saw little of her after their marriage."

"I barely think of her now," Katherine said. "My childhood seems so long ago. So much has happened."

Caroline had stayed away from Charles Patterson's memorial service on the previous day, feeling unsure of her welcome at the small chapel in Newport from the woman whom she had been responsible for turning in to the authorities. Louise had decided that she should go, and had introduced herself to Katherine after the service. It was with some astonishment that Caroline had answered the telephone that morning to be asked by Katherine if she might call at Kenwood.

"Your life is very different now," Caroline said. She still felt uncomfortable, and uncertain as to why Katherine was here.

"I love my life," Katherine said. Suddenly the eyes flashed in the same artful way Caroline had seen Will's look that terrible day in their father's bedroom at Windward. "It has meaning."

"I'm sorry," Caroline began. She needed to get it out, and she was having difficulty framing her thoughts. "You must be very upset with me. The FBI finding you—"

"Oh, don't blame yourself, Caroline," Katherine said easily. She drained the last of her tea and put the cup down on a table. "It was bound to happen. Honestly, I don't know why our stupid government never realized who Kate Patterson was all these years. It only made me bolder, I think."

"What will you do now?" Louise asked.

"Oh, I've got this awful trial and all, but Stone says not to worry, and I'm not. In the meantime, I'm free to continue my work. The government can't stop me from speaking out. It's all right with me if they want to make me into a martyr."

"Is that how you feel?" Louise asked, her eyes narrowing.

"It doesn't matter what I'm feeling. It's all for the work I do. The more I'm persecuted, the more people will listen to me."

"I see," Louise answered. "But what happens if you do go to jail?"

"I could tell you about the people whose lives have been ruined by exposure to nuclear waste, radioactive sludge in the rivers. Children with horrible diseases. Adults whose lives have been cut short. All because they had the bad luck to be living near places like Oak Ridge and Idaho Falls, and Hanford in Washington state. And as for what's happened to the people who actually worked in those plants. Well, I wish you could see the statistics." She turned to Caroline. "You must have read all about this when you did your research on the web. Yucca Mountain can't be allowed to become a permanent nuclear waste repository." She paused and stared straight into Caroline's eyes. "So you can see what happens to me is not important at all."

Caroline nodded. Why was she getting the feeling that, on the contrary, it was very important to Katherine?

"Our government has got to be held accountable. I'm sure you and Louise both agree. I'll never stop until the government's policy is to close all these plants."

The rhetoric hadn't changed since 1991. Katherine's father had not been moved to help his daughter, but the fight went on. It had to go on. The bomb was ticking.

"Have you seen your brother?" Caroline asked. She knew that Will was confined to the psychiatric ward, his behavior becoming more erratic and confused each day.

"No," Katherine answered. "I'm going back to Tennessee tonight. Those are the terms the government set, and Stone says I must obey. He's here with me, you know."

"I didn't know," Caroline murmured. She was suddenly thinking of Will, all alone in the mental institution.

"There's nothing I can do for Will. He was always a strange little boy. How could I help him? He was a child when I went off to college. I don't know him, and I don't think he's amounted to much. Sort of a drifter they tell me." She shook her head and stood up impatiently. "I do have to get going. I've got a plane to catch."

"Thank you for stopping by," Caroline said, also rising from her chair. It was a trite remark, but she had to say something to keep from speaking her real thoughts. She hesitated. "Meredith and I were friends . . ."

"Meredith?" Katherine looked perplexed.

"Phoebe Harrington. She called herself Meredith Hackett when I knew her."

"She didn't want to get involved with us, you know. She didn't understand at all what we were doing. But Phoebe couldn't bear to be left out. She was like that. She didn't know anything about politics and could have cared less what the government was doing. But when Josh and I were planning the whole thing, Phoebe had to come along. I think she thought it was going to be fun." Katherine laughed.

"Fun?" Louise repeated.

"Well, something different. She wasn't happy at school. She and Darnell were homesick, and they both wanted to leave college. I knew she had that aunt with the summer house in New Hampshire that would be perfect for us to hide out in. It was easy to talk her into helping us. She wanted to believe we were right." Katherine looked knowingly into Caroline's eyes. "So Josh and I, we convinced her."

"It certainly changed her life," Caroline said sadly.

"It was meant to," Katherine Patterson said crisply.

"She didn't mention her father once, Hank."

"She also didn't ask to see her brother while she was here," he answered.

"I know. I don't understand Katherine Patterson at all," Caroline said, shaking her head. "Why did she bother to come to Newport in the first place?"

Caroline and Hank were sitting on the terrace at Kenwood on the evening of Katherine's visit, watching the last of the sun's rays disappear in the sky. Caroline had brought out two glasses of wine, and they were enjoying the cool taste of an excellent dry white vintage from France.

"What is this?" Hank asked, holding up his glass. The hint of yellow in the wine's color caught the last light from the sun.

"It's a Muscadet. Do you like it?"

"It's different. Yeah." He took another drink.

"I should have brought out the bottle."

"I'll go back for it in a minute. Let's talk about Katherine Patterson."

"I asked you why she bothered to come back here."

"I've thought about that. I had a call yesterday from Stone Sumner, asking about Will's case." Caroline raised her eyebrows, and he continued. "We had an interesting chat. Very objective and all. Here's my take, for what it's worth. It was all done for the benefit of the media."

"The media? I would have thought she'd had enough publicity."

"But this was good publicity, don't you see? A memorial service for her father. Get it now? It keeps the story going in her favor. Sumner's going to get the upper hand in the public opinion battle between her and the government. Coming here for her father's service makes the public see Kate Patterson as a sympathetic character."

"Louise said only a handful of people were at the chapel. Mostly some old fellows who served with the general either in the Army or in the Bush administration."

"The service was orchestrated so that Sumner could get the public to see how Katherine has forgiven her father. Katherine is such a wonderful do-gooder, you see, that she bears him no hard feelings for not wanting to rescue her from her kidnappers. Sumner's smooth. Very smooth. He's been around a long time. He knows what works in the press. Katherine was the good daughter in the end."

"Unlike Will," Caroline said with a shudder. "Do you think you'll have to prove he killed Meredith as well as his father?"

"We've matched a sample of his hair to the ones found in your car, the ones we couldn't identify earlier. He is our Mr. X. And the medical examiner confirms that the dimensions of the speaker wire Will had in his apartment are consistent with the marks made on Meredith's throat. There's a good chance that the wire was the murder weapon . . . as you suspected."

Caroline shivered involuntarily.

"I'm sorry he is Mr. X, Hank. I wanted to hate the person who killed Meredith, but I can't hate him."

"No, it's no good hating them, Caroline. I've learned that much over the years that I've been a cop."

"I'm just glad it wasn't Spider."

"I guess you realize that after what's happened, he's your friend now, as well as mine."

"He tried to save my life, Hank. Yours, too. He threw himself on Will and the gun."

"I didn't ask him to," Hank reminded her.

"I don't think that matters now. And don't forget. We have to take him out soon for a night on the town."

"He's already called me. He wants it to be this Saturday night."

"That's all right," Caroline said. She reached over and pushed up the down turned corners of his mouth with her fingers. "I can be free on Saturday. It'll be fun."

"Sure," he muttered good-naturedly as she continued to press a smile on to his face. "You, me and Spider. We'll have the time of our lives."